I remember him saying, "Hey, uh... it ripped." I wasn't quite sure what he meant so I asked him to say it again. He said, "The condom, it ripped!" I was a bit nervous now and stupidly asked him, "Is that a bad thing?" I think he almost wanted to smile at the question but still had the panicked look and said, "Uh, yeah!" I started to think what this might mean. I wasn't on birth control yet, my mother refused to let me get on it, and my father was still looking into it for me.

Sixteen-year-old "Katie" was half way through her junior year of high school when she became pregnant. Throughout her pregnancy and for several months afterward, she kept a journal. This is her story as told in that journal.

Katie is not one teenager dealing with unplanned pregnancy, she is one of many. She may be the girl next door or the girl in the next block. She may be your daughter. She may be *you*.

Teens are more openly sexually active than in past generations and unplanned pregnancy is not the social stigma of years ago. The pregnancy of pop idol Britney Spears' 16-year-old sister, actress Jamie Lynn Spears, was good fodder for the media but it didn't cause her to lose a starring role in *Zoey 101*, a television show drawing a large viewership aged 9-14. When vice-presidential candidate Sarah Palin announced her 17-year-old daughter, Bristol, was five months pregnant, it gave teen pregnancy even more of a stamp of "normalcy."

What is it like to be a pregnant teen? Let teen mom Katie tell you about it. She is one of more than half a million teens facing unplanned pregnancies each year according to data from *The National Campaign to Prevent Teen and Unplanned Pregnancy*.

TEEN MOM
A JOURNAL

Also by Pat Gaudette

*How to Survive Your Husband's Midlife Crisis:
Strategies and Stories from The Midlife Wives Club*

Advice for an Imperfect Single World

Advice for an Imperfect Married World

Midnight Confessions: True Stories of Adultery

Sparky the AIBO: Robot Dogs & Other Robotic Pets

TEEN MOM
A JOURNAL

Edited by Pat Gaudette

Home & Leisure Publishing, Inc.
Lecanto, FL 34460

Published by
Home & Leisure Publishing, Inc.
P O Box 968
Lecanto, FL 34460-0968

Copyright © 2008 by Pat Gaudette

All rights reserved. This book, or parts thereof, may not be reproduced in any form without permission; exceptions are made for brief excerpts used in published reviews.

First edition: October 2008

ISBN-13: 978-0-9761210-8-4

Library of Congress Control Number: 2008938269

This is a work of nonfiction. It is based on the actual, very personal, journal of a 16-year-old girl. It is hoped that her thoughts will provide an insight into the complicated world of teen sex and unplanned pregnancy and parenthood. The journal entries have been edited liberally for clarity and conciseness. Names, locations and other identifying features have been changed to protect anonymity. Any similarity to the real name of a person or member of their family is coincidental.

Printed in the United States of America

"It's hard to raise a child when you're still a child."
– Anonymous

Contents

Foreword 13

Introduction 15

TEEN MOM – A Journal 19

Katie: My thoughts for the past year 257

Epilogue 261

Glossary 263

Additional Reading 267

Web Resources 271

Hotlines 275

About the Author 279

Foreword

Teens becoming pregnant is not a new phenomenon. In fact, depending on the life expectancy for each era of time, it was commonplace for girls reaching adolescence and puberty to become pregnant then. It was an accepted practice that usually marked a girl's passage into adulthood and marriage. However, what was once a norm in other eras is now a societal problem today.

Nationally, nearly one million young women under the age of twenty, become pregnant. That translates into 2,800 teens getting pregnant per day (Source: *Teen Sex & Pregnancy, The Alan Guttmaker Institute, New York, 1996*). The good news is that there have been trends of teenage pregnancy rates dropping with the advent of more education, contraceptive use, and celibacy pledges. Yet, the United States still has the highest teenage pregnancy rates among all of the western industrialized countries. The problems that arise with teenage pregnancy include high dropout rates in high school and college, many ending up on welfare. And, babies born to teenage moms tend to have lower birth weights that can cause future health problems.

It is my opinion that educating teens about the realities of teenage pregnancy is the real key to counteract this growing trend. Today, with sex being shown on popular TV shows and in movies, teenagers may not connect the "fantasy" with the "reality." Parents of any teenage child, whether male or female, need to have equal concern that their child may end up as one of the statistics of the teenage pregnancy fallout.

Perhaps, one of the best educational approaches to stamp out unplanned teenage pregnancy is hearing the truth coming from one of those "statistics" who ended up getting pregnant. Teens, both male and female, need to read *Teen Mom: A Journal* which will offer them a blow-by-blow account from the perspective of a teenage girl named Katie who finds herself pregnant at age 16.

When you read Katie's journal, you will feel sad, angry, curious, and shocked. Katie may not be the most likeable person as she presents herself in the journal, but underneath all the bravado is a real girl struggling with emotions and events that are way beyond her age ability to handle them successfully. Whether you end up hating or liking her, the truth that emerges from reading her journal is that casual sex ended with a pregnancy that changed her life, and all those involved with her, forever.

My experience, from working with families and children of all ages, is when you deal with events that evoke highly emotional responses that will impact your life in some way, whether now or in the future, that you stop and fully assess the situation before a decision is made that you may regret.

I highly recommend both male and female teenagers read this book before they think what happened to Katie could not happen to them.

—Andrea Goodman Weiner, Ed.D.
Author of *The Best Investment: Unlocking the Secrets of Social Success for Children*

Introduction

Several years ago I began a casual friendship with a teenager as the result of an eBay purchase lost in shipping. We exchanged several chatty emails during the time it took for the package to finally make it to the correct destination. After a few months of silence, "Katie" emailed to ask advice in dealing with a less than trustworthy seller. I made some suggestions then asked how everything else was going. Her response was completely unexpected: she thought she was pregnant.

It was difficult to know what to say. She was 16, midway through her junior year in high school, facing the possibility of unplanned motherhood. I tried not to respond with anything other than optimism and said she could email me if she needed someone to talk to. I didn't see that there was anything else I could do; her parents, family, and friends would have to provide the bulk of support should pregnancy tests be positive.

She appreciated the offer to share some of her thoughts with a virtual stranger instead of possibly saying the wrong thing to those closest to her. Her emails were introspective and candid. On some subjects I found her to be surprisingly intuitive, yet, as far as relationships, I couldn't help thinking she was far too trusting and somewhat emotionally immature.

I thought of her as "every girl" in a decade of war, extravagance, virtual reality, and Botox. As a writer always in search of a good story, I wasn't sure if hers *was* a good story but I thought it might be. When she emailed to say that, yes, she was pregnant, I asked if she would be interested in journaling her thoughts during the coming year for a possible book about her experience. My plan was to set up a private online journal for her use and send her a small monthly "fee" for her journal entries. She could write about anything she wished, there would be no set schedule, and no minimum number of entries. If something needed clarifying, I would ask questions and she could respond, or not, with as much or as little detail as she wished. She would be able to stop at any point and the book project would go no farther. I also asked that she tell her parents about the journal and possible book.

Throughout the journaling process I wasn't sure how I would use her words or even if there was a book that deserved to be published. When journaling ended, I assembled the raw material and read her entries in their entirety. It was then that I knew this book had to be published.

While there were several ways to present Katie's story, my choice was to edit and publish the actual journal entries. I felt that rewriting into another format would have changed Katie's "voice" and her voice is quite compelling even if readers won't always agree with her thoughts or actions.

Entries in Katie's journal were edited in an attempt to preserve her anonymity as well the anonymity of other persons mentioned. Further editing was done, when necessary, to make the narrative easier to follow and to blend in responses to various questions I had during the journaling process.

—Pat Gaudette

"If I was an anime." - Katie

TEEN MOM – A Journal

I was in my History class eagerly waiting for it to be time for my boyfriend Shawn to pick me up. I am 16 and a junior in high school; Shawn is 19 and a freshman in college. Not too long before class, I was talking to my friend, Andrea, at lunch about how tonight would be "the night," the time I was to finally lose my virginity.

Class was almost over when the office summoned me over the intercom. I was so excited! I hurried to my locker to get my things and went straight to the office, almost running but trying to look normal all the same. When I got there I looked in through the glass wall at the front to see Shawn waiting for me. I walked in and tried to act casual as I signed myself out. Shawn was doing his best not to hug me in front of school personnel.

We walked out of the office and around the corner, and he wrapped an arm around me and gave me a kiss as we headed outside to his car. Once we were in his car, Shawn gave me a kiss, and said how much he missed me. I told him the same. Before going to my house, we stopped at the elementary school to pick up my younger brother and sister as I had to babysit them until my mom got home from work.

When we got home, the kids went to play with neighbor kids which left Shawn and I alone in the house. I wanted to fool around and so did Shawn but we decided to wait until later that night when we were at my dad's house so we could really be alone instead of having to worry about the kids coming inside or my mom catching us. We passed the time by watching some television and going online.

Finally my mom got home and Shawn and I left. I told my mom I'd be at my dad's that night and I don't think she realized Shawn was staying there, too. At my dad's house we ate supper and watched television, waiting for dad to leave. Finally he left to spend the night at his girlfriend's house and Shawn and I got our chance to be alone together until morning.

I was very anxious to "eat the forbidden apple," but was also very nervous. I didn't want to be bad at sex and I didn't want to seem weird. I wanted things to just flow. Shawn, having slept with a few girls before, knew what he was doing and quickly helped me undress. I asked him again if he was sure about this, and, of course he said he was. I also asked, for my reassurance, if he'd been tested recently and he reminded me that he's in the Army reserve and so he was tested and clean.

After a little persuasion, I finally gave in and Shawn and I had sex. Afterwards I felt no regret, although I was a little sore during and when done. I remember telling him that it hurts a little and him saying, "That's because I'm popping your cherry, baby." I always liked how he called me "baby" or "babe" or "sweetheart." We went back to watching a movie, happily lying next to each other.

Soon, Shawn wanted to go again. I was a bit unsure about a second time, being so nervous the first, but I did enjoy it and couldn't say no. We were very safe about it; I made him use a condom each time. I was not on birth control yet, but figured I'd be okay with doing it once, twice, however many times, so long as he used a rubber.

After the second time, I snuggled with him and fell asleep. I remember waking up and looking at the clock. It was 1:30 in the morning. I couldn't go back to sleep so I rolled over on top of Shawn and woke him up. I began to "play" with him, which lead to me giving him oral sex. That managed to get us both back to sleep for the rest of the night.

The next morning we had yet another round of sex before breakfast. We left early to be at my mom's house when my step-dad left for work since we had to watch the kids until early afternoon. After my brother and sister had lunch, they found friends to play with and I told Shawn I wanted to take a shower because I felt grimy after going at it so much.

I went in the bathroom and he followed me in, closing the door and locking it. He kissed me and took off his shirt. I asked him what he was doing and he said he was going to join me. Being very self-conscious, I didn't know if I wanted him seeing me naked in so much light, but he insisted. He said he saw it the night before, so it was nothing to worry about.

With more words of encouragement, he managed to get me in the shower, and we bathed together. He "poked" me while in there, but not enough for him to ejaculate, so I figured it was okay. We finished showering, I got dressed and brushed my hair, and then we waited for my mother to come home.

Mom was happy to see Shawn as she thought he was nicer than some of the guys I'd dated. After mom got home, Shawn and I went to the mall to meet my dad. Dad met us a couple hours later and bought us dinner at a Chinese place and then suggested that we all go to see a movie.

While we were at the restaurant, Shawn kept talking to me and teasing me to ask dad if we could just go home. I was wearing my dog collar with spikes and Shawn kept pulling on it to get me excited. Finally I gave in, as I tend to do, and asked my dad if he'd mind if Shawn and I did something other than going to the movie and he said it was okay.

I had a key to my dad's house, so we headed back there. Dad was again spending the night at his girlfriend's house so we had the house to ourselves, once again, until the morning. No sooner did we get in the door than Shawn tightened up my collar a bit and then helped me get undressed. Once he got undressed everything went so fast I didn't even think about protesting.

Things started getting a bit hot and heavy and Shawn "poked" me a bit before I told him he had to put a condom on. We had sex, yet again, this time pretty rough with Shawn tugging on my collar and doing me in a couple different positions before he finally climaxed and pulled out. That's when a look of panic struck his face.

I remember him saying, "Hey, uh... it ripped." I wasn't quite sure what he meant so I asked him to say it again. He said, "The condom, it ripped!" I was a bit nervous now and stupidly asked him, "Is that a bad thing?" I think he almost wanted to smile at the question but still had the panicked look and said, "Uh, yeah!" I started to think what this might mean. I wasn't on birth control yet, my mother refused to let me get on it, and my father was still looking into it for me.

Shawn put some clothes on and sat in the chair, watching TV to distract himself while I got dressed as well. I sat in the chair by him and asked, "Are we going to be okay?" He reassured me that he thought we were, but still wasn't 100% positive. But, even with the scare, we still managed to have sex again that night before going to sleep.

We woke up bright and early Sunday morning, fitting in another round of "play" and Dad arrived not long afterward. We were all going to the movie we missed the night before, but Shawn's mother called him just after lunch saying he needed to head home right then and there. He gathered his things and we said our good-byes, Shawn again saying no matter what it'll be okay. He drove off, leaving behind only a can of his spray deodorant (because I was so fond of the smell). My dad and I went to the movie.

January 31

Yesterday at school I told my best friend, Andrea, what had happened. I asked the school nurse about the odds of my being pregnant and told her my last period had been two weeks before and my next should be in about two weeks so I figured I was right in the middle. She said I was at my most fertile time and I should get the emergency contraceptive.

After school I asked Andrea if she could take me to the health clinic to get the morning after pill, which is supposed to be able to work up to three days after the questionable incident. After some difficulty finding the clinic, I went inside and explained why I was there, feeling very uncomfortable. After a lot of paper work and a long wait,

I was sent into a room. The lady that came in explained about the morning after pill, how I should take one pill at maybe 6:00 PM and then again in 12 hours at 6:00 AM and to come back if I threw up at all. I did as instructed, not even feeling a little nauseated, and think I'm fine.

February 18

I have a bad feeling about everything. Even though I took the morning after pills, I still feel that something isn't right. I started to get mild cramps, like I normally do a few days before my period, so I was a bit relieved. A week has gone by, but no period. I've talked to the school nurse and Andrea.

I've called Shawn almost every night and chatted with him online whenever I can. He tries to stay positive, and we both think it may be stress making me late, even though I have *always* been very regular.

As soon as I got to be a week late I asked Andrea to take me after school to get a home pregnancy test. I told my mom that Andrea wanted to go shopping for some clothing and I was just riding along, so that she wouldn't know my true agenda. I got home and had the pregnancy test kit, supposedly 99% accurate, hidden in my book bag. I read the instructions and hid the test in my pocket, disposing of the box and papers in my garbage in my room sort of in the middle kof everything else so it wasn't easily seen. I went to the laundry room bathroom while complaining of feeling a bit sick (an obvious lie) -- it was the closest to the garage that had a garbage can I could easily dispose of the test in when I was done. And by saying I wasn't feeling well, that would buy me the otherwise unexplainable extra time for the test to set.

I went in and used the test as instructed, making sure to get so many seconds of mid-flow urine on it, and then placed the cap on and put it in the bucket next to the toilet to set, the surface being plenty flat as it was upposed to be. The designated time went by and I checked the test. It gave a very solid "negative" symbol with a *very* light line making it a positive. I remembered looking at the box and it showing that a light line that forms the positive symbol out of the dash is still read as a negative. I threw the test away in the garage, getting a drink of our bottled water to further eleviate any suspicion of my actions.

I went to school and told the nurse and Andrea and everyone was happy, the nurse even saying, "I knew it would work out for you." But, even with those results, having done everything I could, and all the people around me saying it was okay now, I still don't feel right. I still feel that I might be pregnant. I've told Shawn everything, except my feelings that I might still be pregnant, and he is relieved.

February 21

A few more days have gone by and still no period. An online friend told me that sometimes you can miss a period with stress and I really hope she's right, but don't really believe that's what it is.

February 28

Yet another week with no period, and my dad, who doesn't know anything about what happened or is happening, set up an appointment for me at the health clinic to get on birth control. When I went with him, I filled out the papers again and acted like I'd never been there before.

My dad was in the waiting room while I went to the back with the same lady who gave me the morning after pills. She was ready to give me my birth control when I mentioned about being there before and filling out so many papers. She said, "Well, you wouldn't have had to do the paperwork again if we would've known you were here before!" I explained my dad didn't know I'd been there before and that's why I didn't say anything. I reminded her why I was there before, about the emergency contraceptive, and she said that she normally wouldn't test for pregnancy, but because I did come in being unsure, she had to test.

A short time later she came back in the room with the test in her hand. She asked me about taking the pills, if I took them right, and I told her I did. She said that normally they work and she's only seen them not work maybe twice and then told me that mine didn't work. I was, in fact, pregnant. I began to cry and she apologized that she couldn't send me home with birth control, taking the bag they were in and moving it away from me. I told her, "I'm not so much upset at the fact I'm pregnant, I'm just upset because I know I have to tell my mom and dad and I don't want to disappoint them, especially my father." The lady offered to bring my dad back and said she'd tell him for me while I sat there. I agreed because I just couldn't do it.

Dad came back, kidding with the lady, still unaware of what he was about to hear. The lady, so bluntly, told him I was pregnant and went on about counseling and groups and how I will need support. My dad just sat there, silent. I couldn't look at him, but I could tell his face was red and he was in shock and very disappointed in me. We left the clinic and sat in his car. Dad asked me if it was my ex-boyfriend's, but I explained that it was Shawn's.

My mom called right then asking if I was coming home because she needed me to babysit. Dad said I was on my way and told her about me being pregnant. Mom sounded upset and said she knew I might be because she hadn't needed to buy "girly things" for me recently.

Dad drove me home and was very quiet. He still had a red face and his eyes were watery. He asked what I planned to do and I wasn't sure. My mom mentioned abortion as soon as I got to the front door and so I, later that evening when she got home, mentioned it again along with adoption.

I finally got hold of Shawn and told him everything. He was very shocked and speechless. I told him his job for that night was to just breathe and let it sink in while I talk with my parents. He still said he loved me and was very supportive.

My step-dad and mom both said I could keep the baby and raise it, but said they wouldn't help financially. I'm still unsure about everything and feel very confused. I'm glad my mother calmed down and was talking like a normal person, but I know I can't afford a baby, even with Shawn's help. He lives at college, three hours away from me, and it just can't happen. I cried a lot and went to sleep with way too much on my mind.

March 6

Over the past week I've talked to my mom and Shawn about the whole situation. My dad is still too quiet and not himself. He called once and was really weird on the phone, asking why I "lied" to him, I guess about being sexually active, and I started to cry and handed the phone to my mom. She told him, "It's done and over with, now we deal with it." She is really being quite supportive. My dad finally came around and is okay.

After talking to Shawn, once it all sank in, we still don't know what we want to do. Shawn and I would love to keep the baby, but don't know how we'd afford it.

Prior to this I had asked my mom if Shawn could stay with us for a week during his spring break, and she had said no. Now, she talked my step-dad into allowing him to stay with us for that week, sleeping on a couch in the basement, so that he and I could talk face-to-face about the baby.

March 12

Shawn arrived Wednesday evening and will stay until next Tuesday. He will take me to school and pick me up each day. Many of my closer friends already are aware of what is going on and are actually very excited for me.

Shawn told his mother and father about the baby. His parents are divorced like my parents, and his father lives out of state. Mom and Shawn's mom talked on the phone about the whole situation. That's when mom wanted to know details of how Shawn and I met. I felt very uncomfortable explaining we met on the Internet, but she was surprisingly okay with it.

Shawn and I met online and had gone on dates before, almost a year prior, so that may be why she didn't judge it so much. Both our moms ended up agreeing that we should all meet at a local restaurant to get acquainted and discuss the situation.

March 18

A couple days after Shawn arrived, we all met for dinner: my mom, step-dad, little brother, Shawn's mom, and Shawn's step-dad. Shawn and I haven't had a lot of time to talk about our options but we told everyone that we are leaning towards keeping the baby.

Shawn's mom, Nora, immediately began saying how she was adopted and how we can't afford a child, that we are too young and how Shawn isn't that responsible, and then apologized for being such a rag. My mom and step-dad are trying to be supportive no matter what we decide, so they didn't say much in favor of one idea over the other, but still said that we could keep the baby.

Shawn and I were fairly quiet. Shawn wanted me to speak up more, but I wasn't sure what to say. Meeting his parents for the first time under such conditions wasn't that easy. Then to say "I want to keep my baby" felt like it would've been an impossible thing to do. Shawn put his arm around me from time to time and told me he loved me, and was very nice even if I was being quieter than he wanted me to be.

When we were done eating, we all headed out to the parking lot. Shawn's mom again said she didn't mean to go on and on, but her opinion is adoption would be best. My brother, Shawn, and I got into my mom's car while my mom and step-dad talked a bit with Eugene, Shawn's step-dad. Shawn's mom went to their car, which was parked in front of ours, and called Shawn over. He got some papers he needed for the Army reserve and a small box. When he came back, he opened the box revealing a small diamond ring that belonged to his mother.

Before any of this happened, Shawn had asked me to marry him when I turned 18 and I had already said yes, and now he was actually giving me a ring. I told him to show it to me again when we got home so I could see it in better light and try it on.

We got home and Shawn and I headed downstairs. I tried the ring on and it fit although a little too tight but I could get it on and off. Then Shawn said, "Katie, I think we should give the baby up for adoption." I began to get wet eyes and even though I knew it would probably be best, I still couldn't handle hearing the idea, especially from him.

My mom and step-dad came downstairs and asked if we had any idea what we wanted to do, knowing we previously wanted to keep the baby, and I told them we think we're going with adoption. Neither my mom nor my step-dad was happy with this and my mom later said that I was brainwashed into the idea and too easily persuaded.

March 30

Over the next week, Shawn and I talked a bit about the baby, but sort of let the idea of adoption settle in. He took me to school and picked me up every day. We played Scrabble every night and had sex almost every day, at least once a day, knowing we couldn't screw up any further.

We enjoyed being together and didn't want to dwell on our options anymore, thinking it would make it too hard to go through with our plan. Shawn mentioned that he and his mother knew a few people who couldn't have children and who would be willing to adopt our baby.

Now that Shawn has gone, I feel a little unsatisfied. For one, I'm unhappy he couldn't stay longer. It's really hard being in a long distance relationship, especially with a baby involved. Secondly, I still am unsure about the whole pregnancy thing.

It is hard to believe I am having a baby and the thought of giving it away makes it seem even more unreal. I'll carry it, and then it'll just be handed over to someone else and gone. My mom and step-dad still insist that I can keep the baby, but at the same time want to be supportive of Shawn and mine's decision.

April 17

For prom night, Shawn drove up to go with me to my prom. I'm a few months pregnant and already showing a little, making fitting into my dress a bit challenging and very uncomfortable. Shawn wore his fancy uniform from the Army reserve and looked very proper.

We were supposed to meet people for dinner before prom but couldn't find their house, ended up eating at a fast food place, and then got lost on the way to where the dance was being held.

I began to feel ill not long after getting to the dance due to my dress being so snug. We headed back to my dad's house and I changed my clothes and got into bed. My dad was working and then planned to spend the night with his girlfriend.

Shawn and I had sex, then he put a movie into the VCR and shortly after that I fell asleep. I woke up a couple hours later and told Shawn that I had wanted to go to the after prom stuff because I had paid for it but was much happier to just sleep with him next to me.

Today we went to the mall and after a while I called my mother. She wasn't happy that I didn't tell her I was going to stay at dad's with Shawn. I figured she knew where I was since I took a bag of clothing when Shawn and I left to go to the prom. Shawn called his mom to let her know he was with me, even though he had already told her, and his mom said she had a "pleasant" conversation with my mom earlier that morning.

We were going to see a movie with my dad later that afternoon. We told him we wanted to go to the mall and then we'd meet him there. We looked around in different stores until I got really warm and wanted to sit down. I asked Shawn, "If we could afford the baby, you'd want to keep it, right?" Of course he did, we both would like to have our baby and be a family, but know it can't happen.

May 3

Shawn headed home that evening after dropping me off at my mother's house. I got grounded from the phone for a while, which is unpleasant because I won't be able to talk to him even though I really feel the need to. Being pregnant makes me upset a lot.

I've managed to call him occasionally from my dad's cell phone and sneak some Internet access on my PSP, so I'm not completely without contact with him.

May 30

This month has gone by pretty quickly. I still have moments of depression where I want to be with Shawn and where I don't want to be pregnant and then other times I feel I want to have the baby and keep it. My mom had me talk to a neighbor that gave a child up at a young age and the lady explained how much she regretted it.

My doctor says if I make a decision to either keep the baby or give it up for adoption to stick with it, don't dwell on a decision once it's made. I am very confused whether I should think about it or not and have decided I am better off just not thinking about it.

We have an adoptive family picked out and they are very happy to be getting a child. They are distant relatives on Shawn's side and have already gotten the paperwork going and the background checks initiated. I think maybe this "big mistake" was meant to be and I am meant to give a family a baby.

My mom's comments and criticism upset me and Shawn being so far away leave me feeling sad and lonely much of the time. I call my dad upset a lot wanting to see him, because he is very much back to normal and being my best friend. I also call Shawn whenever I can telling him how much my mom upsets me and how I really want to see him, even though I can't.

The last day of school is also my 20 week doctor's appointment. I finally figured out why it is considered 20 weeks when I figured more along the lines of 16 or 17 weeks. The count is from my last menstrual cycle.

This appointment I am to have my first ultrasound. At my last appointment I was told the ultrasound is required, which meant insurance would cover it so I was okay with that, because I am measuring big.

The doctor mentioned the possibility of twins and I immediately began thinking that was the reason I am so big. I just had a feeling, like when I knew I was pregnant, that it is twins. My mother said it may be my generation's turn to have them because fraternal twins run in our family and Shawn's family has identical twins.

June 1

My dad came up for the ultrasound, so he and my mother, brother, sister, Shawn, and I all crowded in the room with the lady who was to handle my stomach. I lay down on the little bed and the lady gooed me up and no sooner put the thing on my stomach when we saw two babies up on the screen.

My dad was quiet, my mother was excited, and Shawn was in shock. I knew it was going to be what it was, my instincts haven't ever failed me, but it still was different seeing them. Everyone kept making me laugh during the ultrasound, so it was difficult to get good pictures sometimes, but I think everyone was just excited, especially my mother. I think Shawn was a bit emotional. He held my hand and stroked my hair, but he still claims he wasn't.

When we came out of the ultrasound room we saw my school nurse in the waiting room, and I told her the news. She was surprised, but seemed happy. Shawn called his mom and told her, but she didn't believe him, so my mother had to take the phone and tell her it's true, I'm pregnant with twins. Shawn and I immediately began to kid with each other, calling the other "over fertile" and that's why it happened.

June 4

After the ultrasound, I told my mom I'm staying at my dad's a couple days, which is true, but didn't tell her that Shawn was staying that night with me.

The next day we went to the mall. After visiting a few stores we sat down on a bench because I was getting really hot under the lights and we talked about the twins. We're both amazed and I just laughed when we joked about being really good at breeding. I asked Shawn, "If we could afford to keep them, would you want to?" He of course told me yes, but we know we can't. If we can't afford one, two would be impossible. We enjoyed the rest of our day together until he had to go home.

The next morning my mother called me and asked if having twins changed my opinion of anything. I could feel myself getting a bit upset, but told her not really. She brought up keeping them again and I started to get teary-eyed saying, "If we couldn't afford one, how can we afford the two, Mom?" Mom said she and my step-dad had been talking and if I still want to give the kids up for adoption, they'll take them. Or Shawn and I could keep them and if we need the financial help they will "pay for everything for the next 5 years" while I get through college. I said I'll have to talk to Shawn, but it is a very promising offer.

It was early in the morning and I was crying when I called Shawn, waking him. He asked what was wrong and I told him I want to keep the kids. He was a bit taken back by it and started to say how we can't afford it. Then I told him everything my mother had just told me.

He asked, "She'll pay for everything?" I told him she would if necessary, but of course we should put money in when we can, and he agreed. But then he said, "Okay, we'll keep the babies." I asked if he was sure because I don't want to force him into it. Even if I do want them, I believe keeping them should be *our* decision. He said he is sure and I asked him about wanting them all along and he wanted to keep them all along, he just knew we couldn't afford it. I told him I loved him and let him get back to sleep, promising to talk to him later.

I called my mother and told her I talked to Shawn and that he wants to keep them, too, if they are helping with money. Mom said she thought Shawn looked emotional at the ultrasound so she thought he wants them like I do. Shawn claimed he wasn't emotional, but the way he was acting made me think otherwise. I explained to my mother how I always wanted to keep them, but finances threw me off and what Shawn's mom had said at our meeting.

I asked Mom about the adoptive family, the one we have picked out, since they are getting a background check and the paperwork ready. Mom said that they knew this could happen, it's a risk someone takes, and even if they are bummed about it they'll most likely understand as the decision is Shawn's and mine. We can't base a decision on whether or not we'll upset the adoptive family. We know they'll be upset particularly after Shawn's mom told them about the ultra-sound. They are ecstatic about the twins.

My mom emailed Nora, Shawn's mom, telling her we think we are going to keep the babies.

June 5

I was at my dad's house checking my email, and I had emails from Nora. One was from yesterday, the other from today. I read the newest one first and it was a big rant about how we have to think of the children and there's nothing wrong with adoption and how we should still give them up and how I had told Shawn my mind didn't change about adoption so why change it now? I felt very threatened when I got done reading it, especially because I thought Nora seemed so nice to me. Before replying, I read her email from the previous day and it was the exact opposite of the newest email. She said she and Eugene, Shawn's step-dad, support our decision and will help however they can. It was totally supportive of whatever we do.

I hadn't even talked to Shawn's mom and she sent me two emails with completely different messages. I printed them both and saved them so I could reply later at home. I showed the printed emails to my dad and he told me not to think a lot of it, which made me upset that he doesn't understand. I am very confused having those two emails in hand and dad's neutrality doesn't help me any.

When dad and I got back to his house I called my mom. I told her about the emails and read them both to her. I was crying and told her I was very confused by it all. Mom agrees that there is something weird about the change of tune from one day to the next particularly since I haven't talked to Nora. She said she was going to write an email asking Nora to stop sending me weird emails like that.

June 7

For the last two days, Nora has been sending emails to me and my mom. Then they got into sort of an online argument and mom ended up blocking Nora's emails. I still get emails from her where she goes back and forth saying how she doesn't necessarily think that Shawn and I are bad for the babies, but we have to think of what's best for the babies, implying that we aren't it. Then she turns around and says how she'll get them some things, asking what we need and what we expect of her and Eugene. When I say we don't need anything right then and not to worry about it, she takes it that we don't want her help and then rants about how she is being used and that we think she's all about money.

I am very confused throughout all of the email exchanges and told my mom I almost want her to adopt the twins so that she can tell Nora to go fly a kite and to stay out of their lives. We still figure it'll be best if Shawn and I keep custody because we do want them as our kids.

Through all of this, Shawn keeps insisting his mom is trying to help. I told him I think that she doesn't like me. In the end, once Nora and I stopped talking to each other, Shawn finally agreed he thinks the same. It is just one more complication to add to the mix of a twin pregnancy.

June 8

Before Shawn, I dated Eric. We started dating when I was a freshman and he was a sophomore (I was 14, he was 16) and were off and on for two years. Sometimes it was good, sometimes it wasn't. He'd say he loved me and then he'd turn around and say he just wanted to be friends, until he couldn't get another girl and wanted someone to fool around with, and I was dumb enough to go back to him. It finally got to the point where we both got tired of back and forth and it just ended. It was pretty mutual, but he takes credit and says he dumped me.

He was the only serious relationship I had before Shawn because I tend to get scared of commitment, and would always end up breaking it off with a guy after only a short time of dating. Eric and then Shawn were the only ones I ever felt I wasn't afraid to be with, but Shawn was the only one that was worth the time and actually loved me back.

Eric, being the only one before Shawn, was also the only one I ever really did anything sexually with. The farthest we went was oral sex, me giving him, not the other way around as he refused to do it to me. He'd only use his hand on me. I personally did want to go all the way. I have always had an interest in sex and sex-related acts, and I also did love Eric at the time. But, Eric didn't want me to get pregnant and had a huge fear about that, and, he was Catholic. When we first met, he didn't even want to mess around other than kiss, but as time went on I guess I broke down those barriers. Eventually, we just stopped dating and had never had sex. Now that I think about it, I'm glad Shawn was my first and only as far as actual sex goes.

I never really thought about *why* I don't consider oral sex the same as *actual* sex. I don't get anything from it other than the knowledge I made a guy happy which is nice, but not as nice as what he got. So I guess it's not considered the same as sex because sex is mutual. But then you could open the broader field of 69. Both people are getting pleased, yet I still don't think of that as sex. I think it's just because of everyone else around me: sex is sex. Everything else these days is just common alternatives. I was never really raised knowing about oral sex; it was something I heard from friends and TV and the Internet. So, because I was not told about it and warned that it's "bad" too, it's not the same.

I always liked Shawn, even when dating Eric. While Shawn was in basic training for the Army reserve we actually were dating (this was in between dating Eric off and on), but as soon as Eric came back, I left Shawn. That was a stupid mistake right there.

Finally when Eric and I were over for good, I cried on Shawn's shoulder. The same day it ended with Eric, I was talking to Shawn on the phone. I told Shawn I thought it was going to be over with Eric, called Eric and it ended, called Shawn back and sobbed. He immediately offered to come up the next day, a six hour drive because he was at college, and stay a couple days to make me feel better. He even went with me to school one of the days.

I should've been with Shawn sooner, because Shawn and I have a ton in common and he has all the things I liked in Eric *plus* all the things I wished Eric had, so it felt right to be with him. We had already fooled around (oral sex on him, hand on me) and we were comfortable with each other in that way, so, after we were dating a month or two, I told him I wanted to have sex and he of course wanted to as well. It was definitely a mutual idea. I loved him, I still love him, and he loves me. He's loved me longer than I've admitted to loving him and he's always been there for me, even when I was too stupid to be with him.

June 10

Being pregnant hasn't changed things much at school. My friends are about the same although none of them have been pregnant; they all tell me they're amazed how well I handle things.

There are some students who have babies or are pregnant but I really don't know much about them and never have a chance to talk with them since we don't have classes together. Sometimes other people joke around about pregnancy, not necessarily about me, and I just laugh with them. So, because I don't really let the outside world get me down, everyone else just goes with the flow as well.

Other schoolmates haven't really said much that I know of. I've heard of a few people asking my friends if it was true that I'm pregnant and they've been told either "yes" or "it's none of your business," but I haven't heard anything bad. Most people say they're surprised it happened to me as not many students really think I'm into sex.

It is sometimes talked about with people other than friends, but I will admit I still feel weird saying "I'm pregnant" or "today the baby was kicking a lot" or things like that. So it's not as talked about as it could be. The fact that, towards the beginning, we were going to give the kids up for adoption also made me talk less about it, sort of a "I don't want to be attached, so I'll pretend it's not there." So unless somebody asked a question, which I was always happy to answer, I didn't bring it up. Nobody really said anything bad about me or the situation, which was shocking because the other girls at school I know I've heard negative comments about when it happened to them.

June 14

Right now it's unknown what kind of money support Shawn will be providing for the babies, if anything. He was told yesterday that he'll be doing security work out west in the fall and he could be there anywhere from ninety days to two years. He'll be making a bunch of money and probably will be able to send some my way for the kids. Whenever things go back to "normal" and he goes back to his regular job, he won't make as much and probably can't afford to support money-wise.

Basically, he'll help if he can, but if not then we'll deal with it. My mom has said that she understands he may not be able to provide right now, but one day he will. It just depends on what we do. When I turn 18 I hope for Shawn to be active in the military so we can live on/near a base and have a lot provided for us, like free insurance, so then he'll be making good pay and covering us with insurance. But again, that depends on the security job.

I think the babies will affect Shawn's schooling and his career choices; he is taking this year off from college and was planning on going back next year, until my mom and I mentioned him going active. If he does that, which would be the best source of income, he probably won't go back to school and will just settle with his one year of college. Because of the babies, he'll likely do what'll make the most money for us to be a family. He's very concerned about him and me and the kids living together, so he'll probably do whichever allows that to happen soonest.

I also think the babies will affect my schooling and career somewhat. I still plan to go to school no matter what, but where I go is a big question right now. If I move with Shawn because of him being active and living on/near a base, then I won't be going to school around here like originally planned. If that doesn't happen right away, then I'll have two years' community college here and then two years' regular college elsewhere, unless he does not go active at all. Then I'll do two community and two regular here.

When the babies are born, I will likely see less of my father. He works a lot anyway, especially during the school year, so our time will become limited whether I move in with Shawn or stay with my mom. It all really depends on where I live. Shawn and I want to live together, but now with this security thing it's hard to say when that'll happen although it will eventually, if not right away.

If we can't right away, then I'll be living with my mom. The community college is in town, so is the daycare, so I can get my general education classes out of the way while I wait for Shawn to be done with his security job. But if allowed, we will be getting legal papers when I turn 18 so that we're considered husband and wife and he'll go active. Of course, Shawn going active may not happen, either. It's something we're both interested in, but by the end of this coming school year, he could find out something about being active that'll change his mind, even if it does produce higher income. We have plans and back-up plans, but nothing can be carved in stone at this point.

Shawn said that his mom told him she'll buy a couple things for the babies, but that's it; she will not help financially at all. Eugene, Shawn's step-dad has said little, as far as I know, and Shawn's real dad, Cal, lives out of state and seems to be okay with anything Shawn and I decide. So, Nora is not very supportive at this point in time.

June 17

We're still planning on getting married when I turn 18. We won't have a fancy wedding, I don't really want one anyway; maybe someday when we can afford it we'll do it "right," but I'm not worried about it. We'll be getting the legal papers saying we're husband and wife. That way insurance will be taken care of through the military. But, even if the babies weren't in the picture, Shawn and I planned on getting married when I turned 18.

He'll be 20 next spring, so he's getting to that point in his life anyway. He had asked me if I would marry him before we even slept together and gave me a ring the night we met with his parents. I'll be getting a new one eventually because this one was his mother's and he knows I don't get along with his mom and don't feel right having it.

June 20

Right now I have lots of aches and pains. I know if I walk a lot, my feet get bruised under the front pad. It's harder to get up from sitting or lying and I can feel it strain on my knees because of all the weight. I'm a small person, so this is very new to have so much extra weight brought on so quickly.

If I lay on a very flat surface on my back, my stomach makes it so I can't breathe well. If I lay on my side certain ways it makes me hurt near my hips and lower stomach. I get headaches from time to time and although I haven't gotten morning sickness, I have had upset stomachs from foods and had to go to the restroom. If I sit for too long it puts a lot of stress on my tailbone area, so it's really sore when I get up. Basically, I can't sit, lie, or stand for too long without being in pain. Also, I get out of breath very easily and find myself wanting to sit after just walking around a store for a little bit.

Before pregnancy I weighed 137 and had just started to lose weight again because I used to be overweight and lost some weight, making me average, but gained about five pounds back, but by that time found out I was pregnant and started to gain weight. Now I weigh about 174.

I hear up to 45 pounds is normal for a twin pregnancy and I only have four to six weeks left because they'll most likely not go 40 weeks, only 35 or 36. So I'm pretty average for carrying twins and most likely will be within the average weight range (35 - 45 pounds). Also, with it being hot out, I feel even hotter. Having the extra pounds on me feels really warm and I can't stand being outside much.

As sad as it sounds, I've sometimes wished I had decided to abort instead of going through with the pregnancy. I know I never could have aborted, even though sometimes I really just hate being pregnant and am scared of having kids and all that'll happen once they're born.

Sometimes it's just hard to think I'll have kids and I know I am very self-conscious about my very large stomach as well as swollen everything else, so I just wish I would've gotten them out and never dealt with it. But on the same note, knowing I "bred" with Shawn and that we'll be a family and all the support I have and the fact that they're *my* kids makes me sort of glad I didn't abort them. How I feel after they're born may be a different story.

As with my thoughts about abortion, I've thought that I should have opted to put the babies up for adoption. Sometimes I just am scared of the idea of having my own kids, two of them, running around. I figure it'd be easier if I just gave them away. But, they're *my* kids that I conceived with Shawn and I couldn't give that up and deep down never really wanted to. Sometimes it's better to ignore the easy route.

July 8

None of my friends have thought poorly of me being pregnant and I haven't lost any friends. On the same note, I haven't really gained any either. I know some people talk to me a bit more on the subject of kids, especially neighbors that I didn't previously associate as much with, but nobody completely new has stepped up and wanted to be friends based on my situation. I go to the pregnancy center, so I guess the girls that work there are sort of new friends, but I really consider them more like acquaintances; they're helpful, but at the same time they seem to push their religion too much for me to feel comfortable calling them friends.

There are days when I feel like everything is hopeless. Sometimes I think it's just not going to work out. I'm going to have no idea what I'm doing, things will fall through with raising these kids, I won't be able to finish school, I suck at being a mom, Shawn will be away forever and we'll never get to be together. It just goes on and on! But talking to Shawn or asking my mom questions to remind me of how it's going to work helps with that.

I normally wear pajama bottoms and large t-shirts. I don't have a whole lot as far as actual pants and shirts while being pregnant. I have some, but most of them no longer fit because my stomach has gotten bigger than it would have with one baby. I got most of my clothing from Goodwill, only a few things came from other stores. But, most of that stuff is a tough fit.

We have some baby stuff, a couple outfits and toys, a bumper pad for a crib (no crib), a double stroller (although it'll most likely be a backup because it was free from a garage sale and not in the greatest shape). But we're waiting to get a lot until after the baby shower which is next week.

We have a few people offering to lend us things. We have two baby swings, two bouncy chairs, and a pack 'n' play on the way from someone. We're still looking for cribs, have one double stroller that we'll use if we don't get a better one, and a few hand-me-down toys and a couple things I got from Goodwill such as a Glow Worm. I had one when I was a baby, so I figured they should have one as well, but unfortunately I only got one; there were two, but someone got the other one.

I go to a class at the pregnancy center and I get "mommy dollars," three a visit, and one equals one dozen diapers. I have 21 right now, so they'll probably all go for diapers. We haven't stocked up on them or formula at all yet. Whenever I'm through with the maternity clothes I have, I've already decided to donate them to the pregnancy center. I'll be getting some stuff from them with my "mommy dollars," so I feel it's nice to give back.

July 29

Shawn asked my mother if she'd sign papers for us to be married now, but she said she'd rather not and that we can wait because we're going to do it later anyway. I'm not exactly sure of *why* she won't sign, but I think she'd rather us be sure that's what we want by giving us this next year than her deciding it's okay and us not wanting to be together later, although I doubt Shawn and I will have that problem.

August 2

I went with my dad yesterday to spend time with him. I started to feel sort of sick while outside a lot in the heat. My dad had a big argument with some cops and a meter maid over parking tickets, which made us stuck outdoors even longer and I ended up missing my pregnancy class. So, due to my father being such a "fugitive of the law" for not paying parking tickets, I was outside in the extreme heat for way too long. I started to feel sore in my abdominal area, which made any moving or even sitting/laying painful.

I couldn't sleep at all last night and ended up waking up and showering, only to pass out in the recliner in the living room later since my dad has no air conditioning, just fans. Today I didn't feel much better. My feet and ankles were very swollen and the pain seemed worse. Even after being cooled by a fan for a while, I still hurt.

I called my mom to ask if she could come and get me, after telling my dad I couldn't help him work tonight, and she told me to call the clinic nurse first to see if she could avoid that since my dad was going to take me home at 5:30 anyway. I called and explained to three different people, while standing outside in the sun where the phone was, what was wrong and they told me to come in. After going to the clinic, they sent me straight to the hospital. They made me put on a robe and lie in a bed while attaching things to my stomach to monitor both babies' heart beats as well as my stomach to see if I had contractions.

I had to give a urine sample, that was "contaminated" probably because my stomach is so huge and the past couple days I was sore, so it's hard to clean down there. They ended up putting in a catheter to get some urine out, which they barely got any. They poked a large q-tip into my vagina and rectum, and a lubed finger into my vagina to see if I was dilated, which I was by one finger. The catheter and finger poke both hurt and I cried as my mom stayed nearby. They told me they'd be back in an hour for another finger poke, which didn't take as long so wasn't as bad, and said I was still the same. She said I had minor contractions, after looking at the monitor I was hooked up to.

After a long wait, they came back with the results of the testing on my urine and said I have a bladder infection, which is causing the soreness and small contractions. They said to drink plenty of fluids (water and juice) and to take a prescription twice a day. The contractions will go away and the soreness will go down a lot if I do what I'm supposed to. After going through all that just for a bladder infection, I am very nervous about when I have to give birth.

I've kept my dad and Shawn updated by phone and both are glad to hear I'm okay. Mom told me I can't spend the nightat my dad's anymore, just to see a movie or dinner, and that is disappointing. I know I shouldn't be in the heat, but I will miss being with my dad.

Tonight when I talk to Shawn I think I'm going to tell him I don't want any more kids. If he wants to have a second son, as he told me before, he can get it elsewhere (which I obviously don't want him to do).

August 3

Last night didn't get a whole lot better. My chest hurt all night, causing me to wake up every half hour to an hour. It felt like pressure and heartburn combined. I've had the feeling before and I always compare it to a "heavy heart." Before bed I started to feel like I had a bit of the flu, which has been going around our house, on top of my bladder infection and chest pain. I get chills easily and feel really run down.

This morning I am not so sore abdominally and the flu feeling isn't so bad, but the chest pain is still off and on. I called my mother at work to see about taking a bath to soak my muscles, but she said because I was one finger dilated it would probably be a bad idea. Now I can only distract myself by being online to help ease the pain. Besides all that, I'm still tired and wish I could go to sleep.

My brother decided to get everyone up this morning at 6:30 a.m. for no apparent reason. I fell back asleep about an hour later, but got too warm and woke up. Now I am tired, yet not tired enough to sleep through the chest pain. It's so complicated!

I read the sheet that came with my bladder infection pills which I should have read sooner and it said side effects include nausea, headaches, loss of appetite. And then it mentioned chest pain being something to call the doctor about, but now that it has passed I figure I don't need to worry about it. So at least I know it's the meds messing me up and making me feel like I have flu. It also said on the sheet that the symptoms may go away during treatment. My treatment only lasts a week anyway. So hopefully I'll be feeling better soon.

As of now, chest pains are gone but still feel like I have flu. Very drowsy and achy and my stomach feels sick a lot. Sleeping tonight is going to be another adventure. Tomorrow I'm going with my dad to a movie and then coming home, so at least my day will be broken up and not so boring.

Shawn has been reminding me to drink lots of water (which I have been, even though I feel sometimes I'm forcing myself) and he keeps saying he hopes I feel better. Obviously hearing it from him always sounds so much nicer than anyone, but it's still good to hear from others. I probably should have assumed my pain from the bladder infection wasn't normal; I had it the day before.

I called my mom and the clinic nurse. I told mom about my symptoms now and she's the one who found the sheet that came with the pills and we both read it, so we both are in agreement that's what was causing my flu-like symptoms.

August 4

Today I don't feel as sick, but I did just take a warm shower as that tends to help me feel better. I can't wait to be able to take a hot bath again. I guess I had contractions the other day, but they were mild and with hydration and such getting me back to normal, they went away. It was definitely a bit of a scare because the babies would be quite a bit early, by at least a few weeks. I have to go three more weeks for the doctors to be happy, about five more weeks for them to be really happy.

I've already told Shawn that he can carry the next baby if he wants more. He wants us to one day try for another son. He's happy we're having one of each now, but he still wants to have two boys, why I don't know. I personally am happy with two kids and don't really want more, but I am sure years down the road I may change my mind or maybe he'll change his. Either way, I don't like being pregnant, so I'm not very ready to do it again especially with how compatible Shawn and I are at making twins. It would be sort of funny, but sort of a pain, to try for a son and then end up with twin girls or something.

Time already has gone quickly, I can't believe Shawn will be here tomorrow and it's just a matter of a month or so and I'll be giving birth. Still not sure which route I'm going, but the more I talk with my mom the more I honestly think pushing them out sounds better. I won't lie, part of the reason I didn't want to was for selfish reasons. I don't want to be stretched out "down there" because I still plan on using it! But the other part was because of pain and I thought it may be safer having had at least one relative who almost died giving birth.

My mother has had three C-sections, one for each kid, and only tried pushing with me until I got stuck in her pelvic bones. She said there is definitely a lot of pain and discomfort and scarring with C-sections. She remembers when she did try pushing me out, it wasn't that bad and she tells me that I can handle it. I figure if I have medication I should be okay. But it's still scary!

August 13

My mother called the clinic nurse to ask about my excessive swelling from my thighs down. She just wanted to know if there was anything we can do for the swelling because of how huge I am and the nurse said she'd call back to let us know what the doctor thinks.

About an hour later the nurse called back. By then everyone but me had gone to the mall and my grandma was on her way to sit with me in case something happened. The nurse said that I was to come in for the doctor to look at me and I told her I'd be in when my grandma showed up.

At the doctor's office they got me in right away, asking for a urine sample and weighing me; I'm 199 pounds which is outrageous for me! I was only 176 pounds a couple weeks before the swelling came on. I went to wait in the room for the doctor, having changed into a robe.

He came in and checked me to see if I was dilated, did not tell me one way or the other, and told me that my urine sample had too much protein. He said 1+ they do not worry, but 2+ or above is something to get nervous about and I was a 4+! He told me I needed to go over to the hospital immediately. I asked to use a phone to call my mom but we couldn't get through to her.

My grandpa drove my grandma and me to the hospital and we went in the emergency section as we were told to by the doctor. I gave them my information and then they took me by wheelchair to a room where I changed into yet another robe and got into a bed. They got me set up to check my blood pressure and said it was very high. They told me about Toxemia and Preeclampsia, a disease that's brought on sometimes while pregnant and can only be cured by delivering the babies.

They said I had Preeclampsia and would need to be transferred to a larger hospital in the next town. My grandma kept trying to find my mom until she finally walked in the room where I was. After my mom came in they asked which ambulance service we wanted to use and we just said to go with whoever they use most. It wasn't long and two men came in to move me over to the stretcher. Both were really nice and easy to talk to, but it felt odd being pushed down the halls into the garage where the ambulance was, and then loaded in.

The drive took about an hour and twenty minutes, or at least that's what they said when the nurse riding with me asked, and my blood pressure was still really high the whole time. They hurried me into the building and into a room and switched me over to the hospital bed.

Soon Shawn arrived; my mom had called him right after they asked us which ambulance service to use. He said he took 45 minutes to get there and it's supposed to be an hour and a half drive for him. I told him to stay behind the curtain by the door at first, though, because they were coming back to put in my catheter and I felt awkward peeing in front of him.

After that got situated and I got used to the idea of just "going," he came and stood by me, petting my hair and being all around friendly. It was nice to not be there by myself. A little while later my mom and grandma arrived; they had stopped at home to get clothes because they figured it'd be a long night.

They kept monitoring my output of urine, the babies' movements and heartbeats, and my blood pressure. They gave me an IV and I eventually began having contractions, so they gave me some medication through the IV that immediately made me light-headed. It got to the point where they said one baby wasn't moving as much as they liked and I wasn't outputting enough urine, so they wanted to monitor the baby for half an hour with an ultra-sound machine.

The time went by, with the other baby kicking, but the one causing worry still barely moved at all even though her heart was beating fine. They said they had to talk to a few other doctors, but there's a good chance they'd be coming out. My grandma insisted they'd be out before long and mentioned them having a lot of hair because of me having a lot of heartburn. Grandma is always very sure of herself when it comes to babies.

I ended up getting an epidural. The anesthesiologist was really nice and warned me of holding still so he didn't mess up. As soon as he poked me I flinched, but he said that was normal. Luckily I didn't have any problems from it, it just really drugged me.

It wasn't long after and they came in to say that I needed a C-section. I woke up Shawn, who had still been sleeping on the floor, and asked him if he was coming with me to the operating room or if my mom was. He immediately said my mom can go because he didn't like the idea of me being cut open. My mom was all for it and very willing to hold my hand.

Being wheeled into the room with everyone putting on gloves and masks and me getting moved to a table was all very scary. I was very nervous and felt a bit awkward having them put up the curtain and lift my gown, but I knew they had to.

They used an alcohol wipe on my arm and said they were going to increase the anesthesia and to tell them when it felt cool on my leg like it did on my arm. Finally it got to the point where they could rub it from my thigh up to my lower ribs without me feeling it at all, so that's when it was good enough. They gave me something else to make sure there was no pain, because when they poked me I could still feel it like a needle prick, but it really made me unaware of everything.

I could hear people talk and see things move around, but I didn't feel like I was there. I talked to my mom and the anesthesiologist, but it didn't feel like me talking.

Finally they got one of the babies out and I heard a cry and I looked over but I just saw blurred pink and couldn't comprehend what I was seeing. I threw up a few times and got it on my mom and her hand instead of in the tiny kidney bean-shaped container they held next to my head (that thing's a joke, let me tell you).

Towards the end when they were really pulling, I could sort of feel it. It hurt a bit and I remember whining and my mom even mentioned later about how I must not have had enough drugs because I felt it, but I figured they could only give so much without overdosing, me being a small person, I'm sure that was a concern to them. Also, even though I don't remember what I said to anybody for the whole thing, the one thing I do remember asking is "a boy and a girl, right?" once they were both out. I wanted to be sure we were right the whole time, and we were.

They finished me up, stitching and stapling whatever needed it, and got me put back onto my bed to be wheeled back to my room. The kids were officially out at 6:24 AM.

I was still out of it, but Shawn was there asking how I was feeling. I told him I was drugged a bit yet, but was okay. My grandma insisted on a photo of him and I together and it turned out looking like I was passed out and Shawn was standing over me smiling like an idiot. It was not one of my better moments.

After I thought I was a bit more with it, I called my best friend Andrea and told her the kids were out. I apologized for sounding off and told her about the medication and left it pretty blunt.

It wasn't long and Shawn, my mom, and my grandma were allowed to see the babies. I still couldn't until after 24 hours because I had to stay in bed. I wasn't even allowed to eat or drink anything and the magnesium in the IV made me really warm and really dry in the mouth. They all came back saying the babies have a lot of blonde hair which is Shawn's quality, not mine.

Over the next 24 hours I had to remain in bed. I eventually was allowed to have ice chips and water and Shawn's mom came to visit and see the babies. Finally when 24 hours was up they moved me to another room and I was allowed to try walking and to go to the restroom without the catheter in me. I was wheel-chaired to see the babies and my goodness! So much hair! It was a bit unbelievable seeing children that came from me and letting it sink in that they were mine.

For the next few days Shawn stayed with me, helping me when I needed it and wheeling me if necessary. We went down to see the babies whenever I wanted to and it was overall a decent experience. Once I was allowed to eat, after the first 24 hours, the food wasn't half bad and set with me just fine.

I always felt a bit weird when the nurses asked if I had gas okay, but I didn't lie; that hospital food definitely makes you gassy and I'm glad I was able to release instead of having a problem.

By Saturday Shawn had gone. He had to leave Friday night so he could get up for drill Saturday. I was okay enough to get around on my own, even though I was slow, so it wasn't so bad. I was released in the afternoon when my mom came to get me.

August 19

If my life from this day forward could be anything I wanted it to be I guess my life wouldn't be that extravagant. I'd just want it to include Shawn, the kids, and me living in a house somewhere, not even picky where, happy, both having jobs we enjoy, the kids happy and healthy. That's about it.

Sure, there are little details like "I want a dog" or "I want to lose weight" that I guess are part of life, those little wants, but in general I'd just be happy with us being a family with a life that we can afford.

August 25

Today is my 17th birthday.

Both babies are off of the CPAP and are in incubators. If they're doing well through the weekend they'll be allowed to transfer to the hospital closer to home on Tuesday.

It has and hasn't sunk in that they are actually my children, that I'm actually a mother. I mean, I have pictures, people talk to me about it, and I do talk about "my children." But at the same time, without them being home it's hard to really click with it. So, I realize I'm a mother and they're mine, but the feeling still is weak. It's hard having them away because I can't get a feel for being a mom yet.

Mom doesn't mind being a grandmother. She kids around about being young and such, but overall she's really excited about the kids. My dad was pretty quiet about everything; he likes the kids, but almost wouldn't show that he was happy. Now he goes around saying "I'm a grandpa!" so he's more excited I think.

Shawn's mom pushed for us to give the kids up, now she is very attached and is always offering to help when we need it and even got teary-eyed in their room a few times because they couldn't come home. So she's happy about them, too.

My incision is fabulous. I still have steri-strips on there, none have fallen off, they've just peeled a bit and I trim them as I was told to, but I think it's at the point that if they did fall off it wouldn't matter.

My weight isn't perfect, of course, I still have a tummy that is stretched and a bit swollen and I'm sure some of it is fat, but I lost 27 pounds with the swelling going down from my legs, hands, and a bit from my stomach and of course the kids coming out. Sounds like a lot, but considering I got all the way up to 199 pounds, that's really not that much. My original weight was 137 pounds, so I have a way to go.

As far as having another child some day, I already told Shawn he's not getting any more children out of me. He might want a second son someday, but I am very much afraid of surgery or other things, like the risk of twins again or Preclampsia. He settled for the idea of adopting if possible and affordable.

It wasn't too bad going back to school. It was a bit weird having so many people asking questions, but everyone is really excited and supportive and just plain curious. Nobody is being rude about anything, so it made the transition fairly easy.

August 27

Shawn spent last night at my dad's with me, which was wonderful. I love having him there at night! And we drove to the hospital today. I had to get my blood pressure checked again, it's still high but coming down so I still need meds, and we visited the babies. Both are back on CPAP, so they can't transfer to the closer hospital yet. It's a bit disappointing, but at the same time normal I guess. They keep saying it's not uncommon for them to go back and forth with these things. They said in a few days they'll try again, so maybe next week they'll do better.

Shawn and I are back to some forms of sex, but now are being a lot more careful about regular sex. I am not allowed to do it until after my six week checkup and we won't be able to anyway until a bit after when I get on birth control. I am almost scared to have sex the "normal" way now because I really don't want this to happen again, but hopefully birth control and a condom that has spermicide will do the trick. I don't want to be afraid to have sex, but it might take a bit to get over that whole idea of getting pregnant again.

August 30

My life is crazy and complicated and the only way to stay calm is to take it a day at a time. When the babies are home, my life will change somewhat, I think. I won't be able to go with my dad as much or go out with Shawn a lot, but that's all the going out I do. So I don't feel like I'm losing out on much. Eventually things will settle down and I can go out now and then and by the time I'm in my 30s, the twins will be old enough for me to go out if I want.

We're still planning on getting married when I turn 18. I don't know if Shawn will be returning to college. He wants to take a few classes but may not bother because of prices for school. Now they're telling him he may not even have to do the security job and if he does it'll most likely only be the ninety days. He's looking into a job as a guard, but that's not for sure either. So, he may just end up working a few rinky-dink jobs to afford living here and that's it.

August 31

I got to hold both babies today. My mom, grandma, and I all went to the hospital. I missed school, but picked up my homework. Holding the babies was a bit unbelievable. I mean, I hold them and I know they're mine, yet it's still hard to let that click. I was happy yet panicked at the same time. Hopefully there are no regrets for either of us.

Shawn applied for another job that pays $30,000 a year plus benefits.He also talked about going to Jamaica to get married when I turn 18, but that's not set in stone; I'm not too worried where so long as we get married. We'll see what happens.

September 1

Shawn told me he didn't get the job, but they told him they'd call him if they had other openings.

Yesterday I got blurry vision and then a headache, so I told the nurse right away because with my BP meds they said any change to let people know. She called my mom at work and she got my dad to pick me up and take me to acute care. They said it was just a migraine and that it could've been caused by a peak in my blood pressure, but that's about all they said and sent me home. So, I had one class yesterday.

September 6

Sunday we visited the twins. Taylor is off CPAP and doing great and Tiffany went from a 5 to a 4 on her CPAP, which I honestly don't know what that means, but it's a good thing. Within the next couple days they're going to try and take Tiffany off of CPAP again and if she does good then they can transfer to the hospital closer to home.

Tiffany weighs 3 pounds 8 ounces and Taylor weighs 3 pounds 11 ounces. They both are taking an ounce of milk each feeding and have both tasted 1cc. from a syringe. Taylor can maintain his own body temperature and now wears a sleeper while in his incubator. Tiffany still has to have help with her body temp.

The two biggest things that happened Sunday was Shawn finally held Taylor and I watched Tiffany get a bath. Shawn loved holding Taylor and wouldn't even let me have a turn; he held him the whole hour we were allotted.

Both my mom and Shawn's said that I was to "make" him hold the babies, even if he said no, because men normally don't want to, but Shawn was all for it and even asked about it. It was really a great feeling seeing them together and knowing he was excited about it.

Tiffany didn't get held more than a moment because of her bath; they didn't want her getting cold. At first they made it sound like I was going to help bathe her, which was just wiping her down with a washrag. I was very nervous, considering it has to be done a certain way with them trying to be careful and Tiffany still has so many wires and tubes. But in the end I only watched, I assume so I know for next time. Tiffany was very mad about her bath and screamed bloody murder. I held her as they changed her bedding, but then she was put back right away.

I'm feeling a bit more like a mom, but I still don't feel right calling myself one until they're home and I am taking care of them. I don't know when they can come home, but they have to be off CPAP to transfer to the hospital nearer to me and they need to maintain body temperature and drink from a bottle. I think that's the only real requirements.

I've been told the weight doesn't really matter and if it's another month before they get home, they'll probably be 4 pounds something if not more, so that's not that bad.

Shawn is looking for jobs and everything is up in the air. He admitted to me he doesn't know what he's doing and is having a hard time deciding whether to get a job near his home (maybe go full time in the Army reserve) or try and come here. His mom told him it's easier to get a job if he has one already, so he's trying to get one there before finding one here, but it's still confusing.

Today he's working for his uncle; his mom emailed me to let me know he won't be online because of it. Shawn still wants to take a few classes, but talks more about jobs than school, so I'm not sure how likely school is.

 Shawn's mom is doing okay, I think. She and I get along and she's in love with the twins. Her main concern is a lot like mine, Shawn and a job. She and I had a long talk yesterday about it all.

 Shawn is doing some construction work with his uncle. I guess he's going to do that for a couple weeks and then maybe try and have some other job for a couple more weeks and then worry about moving. It's still up in the air, but at least two weeks are covered.

 He may or may not be coming this weekend to visit me, so I don't know if I'll see the babies or not. It all depends on his work, which I'll know more about tonight. Shawn definitely has the ego thing I think with a job. When he has a job he seems happier and acts like things are more worthwhile instead of thinking he can't do anything. So I'm glad he has something to do for a couple weeks at least because he has a better attitude and is more enjoyable to be around and talk to.

September 12

 This past weekend I had a cold, so I could not visit the babies. My mom and Shawn's mom and step-dad visited throughout the weekend, so they weren't completely alone. Both Tiffany and Taylor are maintaining body temperature on their own and are off of CPAP, so hopefully they can transfer soon! I keep hoping my cold is better so I can visit this weekend if nothing else.

 Today we had to see a play for school and we sat in the rain all day. My main concern was about my cold getting worse and seeing the kids. I used to feel sort of bad, thinking I didn't worry about my babies enough, but today I really did worry about not seeing them for another weekend, so I think it's sinking in slowly but surely. The more I think about it, the more I want them to come home.

 Shawn told me he has a surprise for me, but it won't be for a couple months. He hinted that it's expensive, so I think it's my new ring. I have his mom's old one on a chain around my neck, but he promised to get me a bigger one of my own. As I was saying to Andrea, being 17 and having two kids as well as being engaged is crazy! Not only that, but graduating in a few months and starting college next fall is a weird feeling, too. Life is moving so fast!

September 13

Lately I feel really upset and depressed. I'm easy to make cry and I don't know why. Maybe it's normal after having kids? Maybe it's a hormonal imbalance? I know I don't like feeling like this and I feel bad for Shawn for getting upset so easy.

September 14

I got home from school today at about 4:00 p.m. and checked the answering machine. The hospital called asking for the name of the babies' physicians when they transfer because they are going to transfer them this afternoon or tomorrow! I called them back and told them the two doctors' names, after calling my mom at work to tell her the news and ask for the names. The nurse said she'd pass the word along to who needed it. I don't think they ended up transferring this evening, but they will probably go early in the morning! It's very exciting!

I called Shawn and told him the news and he said he'd come here tomorrow to visit them. Assuming we have time, I hope he can pick me up from school, because I don't have a 4th period class, and we can go visit for about an hour before I need to be home to baby-sit and he needs to leave to go meet with the military guy. Needless to say, it was quite a surprise for today and is very exciting!

September 15

They're here! The babies were moved this morning to the hospital in town. I had to give a phone confirmation right before I left for school, saying it was okay for an ambulance to bring them. They had an operator record it so that it was on record.

Shawn came up today so that we could go together to see them. He held Tiffany, because he hadn't yet, and I held Taylor. Because he was short for time we didn't stay very long, but I ended up going back this evening with my dad and stayed for about an hour and held them both at the same time.

They gave me an odd semi-circle pillow that made me feel like I was in a high-chair while sitting in it. It was really good support though. Taylor lay in my left arm and Tiffany laid flat in front of me on the pillow, so my right hand was free. There was a little fussing now and again when a light was turned on, but no crying, just some sour faces.

When they took the babies away and put them back so that we could go, I felt like all my body heat was taken from me. It was quite comfortable sitting there with them sleeping most of the time. Even after only being there 20 minutes with Shawn and telling my mom about it when she got home, I got emotional. I was saying how they are so cute, now that they don't have so many large tubes and it's all pretty teeny wires now (not that they weren't cute before!), and started to almost cry I was so happy and excited. I think now that they are here that it's all sinking in.

Shawn talked with the military guy this evening and *is* going full-time with the Army but he's not sure which field. The cell phone call wasn't the greatest. He said he'll get to pick where he goes and obviously when we get married I can join him if it's far away, otherwise I don't have to right away.

Today was very eventful!

September 18

I told my mom about feeling upset and depressed and all she said is "it'll pass." It has gotten better recently, though, so she must've been right. I don't have a problem with it much lately.

The babies have to maintain body temp, eat from a bottle, and gain a little weight. So I don't know when they'll be ready to come home; they're doing bits of each every day.

Shawn is now saying he's going to wait on the army until we're married so that it's easier for the kids and me to move with him. And he wants me to ask my mom to sign papers for us sooner. I didn't imagine this a year ago, but I had a feeling. I always thought "what if" and now I know. I'm still too afraid to talk to my mom about a lot of things in this situation, so I don't even try to imagine how she'll react about getting married.

Schooling most likely won't happen. I already told Shawn that I'm starting to rethink it, but I don't want to not go to school and disappoint my dad. Right now, I really just don't know. I do want to do something school-wise, but I'm not sure what.

September 24

Well, they told us that Taylor will come home this week! Tiffany will be about a week or so yet, she's still learning how to eat better out of a bottle and needs monitoring. Taylor is off of all monitors and last night Shawn and I stayed at the hospital to take care of just him so we could be sure we know what we're doing. That was by request of the nurses. The nurse on duty said we did a really good job and I actually felt like it was easy.

We bathed both babies before settling in our room, and because I had helped bathe them earlier this week I knew what I was doing and felt like such a mom. Even when Shawn fed them I found myself telling him all the little things I was told when learning and now feel like such an expert! Hopefully when they get here I still feel that way.

I know that last night I really liked being with Taylor so much and being with Shawn. We were like a family. Shawn loved spending time with the twins, too. I felt a bit bad that Tiffany didn't get to be in our room, but she'll get plenty of love when she gets home and we'll still visit her in the hospital, obviously! Now we're mainly waiting for Taylor to reach 5 pounds. He's only 4 pounds 14.6 ounces as of last night.

Shawn may have an interview at a convenience store tonight or tomorrow. It pays $8 an hour plus benefits, so he can at least get on his own then. Also, Shawn's mom and I have talked online a lot lately and have really bonded, which is nice. My mom and I are starting to squabble a bit here and there again, but it's not as bad as it used to be.

I am getting an IUD within the next month or so, whenever my next menstrual cycle is. It's not going to be very normal, so I don't know when to expect it yet. I guess having it put in then will make it just feel like cramping instead of hurting. My mom has a plastic/hormonal one, but I plan to get the copper one. I don't need the hormones! Shawn and I have gotten back into having sex. We use condoms with spermicide and although they haven't caused problems yet, I won't feel completely at ease until I have my IUD.

September 26

Taylor will be home either today or tomorrow. We're waiting for him to be 5 pounds so he can ride in a car seat. We'll be visiting him and Tiffany sometime this evening, so we'll know more then. Tiffany had a blood transfusion yesterday because her count was low. She still has a hard time remembering to breathe when she eats, but otherwise is in good health.

Shawn and I live about three hours apart. Overall his mood towards the babies is good. He's been in better spirits these days. I think that I will be okay with full-time motherhood. Shawn still says it's okay if I want to be a stay-at-home mom, which I will do if it's affordable. I don't want to go to college quite yet, maybe later when the kids are in school. Babies and school will fill my time up!

We want to be married before I'm 18, but I doubt it'll happen. I plan to move near him whenever I can. I hope to move after graduation but I doubt my mom will allow it so it may not be until I'm 18 and we're married. It's still up in the air.

Shawn got the job. He works from 11 at night to 8 in the morning, Sunday through Thursday. He makes $8 an hour and has benefits, dental, health, and 401K. Now he needs to work on moving into an apartment as he's still living with his mom and step-dad.

I found out this past week that Shawn has slept with a guy before. I knew he had other women, but didn't know about his one time with a guy. That made a bit of tension between us because I couldn't stop thinking about it. I knew he was slightly more than bi-curious (I'm bi-curious). But he reassured me it was only once and he rarely thinks about that stuff. I don't mind that Shawn has done stuff with a guy, it was only once. It's just that he didn't tell me until now. But I think I'm over it and will stop talking about it now because I don't want to keep thinking about it. And not all men go straight for sex and a lot of gay men tend to like cuddling and such (all of them that I know do) and some women like to go straight for sex (I know a few of them, too).

The one thing I do like about Shawn having a bit of that "bi" in him is he does like cuddling, but at the same time likes sex, if that makes sense. In some ways he gives the best of both worlds. A lot of girls want to date a gay man, but can't because they're gay, so I'm lucky to have one that has a bit in him. We love each other, so it's not like I have to worry about him running away, for a guy or a girl. And I know he's not sleeping with anyone else, he wouldn't even consider it. Not while he has me.

September 27

Taylor had a blood transfusion last night, we're supposed to get a call today about it and when he'll come home. They said he wasn't doing badly, but he's "so close" (to coming home?) that they wanted to give him a boost because it helped Tiffany so much.

September 29

Shawn is still getting used to his job and had to work from 9 at night to 8 in the morning yesterday. Poor thing! Whenever I talk to him he sounds tired, but I don't blame him. Hopefully, for his sake, he adjusts soon.

After school, my dad took me to the hospital to feed the babies. When I arrived, Taylor was already fed and I got to feed Tiffany. The nurse that I really don't like was working and made me feel nervous, as usual. Even towards my dad she was a bit witchy.

They wanted me to stick around for CPR, because they wouldn't let my dad teach me even though he's certified, so my dad was going to take me to get food and come back. They said to call at 7:15 p.m. to be sure no other babies came in and then I can come back, learn CPR for infants, feed the babies, and go home.

My dad did errands and came back and called the hospital for me and the lady said they didn't have the dummy there for me to even do it! I was very frustrated because I wasted a lot of time in town when I could've done my homework and now I have to go back sometime tonight and do it.

When I got back to feed the babies the nurse I do like was working, so that helped relieve some stress. For some reason they said I had to feed them while someone watched to be sure I knew how because I guess staying the night with Shawn at the hospital on Saturday wasn't good enough. I did fine with both babies, the nurse said I did a great job, and then I got home around 9:30 p.m. I had to make the decision of taking a shower or staying up to do homework. I went with the shower. Today, the teachers were pretty understanding.

On a lighter note, the babies' doctor was there last night and said Taylor will be coming home tomorrow! He said he'll check him again in the morning and give me a call although the past three days they were supposed to call with information and never have, I had to call them. He also said Tiffany will be home in about a week or so, she's not that far behind. Taylor passed his car seat "stress test" and they are both over 5 pounds.

September 30

Last night we were surprised to find Tiffany unhooked from all monitors. The nurse seemed rushed and handed me Tiffany, asking me to finish feeding her. So, I sat down and took over while my dad sat in a chair nearby. The nurse wandered around, doing her thing, and then came back and asked, "So, are you ready to take them both home tomorrow?" My dad and I looked at her and simultaneously asked, "BOTH?!" She explained that Tiffany has been doing really well recently and is up to speed, so she can come home with Taylor.

I called Shawn and told him that unless they changed their minds, we'd get to take them both. He was very excited. I didn't get to do CPR last night, but they said they can just tell me today when I go to get the babies. That's right. *Today!* Their doctor just called and said that anytime today we can go and get them. He explained that Tiffany has improved tremendously, and said they'll still need NeoSure formula because it has 22 calories instead of 20, plus they'll still need iron drops. Other than that, it's like bringing home normal babies. I mean, we still will have to watch them, but I feel a lot more comfortable about them now. So, I'm just waiting for my mom to get home so we can go and get them and learn CPR. I'm surprised that I don't feel overwhelmed. And I actually have time to get online.

October 1

We're all home, at my mom's, the babies and me. I had to do a round of changing, feeding, putting them down all by myself with my brother and sister holding the bottle for me while burping and actually managed. It's early to say much, but I think we'll be fine.

Last night wasn't too bad, but I did think I'd get more help from my mom. I'm sure during the school week she'll help more. Time flies in between feedings because by the time you get them both done there goes an hour. My grandma and Shawn are staying tonight to help out, so I should get some sleep.

October 2

Well, last night was still tiring. Even though Shawn fed the babies and changed them all but one time, Tiffany was fussing, so he asked me to feed Taylor so he could tend to Tiffany. I still woke up about every time he came in or the babies fussed. But overall I guess I slept better than the other night although I did take a nap for about an hour at school 4th period because I don't have a class, just can't come home because I don't have a car yet.

Shawn lay by me a few times during the night, but didn't stay long each time because he's still trying to be in the swing of sleeping during the day, being up at night. This morning at about 5:00 he lay down and slept next to me for about an hour and a half, though.

Between my grandma and my step-dad I think I'm going to go crazy. My grandma tells the same stories over and over and she likes to revert to the way she did things "back in the day" instead of doing things the way I'd like. I often find her, along with everyone else, not respecting what I want with the babies and moving them here or there and showing them to everyone. It's really annoying.

Not only that, but my grandma for one keeps asking me about my every move: "Who are you calling?" "What's that on your computer?" Also, Grandma was complaining today to my step-dad, who is home due to dental surgery, about one of my game consoles that was making a little bit of noise so Robert (step-dad) turned it off. I came home and turned it on and asked grandma if she did it and she said no and asked

Robert and he said he did because grandma complained about it. I told him not to do it again and he said it was noisy and he might make it "disappear" if it stays on and I said he can't do that, but of course he said he could. So I sadly turned it back off and turned off the baby monitor in my room so I could sit and cry for a moment.

Now I'm welling up again and the fact these people are driving me insane. I can't wait for Grandma to *get out* for a while and maybe have us find someone else to watch the kids.

It's getting harder and harder to not have a "tone" when talking to them. My mother is going to the clinic after she gets off work because her chest hurts, so who knows with that.

The babies are doing good over all, but I still worry about them being home with my grandma. I worried about that a lot today and tried my hardest to get home a little sooner (talked my ride into it) so that I could be sure they were okay. I think I'm more stressed out from everyone else than I am from the babies! I hate that Shawn left, he was my little bit of sanity.

October 3

Journaling seems to help because now I feel a little bit better, at least towards my step-dad. My mom was getting annoyed with my grandma, too, so I guess I wasn't alone.

Both babies are gaining weight; there was an in-home check while I was at school. Mom said Tiffany is 5 pounds 10.6 ounces and Taylor is 5 pounds 13 ounces. That's a lot more than they were when they left the hospital. I consider gaining an ounce a lot.

I don't think the babies are all that challenging, although the strict schedule sort of sucks, but that'll improve. They're allowed to eat more now if they want and I think that's a good sign of things.

Some people I can definitely see thinking I should be "all grown up" now, and give up the game stuff and things I enjoy, but I hate to tell them, I'm always gonna be a "big kid," just like my dad is. Shawn will be, too. I see nothing wrong with that. But I do understand I have to mature with some things, it's just the way of life.

October 4

Looking back, knowing what I know now, I wouldn't have done anything different. I wouldn't have wanted the babies to go away; I wouldn't have wanted adoption or abortion as an option. I like having them, even though it's going to be a lot of work especially once I'm on my own with Shawn, but I still wouldn't change it. I do love the little things. School's good, I have all A's as far as I know except for civics, which is a C. It's a college class, but the way it's set up I basically can't fail. So that's reassuring.

October 7

Both babies are gaining nicely and I like that we can let them go until they want to eat instead of feeding on a schedule, although they both got up a few times last night.

My weight is okay. I still have some I need to lose and my belly and thighs are still stretched, darn marks on my legs from the swelling like a balloon. It's coming slowly but surely. In a few months I should be fairly normal, assuming I work at it.

October 10

If I wasn't living at home I'd live with Shawn unless he didn't have a place of his own, then it'd be with his mom and step-dad. They've already offered for me to go there and it looks more tempting as time goes on. It would just be me and the babies. I don't think they're hard to handle, only at night when I'm dead tired. His mom would still help where she could.

Shawn and I are fine, the babies are fine, but my mom and grandma still drive me up the wall. Getting up at night is really hard. I can't seem to wake up and often fall asleep during feedings and my mom either won't help at night or if she does, she complains about it because she can't sleep. I'm very tempted to ask her, "And what if you would've adopted them?"

Shawn and I had a miscommunication yesterday. He was "flirting" online on the same site we met on, with other guys with his second account. He said it was just for fun, and because I never let him be the "cute one." So he thought I wouldn't allow him to be the "immature" one in the relationship sometimes and turned elsewhere, but I think we worked it out. I never piped up and said I'd like him to switch roles with me now and again.

October 12

Well, yesterday my mom actually made my grandmother cry. I thought she only did that to me. My grandma wanted a friend to come visit because it gets boring sometimes sitting at my house all day with the babies, I understand that, and my mom freaked. I was in the other room watching a movie because the babies were just fed and grandma came in bawling her eyes out. She sat on my sister's bed (I was in her room, she has a DVD player and I have no TV) and I hugged her and she explained that my mom was mad about germs, although she has her friends in the house and my siblings' friends. I didn't understand.

Now my grandma and mom aren't talking and my step-dad is really pissy this morning. Grandma was going to just leave now, but stayed for my sake. I am asking the guidance office today about doing schoolwork at home and that way grandma won't have to do it anymore because even if she doesn't leave, mom will find someone else and I don't trust that. Things are just hectic!

October 13

Grandma, Mom, Robert, and I were going to "conference" last night, but it never happened. I hope to talk to my mom tonight more. My grandma said she's going to pretend nothing happened until after she's not needed so that things are smoother for me. I talked to the counselor yesterday and she is asking the principal about me doing my work at home so I can be a full-time mommy.

Shawn was telling me about some drunk guy who came into the store with a gun and was arrested. There was more to the story but a baby is crying and my mind has gone blank.

October 14

I talked to my mom last night. They're trying to work it at school so I can study at home and still graduate at the end of this semester.

My mom also told me that after I graduate I'm free to move with Shawn, which Shawn was very excited about. I'm a bit worried about Shawn's job now, but he needs work and money so not much can be done.

October 23

Things at home are so-so. It varies a lot. Sometimes we all get along; sometimes people are annoyed with each other. I have heard my mom and grandma tell me about the other and how they hope I can do school at home. I get annoyed with both at times as well and really hope it all works out for home at school, too. School is okay. I fall asleep in class sometimes, depends on my night before.

I am adjusted to the babies during the day, but at night it's still hard. Last night I went to bed at 7:30 and was up at 8:00, 8:15 (they both whined), 12:30, 1:00, 2:00, 4:00, 5:00, and 6:15. It was a constant awakening. Good thing my grandma took them towards this morning and the 8-ish ones last night my mom held them so I could go to bed. When Grandma's not here, then it's mainly all me. My mom whines a lot about helping out and only does if she really has to but then complains if I'm feeding one and the other's crying for food. I don't ask her for help because there's not much more I can do, let one wait or ask my mom. At night is the hardest part and I fall asleep in class sometimes.

I think my mom and I are getting along better again, though, and if the school thing works out I will have more rest time, so I won't be so edgy.

I plan to move to Shawn's apartment, assuming he gets it, in January and stay home with the kids. The counselor at school gave me an application that could get me a free ride to school, free daycare, and help me get a job after school. If that works out then I'll do that, so long as it's free.

Shawn still is going to stay at his job. I asked him last night if he plans to try and move up positions and he wants to try for management there, so we'll see what happens. He hasn't mentioned military any more and said he doesn't plan to re-up after his term in the reserve, so I assume that's no longer a plan for him. So far he's content where he is.

We are getting along really well, actually. This past weekend I went to see him and took the twins. Shawn's mom picked me up and drove us there. She watched the twins all weekend so he and I had "us time." She told us to get a hotel room Friday night, so we did, and we had a lot of fun.

Saturday we looked at a couple apartments that are a few blocks from his mom's house and he's getting one of them. I even got to sign the paper because I'm moving in with him in a few months, and it's really nice. It's a corner apartment, so it's a little bigger and it allows my two cats. I can do laundry at Nora's house and we can eat with them sometimes, too.

Also on Saturday, Shawn had me pick out my engagement ring and wedding ring; they came in a bridal set. It'll cost him $800 in payments, but it's really pretty. He is picking it up today and I'll get it Friday when he's up to visit again.

Shawn said that he wants me to know we'll fight more living together and that he loves me, he wants to tell me that now before we start fighting. I think we're okay.

The guidance counselor now refuses to ask the principal about me doing school at home unless I have no other daycare, so we can't have it set up ahead of time. My mom is going to call the principal.

October 24

I talked to my mom about me moving in with Shawn in a few months and she's all for it. Shawn and I are very comfortable with each other – I mean, when we had our hotel room Friday we were pretty much naked the entire time, even though we didn't fool around the whole time, that'd be tiring. I am very self-conscious but was still okay with that. I know it's not the same as living together, just saying we're comfortable with each other so hopefully things will be okay.

The twins got their RSV shots today. They would've about a week ago, but the names on the papers were wrong, so they had to reschedule. They had my last name instead of Shawn's. The babies cried, of course, but are okay now, sleeping after having their bottles.

My mom called the principal and he's supposed to call us back.

October 26

It's set up so I don't have to go to school on "B" days, so I only go every other day. I still have to do my reading class homework and go in during my free period on "A" days to do any tests. That way grandma only has to be here maybe 10 more times between now and when I move. I'm very glad because she's really annoying me these days.

Two of my friends stopped by today and saw the babies. My grandma was all in a hurry to go home, but knew my mom wanted her here while my friends were since she's never met them before. Grandma was impatient and kept saying she had to get going, "Robert will be home soon" even though he wouldn't be home for another half an hour. And last night when she was supposed to be helpful she was almost impossible to wake up and kept saying, "I'm so tired and exhausted" whenever she did get up for the two feedings between 3:30 and 5:30 this morning.

I'll be glad when I can move! I filled out an application I need to mail yet for some financial assistance for schooling and daycare. If I get it I can get free school, daycare, and they'll set me up with a job after I graduate. I really don't want to go to school, free or not, but my dad and mom are now saying I should, if it's all free. I guess I'll mail it and see.

October 27

I have to wait until I'm 18 to get married but Shawn is thinking maybe the month after I turn 18 next year. As far as the babies, I do like them. I'll admit, in the middle of the night when they wake me up I find myself chanting in my head, "Shut up, shut up, shut up!" But that's because interrupted sleep isn't very pleasant. During the day they're cake to take care of and I like to watch TV with them, hold them in my lap as they watch the colors on the screen. I am anxious for them to get up and about so I can play with them.

I'll do the schooling if it's free. I'd continue to get child support from my dad from ages 18 to 21 if I'm in school. We'll see what they say about my application.

October 30

Is it January yet? My mom decided to watch the twins for me yesterday so I could go with my dad. She said that hopefully with me leaving early then I could be back by supper time. I went with dad, ate lunch, saw the movie *Final Destination 2*, visited my great-grandma in the nursing home, and then went to my dad's to visit my cats. I was home at 5:30, mom was finishing up supper, and she was throwing a fit. She said I "should've been home hours ago." She didn't make me any supper. She said, "I assume you ate with your dad." I told her, "No, I had lunch before the movie, but no supper." So I ended up going without supper last night because I had to tend to a baby and then both were fussing all evening until bed.

I talked to Shawn and I'm a bit concerned that after I move in with him he's going to tell my mom to shove it. But to be honest, I have no problem with the twins not knowing who she is. Considering my mom makes it sound like such a big deal to do anything with the twins, she sure as hell doesn't need to see them once we're out of here. I mean, at night even when she doesn't have to work the next day, the only time she gets up and "helps" is when she comes in to make sure my butt is out of bed because sometimes I just don't wake up. Then she goes back to her own bed and that's about it. Back while I was still pregnant, right after finding out about twins, she said that Robert would take certain feedings and she'd take one and then I'd only have the early morning one. Ha!

Besides that, she supposedly saved a receipt or two from things bought for the babies that I guess I'm to pay back later. Considering my income is nonexistent, it'll be Shawn's income, and she won't be seeing that. When mom's in a good mood, the world is great and she's really a nice person. But as soon as one thing goes "wrong" in her mind or she isn't getting what she wants, then everyone else is inferior.

Shawn didn't hear from the lady about his apartment, so we assume that means he can move in Wednesday. He's going to call today to be sure, though.

On a happier note, I don't have school today and broke down and got *Animal Crossing* again and added another piece to my collection of

Tamagotchis. And I have a friend that might be giving me some of his Nintendo and PS2 games because he doesn't have time for them.

October 31

When I move in with Shawn, his mom will help some. She said we can eat supper at her apartment if we want sometimes and I can do laundry there so we don't have to pay for it. Otherwise it's mainly us.

Dad said he'll still give me a bit of money and if I go to school I'll still get child support until I'm 18. I am sending in that application for free school/daycare, so hopefully that'll pull through and I can go to school. The counselor says it's highly likely I'll get it, I'm very qualified.

I have really thought about my days there with the kids and Shawn and I really don't see it being that bad. I mean, I don't expect it to be cake or anything, but I do see having time for some fun things sometimes.

It's not like Shawn is never there and Nora offered to take the kids a few hours once a week and all night once a month so Shawn and I have "us" time, but I'm sure we'll find time here and there when the kids nap.

All in all, it's manageable. Not as comfy of a life style as now, but manageable. I used to be such a pessimist and I really don't want to revert back to that. I try to be optimistic and really do think it will be just fine.

My mom is in a better mood today, which is good. The twins are in bed right now. Taylor still has been fussy a lot in the evenings, so hopefully that "phase" of his quits soon. Last night sort of sucked because mom was grouchy at 1:30 when I asked her to feed Taylor. I already had fed Tiffany, but I think it was the lack of sleep talking.

The thing that ticked me off, though, is I asked her to finish feeding Taylor for me so I could take a shower before bed and she refused. I don't know, she was being herself last night and then is all different today. She sometimes says she thinks Shawn's mom is manic depressive, but I think my mom is.

November 1

Things have just been hectic here, mainly with my mother. During the night I hate getting up, but its morning now and I just think, "I survived the night, I'm okay," and move on. Last night my mom said she can't wait to start playing grandma instead of the mom role. And she does pretty much nothing but watch the twins when I go to school, only because she has to.

I can definitely see Shawn wanting to play in the free time and not do work, but I'll crack the whip. I'm not saying I'm great with chores (bit domestically challenged, honestly), but Shawn knows how to do everything and I can learn in a hurry and take over. I hope anyway.

November 2

Last night through this afternoon was very emotional. I tried to talk to my mother last night, but it turned into an argument/fight and her again saying she's the "mother," but branched further into her saying I'm just the "babysitter." Ouch. I talked to both my dad and Shawn and neither had much more advice then "hang in there."

I though about a lot last night and this morning I went to school and got no further then into the gym for P.E. and asked to go to the guidance office to talk to the counselor. I told her about my mother and sobbed quite a bit. I explained how I feel I can't deal with her and I am tired of having breakdowns and crying since the past three nights that's how it's been.

One thing led to another and she asked me if I was happy with my decision to keep the babies. I said I wasn't sure and honestly didn't feel attached as I think I should and still have feelings that I don't want kids. I told her that if I could go back and give them away I probably would and would now, but feel guilty because of my family, Shawn, and his family.

She let me call my dad in and the nurse and the "legal expert" at school came in as well and we all conferred. I was pretty sure in my mind that I didn't want kids and by the end of that conversation with everyone they said it's my decision, one way or another, and I'm not a bad person if that's true. And I am very sure, especially after all that,

that I don't want them. I am just not into them as I should be and don't want them to be "neglected" due to me being uninterested. Whenever I think about the future, I think "Shawn and me," not all of us. I just can't seem to think about all of us and be happy.

I called Shawn and told him that I don't want the babies. He actually said he supports me one hundred percent. He said he loves them, he wants me to know that, but for all of our sakes it'd be nicer for them and us if they were with someone else. I told him to think about it more to be sure, but I think that's the route we're heading.

I didn't want to tell people my feelings before because I don't want people mad. But I'm so unhappy not saying anything it's insane; heck, I'm going insane. Shawn made me feel better by supporting me and even asked if I still was going to move in with him and was glad that I was still planning to.

So, at this point it could still change, but there's a good chance that they are going to an adoptive home after all. My mom and Shawn's will not know until we are more set on the decision.

November 3

I just emailed Nora. I figure she'd be easier than my mom and I'm going to have a mediator when I talk to mine, hopefully it'll be the school counselor. Mom is all about "image" and won't freak as much if someone else is there. I do think this is best and I understand the family and cancelling thing, we already did that once and I am kicking myself for it. I am very set in this and do plan to follow through, even if people get mad at me. Shawn supports me and so does my dad, that's huge because they are the two most important people to me. I'm getting a bit teary eyed right now, so I don't have much more to say.

I still think I want my mom to adopt the babies. I saw my step-dad today talking to Taylor and he really seems to like them, but does little with them because they're not his. I think he'd really be a nice figure in their lives if that worked out.

Well, I just got an email from Nora. She thinks it would be a bad idea for my mom to adopt the twins, that she'd throw the whole thing in my face all the time. Nora says the couple who were going to adopt before, might still be interested, and she and Shawn's step-dad also might take them. So, that's a relief! And she says she's not mad at me and is very impressed that I'm willing to admit my feelings and do something about it.

Now I have to tell my mom although it might be a few days before I do.

November 4

Nora is picking the twins up tomorrow night. She's having Shawn and I sign papers giving her temporary custody which may turn into permanent custody. If Nora kept them, she'd be more willing to let my mom see them than if my mom kept them and Nora wanted to see them.

My mom won't know until Tuesday when we're around a counselor. That way it's more "safe." My dad will be there and Nora might make Shawn come up, too.

IUD getting put in Tuesday, looking forward to that.

November 5

Some people may find it a mistake, but I am very set in my decision. Nora just picked the twins up about half an hour ago. I will probably make sure my game stuff, *Tamagotchis,* and any other expensive items of mine are secure before Tuesday. Maybe take them with me when my dad picks me up.

As far as my mom, I am sure things won't be the same between us, but considering we've never really gotten along except for when she's "in the mood," I don't see how it'll be worse. It was my choice to birth them and at first I wanted to keep them because they were with Shawn, they were part of him. I wanted it for him. Then I didn't want to, because I still feel I'm not into kids and have little interest in raising them. And I feel as if I was talked into keeping them. I gave it a shot, it's not for me. I don't have attachment and don't want to spend that extra time with them that they need.

I know what it's like to be neglected, as in only getting food and a bed, but then not getting the attention and love. And they need better than that. Considering my mom has treated me like crap and different than my half-siblings all these years, I don't want that to happen to the twins and I know Nora would treat them right. When they're old enough to know and to ask, I'll worry about them then and I have no reason to lie to them. I'm not going to be mean and say "I just didn't want you," because it's really more complicated than that, but at the same time I guess that's the reason, if that makes sense.

This week will unfold as it's supposed it, I can't control it. And I'm not going to go against my feelings and my gut anymore to make everyone else happy because I'm tired of being miserable and breaking down all the time. Shawn loves me, everyone, except my mom who does not know, supports me, so I feel okay.

November 6

I don't doubt that my mom will freak and be mad. I think I'm going to box up my "valuables" and take them with me. I hope to stay with my dad if things go bad. My dad is supportive and says he understands where I'm coming from. He says he knows my mom will get upset, but will be there when I tell her.

The apartment is still a go, Shawn has a roommate for right now which may become permanent; I have to meet him first. He supports me one hundred percent and may make a trip for this meeting tomorrow, too. I set the meeting up for 8:30 in the morning; we'll see how it goes. My mom isn't home for me to tell her about it yet.

November 7

The meeting is over and my mom was quite calm. I mean, not saying she wasn't mad at all, but she didn't yell and still hasn't really. Basically I think my mom and step-dad are going to adopt the twins. Not sure, we still have to discuss it further, but that's how it looks. I also might have to live with my dad for a few months until I go to Shawn's place. We'll see.

She isn't "throwing me out," but might. She will still let Nora see them, but is unsure what to tell the twins that Nora is to them, and said Shawn and I will have limited contact with them, which I understand. She also gave me a spiel on how Shawn didn't try hard enough to be involved and how we're not going to make it more than a year together, etc. I was very worried and she did have a look like she was going to blow and some of her comments maybe weren't that nice about me, but she didn't yell and considering it was probably shocking, I can deal with that. I feel a lot better getting it out there and feel better that nobody really yelled or anything. I might still get "kicked out" but it won't be the whole stuff-on-the-lawn thing. So that's nice.

Shawn picked up my rings. I get the engagement ring on Friday because he's coming up here, staying while I baby-sit my siblings, then we're going down there for the weekend.

I got my IUD put in and still feeling a little crampy. It wasn't that bad. I just feel really relieved. Nora said she'd keep the twins as long as needed for us to figure this all out, so they're still there at least for a little bit. My grandma called and asked if she's babysitting a certain day and I told her I was unsure and I'd explain when our household knew.

November 8

Mom and Robert won't be adopting. My mom said they can't handle it and he is getting "up there" so it won't work. Now we're just trying to find a "who."

November 9

Our neighbor, Carissa, was considering adopting, but after I talked to her she backed away. Shawn and I would rather the people be ones that cannot have kids. We figure we can make them very happy and considering they want it so bad, they'll put all the effort into it they can. Carissa was passing word on to a couple that has already done foster care and tried for three kids, but the parents backed out. Obviously they'll take two if they tried for three. We're trying to find people that have the background stuff taken care of so it goes fairly quick.

My aunt passed the word along where she lives; there are a lot of doctors and lawyers up in her area trying to adopt kids from Korea and other countries because it's so hard to get them here.

I talked to Shawn last night on the phone until about 10:30 p.m. Right after we got off the phone it rang again and it was a couple who heard about the babies. I thought, "Wow, that was fast!" because we just sent the word out a few hours earlier. They said they were sorry to call so late, but they wanted to get to me before others did. I guess the "grapevine" was my aunt who told her friend that adopted that told their friend that adopted who told these people. They sounded really nice and I don't want to just settle on them, but I do think that they "earn points" for calling so quickly. We'll see what happens. I feel great. I'm feeling really good that I can help these people and "fix my mistake" so to speak. They sounded so excited.

As far as things between my mom and me, now things are cooled down, she's being civil. I don't want to say we get along perfectly, but it's much better. Shawn's mom is a bit flustered with him, but she's helping work through this. I told the first couple that someone else is interested, but they're not ruled out. And I asked how open of an adoption they will have. It will go through lawyers as far as I know; independent adoption is what it's called. I will make the decision. Shawn and I, that is.

November 10

Today, Nora is bringing the twins because she doesn't trust Shawn driving with them in bad weather. It's raining here right now and I guess snowing there. Shawn will be coming tonight to take me up there and tomorrow I am at least meeting the first family who called the other night and maybe another family from where Shawn lives.

Depending on if another couple gets hold of me or not, I might meet them sooner or later, too. The first couple said that if we signed papers today, they could take the twins as early as next week, for example, which my mom and I think is a very good thing. Nobody else has called yet.

Shawn doesn't work tonight, so he and I get some "time together." I'll be staying at his apartment all weekend and get to meet his roommate and decide if I like him enough for him to stay or not. Because of the weather, Nora is bringing the twins home tomorrow.

I'm not sure if the babies will stay with mom until someone adopts them or not. We hope to have this all straightened out by the time I go to live with Shawn. Nora is talking about taking them for stretches in there I guess, so we're still sorting it out.

Nora mentioned lending Shawn and me some cash to go to Florida and get married because we legally can there. How serious she was, I'm not sure. I did some online searches and read information over the phone to Shawn. He said his mom was serious. So I don't know.

November 13

Well, after meeting with the first couple I think they're very nice people, better in person than on the phone and online. They brought scrap books to show us their family and they treated us to pizza. A lot more people called, though. I guess Shawn and I are now going to sign over rights to my mom and Nora so that they can do the process of picking and then Shawn and I will meet the "final choice" and have a say as to if they are really the right people or not.

November 14

From what I'm told, Nora and my mom are going to be going through an agency; they're just picking which one is right. That way they know what questions to ask, etc. I just want to know who the final choice is, but I personally don't feel the need to be very "hands on." Especially with Nora helping pick a family, I think a good choice will be made. My understanding is Shawn wants people sort of like him, whom he won't find, unfortunately, but otherwise he's pretty much the same as me.

I haven't had any second thoughts. I find myself thinking more and more "are they gone yet?" My mom's friend watched them yesterday because my grandma and I aren't talking, and neither are my mom and grandma. My grandma was going to file "neglect" so the babies were taken away instead of adopted out, but that wouldn't solve anything.

The friend told me when she had her first baby she felt the same as me and pretty much resented the baby for having to take care of it which made me feel a little more normal. She said her biggest mistake was letting her mom adopt the baby instead of finding a family, so I'm glad that my mom and step-dad turned it down. I could see them holding it over me just as mom's friend's mom did to her.

We have a lot of people interested in the twins, so it will probably be a tough decision. My dad hopes that they go to a local family, of course. He's been sick for about a week now and he's losing his voice because he couldn't really talk last night and has been really edgy. I hope he's okay.

My mom and I are getting along okay. When I first got home from my weekend away she was pissed that she had to take care of the twins Saturday night, but now she's cooled off again. She said she might not let me go up to Shawn's, though, until the baby thing is sorted or maybe not even until I move. So I guess we'll see. She almost took my Internet away when I got home because she was so mad, but then she let that thought go.

I got "screened" for postpartum depression today; I don't have it. I think things will go fairly quick, sounds that way. I am hoping everything is good living with Shawn. Staying there this past weekend was different because we were "on our own." It'll take adjusting, for sure.

November 17

It's quarter after five in the morning. And last night sucked. I told Shawn I didn't like the roommate, which led to a big fight. Shawn seemed mad from the start, but claimed he wasn't mad before we talked. I ended up calling Nora and she said to compromise.

I don't like that Shawn's roommate smokes pot and cigarettes, so Shawn and I agreed that if Mark, the roommate, can go without smoking anything in the apartment, not keep drugs in the apartment, and only smoke cigs on the deck then he could stay. Shawn didn't want to tell Mark so I messaged him on *MySpace*. Towards the end of the conversation, which was on MSN Messenger, I asked Shawn if he was still mad and he said "slightly." I asked why and it didn't go anywhere that made sense. I got frustrated because I had to feed Tiffany, who was crying upstairs.

I ended up calling Shawn on the phone after both babies were bathed and fed and we talked. He told me that saying "I love you" didn't have meaning to him anymore, it felt like saying "hello." He said that the last time he tried leaving me when I was a few months pregnant. He kept saying he thought I'd be better without him and I explained I wouldn't be better without him because I love him and he said he loved me too and stayed. He said that time he felt "guilted" into staying.

I don't understand that because he was going to have me live with him and let me pick out my engagement ring/bridal set. I'm wearing the ring now, haven't taken it off since the fight. I can't. He said he wasn't sure if he loved me or sure he wanted to be together. He said we should "slow down" and just be a couple, boyfriend and girlfriend. That's what started this, he mentioned the couple part and I asked why such a drastic change. Going from "I want to be with you forever" to "let's just be a couple."

He said both of our lives would be easier if we end the "drama" now and he wanted a normal life which will be hard to get no matter what. Starting out, single or with someone, is always a challenge. He didn't want things to be complicated. He said I'd be better without him and I again tried to tell him I love him and know I wouldn't be.

He claims I'm a "different person" with him, one that just does things to make him happy. He thinks I make myself unhappy a lot to make him happy. I tried to tell him I'm happy when I make him happy, it doesn't bother me at all. Long story short he told me to tell my mom she was right (she said Shawn would leave me) and hung up. I called Nora again, desperate, and she said she'd talk to him and to just breathe.

Shawn ended up calling me back because Nora told him to and he asked me why I had to bring his mom into it. I explained I didn't know where else to turn when he hung up. Then I said I'd just talk to him tomorrow because nothing I would say could change things at this point, no sense going through it again. But I did ask if we'll still be friends and he said of course, but then I cried harder and said it'd hurt and he told me it's up to me. I called Nora back and explained that last little bit to her and she said all he told her over and over is "She'll be better off without me."

Shawn's dad is bipolar. Shawn himself always felt he needed to be tested, so Nora is setting up an appointment possibly today for him. We think maybe that has a lot to do with it considering he went from "BE WITH ME!" to a bunch of excuses and dumping me. So, we're split up as of now. Whether it'll stay that way or not, I don't know.

I know my name is on that lease for the apartment and I still plan to live there while going to college, so we'll see. Nora said not to think of what he might really mean by all this, but she said she'd talk to him again today. I'm not sure what to think. Shawn said that he's the "nice guy" and didn't want to hear me cry, so he didn't do this sooner. It still sounds like cold feet and a lot of excuses.

All I know is I love him and my life is meaningless without him. I don't care about college, I'm going for a good job and to make dad happy, but I'd be perfectly fine doing what Shawn does, work at a convenience store and live in an apartment. I don't really want much out of life, just to be with Shawn. And that's the honest truth.

November 18

Well, surprisingly as quickly as that happened, it's fixed. It was all an issue about smoking, cigarettes and pot. I told him I don't mind it. I can deal with it later, I can handle it now. So he's good. I love him, cigs and all. And honestly, I'm curious about pot, not smoking, in a brownie. I don't know, we'll see. I was surprised at how quick it was, too, and now I just laugh because it was so dramatic over almost nothing. I knew he was just making excuses. I honestly like the idea of pot more than cigarettes, just don't like that it's an illegal drug. But I'd rather try it before I knock it. I expect more hurdles and drama as time goes on. But I obviously don't look forward to it!

November 19

Nora met with a lady looking to adopt who has a 7-year-old. Nora said she's great, but not as great as the other two families we have in mind. Plus, she already has a daughter.

I talked to my mom yesterday about moving in with my dad after this week when the babies leave. She and my step-dad agreed I could. I still have to talk to my dad more about it, though.

The babies are leaving Wednesday after their RSV shot. Eugene, Nora's husband, Shawn's step-dad, is coming to get them. They're staying with Nora for a while until an adoptive couple is found. This weekend I'm meeting the two prospects.

My mom and I don't get along well and I really get stressed out because of it. I'm at my "breaking point" and so I do feel I'd rather be with dad for a couple months. I had given my mom the address for Shawn's and my apartment, she hung it on the fridge, but I took it down and tossed it out.

I really don't want to see my mother any more after I'm gone. She has her good days, then she's fine, but one thing goes wrong and everyone suffers. She's unreasonable, thinks she's always right, and says things and makes promises and changes things later, claiming she never said it in the first place. On top of all that, she has no sense of humor and can't sense sarcasm worth a dime. I have no idea how the child support thing works. All I know is that mom is making me sign a paper saying I'm leaving of my own free will, which I am, so I don't get it.

The roommate will be staying. Other than him and Shawn smoking, they're good. Mark does not drink and Shawn rarely does. The apartment has two bedrooms, one for Shawn and me and one for Mark. Mark is really cool about everything and I talked to him a bit about the whole Shawn and I sleeping together thing. He knows it'll happen and he said he's okay and comfortable with all that stuff, so long as it's not like a circus in the other room. He understands things pretty well and is very respectful, so in turn Shawn and I are to him. It's funny because he has tattoos and reminds me of some white rapper looking guy who smokes cigs and weed, but he's really a good guy. I didn't believe Shawn when he first told me that, but now I do. Other than smoking, I don't know of any conflicts.

The apartment is two bedrooms, one bathroom, and a combined area that is living room and tiled kitchen. It's not huge, but it's decent. We have a corner apartment, so it has 50 square feet more than the other apartments. Mark is a cook at a fast food restaurant so I kid with him that he'll be cooking. Obviously we won't have any extravagant meals, so I'm sure everything we eat I could make myself. Basically, if you're hungry, make something.

What Mark has in his room is up to him, whether he keeps it organized or not. In Shawn's and my room I'll keep it organized and be sure the rest of the apartment is as well. It won't be perfect, but I don't like the idea of mixing peoples' things together into a big mess. Being an only child for a while gave me a sort of OCD about people touching my stuff, so I'll be cleaning. Shawn has been handling the bills, but whenever I get a job it'll obviously help pay for things and Mark pays his share, too.

Considering I'm the only girl, the bathroom shouldn't be a huge problem. Shawn doesn't take much time to do anything. Being bi he worries about dressing nice and all, but bathroom time isn't that long for him. Mark I'll have to figure out as time goes on, he wasn't around much when I stayed there last weekend. Not enough to tell how long he takes, anyway.

As far as Shawn being bi and having a male roommate, the roommate is very straight. And, I think of it in the simple sense that Shawn wouldn't cheat on me, man, woman, or otherwise. And he leans more toward women, I think, anyway. I make him happy, that's what matters. It's more a question of loyalty, not orientation. And Shawn is a very loyal fiancé.

November 22

Well, things are very back and forth with this moving out deal. Last night my mom told me that my step-dad talked to their lawyer and I was not able to move out *before age 18!* So I would've been here for even longer than originally planned. This morning my mother told me there's one loophole, if I want out that bad. And this way I can live with my dad a couple months and then move in with Shawn. She said she'll sign papers for Shawn and me to be married and then I'm his responsibility. She didn't want to sign me over to my dad and pay child support, which my dad wouldn't care if she didn't for two months, and she didn't want to just let me live with my dad because I'm her responsibility and in case I got in trouble it comes back to her, because I'm such a hooligan.

So, I told my dad, who I still will talk more with tomorrow, and I told Nora this morning on the phone. Nora said it sounds good, but just in case she'll look for other loopholes. I have yet to talk to Shawn, he's been sick and I think is sleeping. I'm not sure if Shawn will want to be married this soon or not, because of what he said the other day. I know I'm ready. I mean, it'll take work and all, but I know we can do it and am willing to put forth the effort. So I guess I'll see what he says.

I talked to Shawn. After a long conversation, he is willing to sign papers and begin a life together. Only thing concerning him is our roommate. Shawn was told we can't have multiple families living in the apartment, so Mark will most likely have to move out one way or another. Shawn has yet to talk to the landlady about it, she was unavailable today. I'm very excited about this, though! Unfortunately, I can't officially leave mom's house until its all "said and done." Papers have to be signed by everyone. I hope to get the papers for Friday when I see Shawn again!

November 25

Before I go on about the meetings with the two adoptive families, I need to mention that Shawn said that his little "down moment" the other day was because of bipolar. He still needs to be tested. Also, Tuesday is when Shawn and I and my mom are going to go in and get the marriage stuff rolling. If it's only a three day wait, then we'll have everything ready Friday next week and just need to arrange for a justice of the peace to sign the stuff.

Now to the families: We met with the second couple first, Troy and April Clark, that Nora found and met, mainly to please her mother-in-law, but they turned out really nice. They were really down to earth and more open seeming than the other family. Troy even cussed once or twice, which the other family would never do. Now, I know that's not normally something people look for in others, but I like that they're more open to the world and not so conservative.

They brought pictures of their house, which seemed fairly empty and more middle class, which was sort of surprising. Troy said April made him clean up a bit before taking pictures. Nora's husband, Eugene, was goofing around the whole time, and Troy was laughing at Eugene's and Shawn's jokes while April was a little quiet, but still appreciated everyone's sense of humor.

After parting ways with the Clarks, we met with the Werners, for the second time. Although I felt they were the best last time meeting them, after meeting them again, especially after Troy and April, I really began to agree with what Shawn said about them being too conservative. They didn't laugh as much and didn't catch on as easily when people were just kidding. They are wonderful people, no doubt, but they just don't seem to be what we're looking for even if they are higher income.

Both meetings took place at a restaurant and we were there from 10:30 a.m. to about 2:45 p.m. When we got in the car with Nora and Eugene, Nora made Shawn and me each write our choice on a piece of paper and we both agreed: Troy and April.

We're still going to discuss it more; I think Nora prefers the Werners. And Nora thinks I might have chosen who I did because of Shawn, but that's not it. I tried to explain that I think Troy and April would be more open to everything that would arise in the twins' lives as they grow up. My example was, what if one of the twins was gay? I think they would be more okay with it whereas the Werners, being very Christian, would be more avoidant of it. Stuff like that I think is important to be open about considering Shawn is bi, even if he leans more towards women, and I'm bi-curious.

We're meeting with Rosemary, the lady from the adoption place about 6. Then we'll hopefully have a final decision and sign some papers that'll terminate control for Shawn and me.

November 26

It all could be settled by the weekend, kids and marriage. We're sticking with Troy and April. Shawn and I filled out the termination of rights papers already, but we didn't tell the family yet. They live about an hour and a half away and Shawn, me, and our parents can all visit sometimes. Shawn said he wants to go to any sports games or plays they're in, so that's kind of cool that he can. They'll know they're adopted, but they won't know it's us for a while. I told Shawn it may confuse them to see daddy in the audience or along side the field and them not be able to go home with him.

Our budget, especially if Mark moves out, will be tough. We'll survive fine, but little extras probably won't really happen. Shawn and I were going to save for a PlayStation 2 and me to get breast implants, a small dream of mine.

November 27

Tomorrow, so long as Shawn's work isn't messed up, we're all going in to be married. It sounds like we can have the three day wait waived and it all be done then. It all depends on Shawn's work. I only need him here for an hour or so to do the paper stuff, and then he can go home, so hopefully I can swing it either way.

November 28

Well, Shawn's work is messed up. So now we're trying for Thursday. After this is finished I'll live with my dad until I'm done with high school. Dad can drive me because I only go every other day. Then when I graduate I will go and live with Shawn.

Mom told me this morning, after I made a comment about siblings stealing my computer paper, that I probably won't have to deal with it in a couple days. And she said Robert said I have to take everything I want with me when I go or else he's throwing it out. I live in such a loving home.

November 30

First, Shawn is on his way! I'm so excited! But, to the real point, tonight, my mom and step-dad are meeting the Clark (Troy and April) family. I guess last night they saw the twins for the first time and Nora said it was just so neat watching them together, so it sounds like all went well.

Tomorrow the twins are going with the Clarks, so mom has to get her meet in before then. I won't be there due to being with Shawn, but I'm sure mom will be okay with Robert and my siblings there.

Well, plans changed, and I guess Shawn is coming tomorrow instead so that we have more time together. While it's a good idea, just wish he would've told me before I went through all the trouble of getting pretty for nothing. So I'll go to the meeting, too.

I haven't talked to my grandmother at all about anything so I have no idea about her thoughts, and I don't plan on doing so. When I move out, I won't talk to my mother either.

December 2

Yesterday Shawn picked me up from school. It was really great getting to see him from noon to after supper. He took a nap for a couple hours and my mom got home not long after. I had to start supper and I went and lay down with Shawn after I was sure my mom was home and informed her of the food almost being done.

Mom came in my room and turned on the lights, blinding Shawn, who was still not fully awake, and yelled at me for lying next to him. She said she doesn't care if I do that when I'm out of her house, but to set an example for my siblings while I was there because sleeping is bad, I guess. I would think it's more dangerous for us to be awake. Of course she cussed a few times in that statement, which echoed through the house, but I guess my siblings' ears don't pick up on that stuff.

Mom continued to complain and bitch and moan and then realized my brother was up at his friends' house. I told her he was there when she came in the door, but she didn't pick up on it until my little sister told her that's where he was.

So, I got yelled at to go and get him, walk him down—the people live three houses up on the opposite side of the street, the street light stretches that far—because he's not supposed to be out past dark. Which hell if I know that, I didn't want him going outside or to someone's house at all, but he throws tantrums at will. I got home quickly; my brother was coming down as I was going up. I went in and sat by Shawn and of course, he hates my mother and this didn't help. He being half asleep didn't help either, but he kept whispering about how she's a bitch. I talked him into getting up and eating the supper I made and then we played Scrabble. Then he left; I gave him my super-drawn-out good-bye and that was that.

Seeing Shawn was good, even if he did nap, but my mother has a way of ruining every moment I ever try to have that's good. I seriously want to know what put her on such a high horse. Besides all that, I wrote a paper for my English class and it was a "voice" paper. I wrote mine about my mother because the subject I picked was a monster I faced and overcame. My overcoming will be getting married and moving out. The teacher I figured would say something, which she did in the comments thing on my grading sheet, but I ended up getting a 100%, which is one out of two I've heard of. So I guess if nothing else, my mother makes for a good story.

Side note on my teacher for that class: She really likes to tie her religion into class sometimes. She tries to do it subtly I think, but I can always tell because I really get sick of hearing religious things. And if I have to hear one more "it's a sign from God," I'm going to scream. On a sheet about future plans we did at the beginning of the year I put for possible careers art teacher, video game tester, and sexologist. She read the careers out loud as she passed the papers back, but all she read on mine was art teacher whereas she read everything on everyone else's list. She bugs me.

Shawn is Wiccan and his religion makes more sense than any Christian-based religion. I mean, to me it does. I still am learning, but I know he believes in Karma, the chaos theory, and Gaia, the earth is alive, we are one with the earth, when we die we go back to it and are reincarnated. It makes sense, the reincarnated part because like Shawn said, we have more people, and we cut down plants for more living space. We have more rabbits; we have less grass, that sort of thing. Basically, there are so many "souls" and everything balances.

My teacher reminds me of a teacher I once had when I tried to conform to the Catholic beliefs. They don't come out and say "this is how it is," but by how they bite their tongue you can tell they're thinking it. I was asked by the other teacher, "What group of people do you think are discriminated against the most?" I replied, "Gay people," and she sort of stumbled with her pause before saying, "Okay, how about black people?" She blew me off and I hated it. My friend Leon was in that class and he's gay, poor guy. He's moved away but we still have some contact.

December 3

I don't want to be an art teacher anymore. I like art, but not the idea of teaching. I love video games, but feel I'm not that great at them. I don't have tons of money to put into them, so I'm sure there are other people that would be better suited for a video game testing job. But, I'm interested in sex and the studies of it; just not sure I want that as a career anymore. I just don't know.

The only goal in life I've decided I know I want is to be, sadly enough, a Suicide Girl. It's not the most pleasing of goals to most people, but I think it's cool and I am very self conscious, so if I can get to the point of wanting to be a somewhat nude pin-up, I've overcame a lot. I'm getting two tattoos for X-Mas from my dad and he's getting one, also. And I'm getting my lip pierced for sure and possibly also my eyebrow and my one ear some more.

That's not really a career, being a Suicide Girl, but it's a goal. I like Suicide Girls. I've considered tats and piercing for a while and finally am going to get them. It's not like I just thought it up overnight although what and where I recently decided on. I know a lot of employers will be picky, but I can always work at some place that's less restrictive. I think it's sad that people are so "fearful" or against expression like that, but I do know that it happens. I mean, why not just accept everyone? Seriously! I doubt I'll change my mind, but it's possible. Piercings I can always remove, tattoos I know won't be that easy. One will be on my back/shoulder blades, the other on the back of my neck, so they won't be that obvious anyway unless I'm half-naked. I can't see myself in a job that's all prim and proper and involves a lot of suits and briefcases, so I'll find me a job that allows me to be *me*. I'm looking into the details for Suicide Girls. As far as I know I have to be 18 because it is soft-core pornography.

I'd like a tattoo of chibi wings, little anime wings that are cute and very simple. I'll also have a barcode on the back of my neck and a fairly standard one but then it'll have different numbers under it. Shawn has a pentacle tattoo on his right shoulder, but no piercings. He wants to get his back tattooed, the whole thing, with angel wings that have feathers falling off at the bottom, turning into devil wings. Neither of mine should take too overly long, not like his which will be huge.

Sometime this week my lip's getting pierced, just not sure when. It was going to be Thursday, but I babysit, so we'll see. I hear the lip isn't bad because it's really fatty, although mine's going to be on the left side, not the middle, so it might be a little worse. The eyebrow, if I ever get it done, or the other ear piercings, on my upper ear, will hurt worse, I think.

December 4

Things went really well the other night. My mom really likes the Clarks and we all had a good time. It was a pizza buffet so how can anyone not have fun? Mom was, of course, putting on her best face. We gave our emails to them and I found out they're renaming the twins. They took the twins on Friday and I'm still filling out paperwork.

As far as the Suicide Girls, Shawn is okay with me wanting to be a SG. My dad doesn't know that's where I'm headed even though I'd still get tattoos and stuff if I weren't going to try and be one. And, of course, my mom has no clue.

December 5

I am still filling out paperwork. I have to have it all done and to the lawyer-lady who the adoption place picked to represent me.

Shawn saw a shrink today, but I have yet to talk to him to find out what happened. His car is still broken down, the tranny is no good, so he rides a bike the couple blocks to work. It's cold! He might be getting online soon; otherwise I'll be talking to him at 9:00 p.m. I think if the shrink says he is bipolar he gets kicked out of the reserve.

Also, I signed on his account on one of the forums where he's a regular, I know his password and he knows mine and snooped (shame on me!) and found he's a bit behind on the rent this month, so I offered to help him out. He won't ask me for money, but if I give it to him he'll take it. Poor boy is having a bad time lately.

December 6

Shawn isn't bipolar; he has depression and now is taking pills. I think that might ruin the reserve for him because he knows a guy who is on depression medication who's trying to get in and he has to be off of it before he can join. Shawn said he has the rent handled and his friend has a tranny he can have for his car. Things are slowly working out, I think.

I'll be getting a job when I move up there, plus if the Suicide Girl thing works out when I turn 18 there'll be some money on the side, too. I know money isn't everything, but I also understand we need some anyway.

I didn't really ask Shawn what was causing his depression. I'll have to ask him tonight if I remember. He's had this for a long time, just finally got around to getting it checked out. His mom set up the appointment or else he still wouldn't have gone. I don't think he's unhappy about getting married. He was always the one pushing it more than me and the only time he changed his tone about it was when he had his "moment" and he told me to ignore everything he said then, he didn't mean it.

I even asked last night if he still wants to get married and he replied with an, "Of course I do!" So I really don't think that's it. He always tells me to speak up if there's a problem and I have told him to do the same and I ask if I think something's up, giving him opportunity to bring it up if he needs to, but he hasn't said a word.

December 7

Shawn's car is getting impounded, so that sucks. I guess his sergeant was supposed to move it for him and a friend had a tranny for it, but nobody ever helped him out, so it was left somewhere to be towed away. Shawn couldn't do anything about it. He can't come here until he gets a car so I might be having my dad take me there for X-mas break. I don't know how that'll work.

He's trying the depression meds for a month and then if they don't work he gets treated for bipolar. He still could be bipolar, but they think he has more symptoms of just depression, not bipolar. Shawn personally thinks it's more than depression. We'll know in a month, I guess, have to give the pills time to work.

Last night he was really mad at the car thing, but even through all his anger he still managed to tell me he loves me and said he's not mad at me and still wants to marry me. And he was nice enough to let me go instead of having us continue a conversation because he didn't want me to feel worse.

I'm still doing paperwork for the adoption, it's so confusing! Tonight I get my lip pierced, though! I think I'm going to get my eyebrow pierced next week.

December 8

Rosemary, from the adoption place, sent me more papers to fill out, to terminate my rights. Shawn is signing new paternity papers because something was messed up with the first ones, and so he will have his name on the original birth certificates which is very important to him.

I couldn't get hold of Shawn last night and this morning he hadn't gotten online and no getting hold of him on his phone, so I got worried. Then he calls asking, "You rang?" He says he has drill all day today, tomorrow, and Sunday. I thought he was laying in a ditch somewhere and he's just at drill. I didn't know he had it today. Makes me feel a little better about the fact he doesn't have a car to come see me today because he can't see me anyway.

I talked to Shawn's friend, Alan, on AIM last night. He's supposed to be visiting Shawn over his X-mas break from college. Shawn and Alan went to college together for one semester, were roommates, and I don't know where Alan goes now. And I'm staying with Shawn over my break, so hopefully our time overlaps somehow, otherwise I'll be telling the boys to make a trip this direction so I can see Alan! He's such a cool guy, majoring in psychology. He does smoke weed, but the more I talk to people, the more I realize how many people do it and I still don't find it that bad. I still haven't done it personally, but we'll see I guess. Anyway, I'm excited to see Alan because I only met him in person once and when I meet someone the first time I'm always really quiet, so I don't think it counts. We talk online sometimes, though.

I got the lip piercing, and so far, no swelling, which is really surprising. The lady said that "there will be swelling," so I'm waiting for it. She actually was really nice. She wore a pink sweatshirt and was maybe in her 40s or so, had a little diamond nose ring, and was very skinny. She didn't seem like someone that would have a nose ring, let alone have had a lip ring though she took it out because her husband didn't like it. We talked a lot, even about the baby thing, which made me very comfortable. I guess she had a baby as a teen and gave it up, but she was sent to a maternity ward and was pretty much an outcast.

After going over care instructions and picking a ring, she found a good spot for the piercing, marked it, and got the clamp on. She asked me if I was okay a few times. I told her if I think too much I won't do it, so I'm fine and to just go and she asked if she should count to three. I closed my eyes while she got the needle ready to poke me and I said no, to just do it. So, she did. I'm not saying it didn't hurt at all, but it wasn't that bad. I didn't scream or squirm or anything. She removed the clamp and needle in my lip, and said she had to put the jewelry in.

She picked out the next size up from the one I'd be having in regularly, in case it swells, and got the ball on. The more I laid there with it in, the better it began to feel. I told her the only thing bothersome is the fact it's big on my lip, which she agreed for me being a smaller person it is a big loop, circumference-wise, not the thickness of the loop itself. She said that she'll send the smaller loop with me and she'll change it for free when I come back in a few days because it'd hurt too much to do it now and it should be swelling, which she doesn't normally do.

My dad was shopping while I was being pierced and came in when it was all over and drove home. I kept waiting for it to swell, but the lady was good about me swishing with salt water and putting ice on it, so nothing showed.

I got home to my mom's and after eating and cleaning it, showed her, and she pretty much just rolled her eyes. I went to bed and awoke expecting swelling, but still nothing. I ate breakfast and cleaned it and it feels fine, just big. I'd do it all again. I won't, because I only want one lip ring, but I mean it wasn't bad and so far so good. Next is my eyebrow.

We're supposed to get married during my X-mas break because Shawn is taking off work for Alan being up. I don't know an exact day. The only way I can leave home is to get married. It'll be just a courthouse trip but Nora wants to throw us a party.

Someone hacked my Hotmail account and then the hacker wanted me to go on webcam to get my account back but I refused. My friend, Jimmy, fixed my account for me and I have a new password. Darn hackers!

December 9

I went out with friends last night, so I talked more than I did the first 24 hours of my piercing. So this morning it is, in fact, swollen. Not terribly, but enough I can tell and my dad noticed, too. I cleaned it and iced it some, though, so it shouldn't get much worse.

I didn't get to talk to Shawn last night because I was in town at the mall. I guess he called twice, but then went to bed. I only talked to him long enough yesterday to have my moment of tears over the creepy hacker-dude. He's at drill, so the fact he had a moment to console me was nice. Tonight when I talk to him I will try and ask about the car and X-mas/marriage.

December 12

Well, I shipped out my old Sega Dreamcast and two games to an eBay buyer. I got enough money for Shawn's ring and phone because the phone went down to $100 with a 2-year plan now and I can fund my eyebrow piercing. The piercing I'm getting tomorrow along with changing my lip ring because it was still swollen yesterday morning, but went away after P.E. and still is not swollen. And I'll even have a few bucks towards my tattoos so that my dad and I can get them sooner. He's paying for them fully, but that may be a while, so I'm going to help pay for them and maybe get him something for X-mas.

I finally finished the adoption papers and mailed them yesterday. The hearing is in two days, so luckily I got the papers out "just in time." I don't know if Clarks did papers, I know Shawn did some. It just asked my personal information, the kids' birthdays, etc. There were a lot of questions about type of case and stuff, but I left them blank because I don't know.

From what I overheard my mother saying, the Clark family had a rough night or two with the twins adjusting, but they still seem head-over-heels. I forgot their email, so I'll have to ask mom what it is because my dad tells me he wants to get photos from them, too. I am not attending the hearing, neither is Shawn, and I have no idea who is doing what as far as the judge, etc.

I talked to Shawn last night online and a little on the phone and he was in a really good mood. Maybe those pills are doing something. Also, I guess his manager at work, who I can't stand, is "cutting his hours back" because he does "inadequate" work. Basically, everyone during the day leaves stuff for the overnight guy and so Shawn has to do his job and everyone else's and is being reprimanded for not keeping up.

His manager is one of the ones even doing the slacking off. From what I hear, she comes in late every day and takes her sweet old time letting Shawn leave and taking over. I guess she has been "looked into" by the big cheese because she's a "bad manager," so Shawn said he was going to talk to the big cheese more instead of taking her word on things.

Shawn has health insurance through work. I don't know much more about him and the shrink until something happens. I don't get the feeling he likes to talk about it.

I may not be moving until after I finish school in January. I have enough credits to finish then instead of going through April. Actual graduation will be around the end of April when the school year is officially ended. I'm getting married at X-mas break, which is next week; it's just a matter of Shawn taking a day off.

I still am moving in with him right after school's done. With Shawn living three hours from here it makes it hard to live with him and finish school. I might move in with dad, but it'd only be in reality a couple weeks, so I don't plan on it any more. Mom may make me, but I don't know.

I guess a bill that Nora said she'd pay and had the "check in the mail" for didn't get paid. Now mom's on a rampage. Hopefully it's a misunderstanding. I guess her debit card transfer was denied and she's on it, so it'll be okay.

Shawn hopes to talk to the big cheese today, assuming he's around, about his hours and about us getting married so he can have a night off. Hopefully it goes well. He said he's often misinterpreted when he tries to have a professional heart-to-heart with someone. I guess he doesn't even know the big boss-man that well because he's never around, so the chances of him talking to him today are slim. I trust that he figures it out.

December 14

Well, my eyebrow is done and it's not sore or anything as of now. It hurt slightly worse than my lip getting pierced, but now I don't even notice it. I told the piercer that my lip ring is most sore after I clean it. She said that's not right, that my soap is probably irritating it. She gave me some liquid soap in a bottle, for free, plus she gave me some lip balm because my lips were getting dry, and took $10 off my piercing this time because I was just in last week. So it cost me about $27. Last time, when I got my lip done, she had given me the loop that I'll get changed to the smaller one for free, also. She must like me or something.

Shawn's car is getting worked on today, so he and I are hoping it's fixed for tomorrow so he can come up, otherwise I'll just see him next week for break. He still hasn't talked to the boss-man, but still intends to. I'll be moving some of my stuff into the apartment within the next week or two. It's weird how it's coming so soon!

My mom just today noticed my eyebrow barbell, only because I mentioned it to her. Her reply was, "You keep putting holes in your face and nobody will want to hire you." Otherwise she didn't say anything which was surprising.

School right now is all right. I have a D in civics, which isn't good, so I'm hoping the test I just took yesterday will pull that up, or at least not bring it down more. I don't understand civics much, nor do I have interest in it. My reading class is my second English credit that I need to graduate and my progress report said I have an F in there which I am not exactly sure why, but I think it's because I still have two vocabulary tests to take. It's the class I do on the side because I don't go to school on those days anymore. I have to figure that out tomorrow. As for my other classes, I'm doing fine.

The lawyer emailed me today and said that everything went well at the hearing and she'll send me copies of the papers. She called last night to get my official okays on everything, so it was just in the knick of time as the hearing was this morning.

December 15

My lip feels much better today; my new soap is helping.

I talked to the teacher that I have an F in his class and I just have to come in Tuesday to make stuff up, then I'll be fine.

The twins, I think, have six months' trial with the Clarks.

December 17

Well, mom still hasn't decided if I can go with Shawn over break or not, so he and I plan to get married Tuesday or Wednesday so she can't say anything. It's all depending on his car. Mom's moving my crap into the basement next weekend and moving my brother back upstairs, so I hope to get some stuff moved out by then so I don't have to deal with it. I have a lot of feelings of hate, mainly towards my mother, right now. I just want to leave.

I talk to Shawn a lot, between online and the phone, and feel much better. His car is still getting worked on, but he said he'd borrow his grandma's car if he can for Tuesday so we can go to the courthouse. So, I guess that's the new plan, assuming his grandma lends the car which I wouldn't doubt that because she's always really nice and trying to help Shawn out. I hope to call the courthouse tomorrow, assuming I get the "go ahead" from Shawn, to find out times and such.

December 18

As I figured would happen, Shawn has no vehicle to come up here, so, no marriage tomorrow. Mom said even if we were married I'd have to be back next Thursday (I can go with him no matter what over break this Friday through next Thursday) as long as I'm in her house. *Bah! Ridiculous!* At least I can see him a little bit. I think I jinxed things by calling the courthouse before talking to Shawn about tomorrow.

Wednesday I get my lip ring changed now that it's healing better due to new soap and Thursday I get my IUD checked. I know it's working, but they have to look at it anyway I guess. I've continued to box stuff up and move it to the garage, hoping to take a lot of it with me this weekend. I'm so excited for break!!

I talked to Nora today. The Clarks sent her the same pictures of the twins they sent to my mom, but I didn't get them for some reason, so I'll have to look at Mom's. I guess one of them got sick a week ago. Not sure what it was they got, Mom called and asked about them but didn't tell me anything really. She's more worried about getting rid of me than talking to me.

Nora said that Shawn is really looking into full-time reserve. I guess there's three months of schooling and then he'll be making $20+/hour. That'd be nice! Then I wouldn't have to work while I go to school, so, hopefully we can be married soon. For security reasons I support full Army reserve, so long as I know I can't be left behind. Maybe a day will work after break with him, considering that late next week I'll be home. Maybe if we come home early on Thursday. I'll find a way for it to work!

December 20

Today I went out with my mother. We went to the mall because she needed to pick up a few ornaments. We browsed around a bunch and actually were getting along, one of those rare moments. We went into Borders bookstore and as she browsed her stuff, I went over to the Manga section. She had gotten me two books, on sale for $5, at the library a few weeks ago. They were an X-mas gift she wasn't supposed to get me because my step-dad told her not to, he just wants me out of the house. She had gotten me book #1 in both series and so I was looking for the seconds.

The one series I wasn't as excited for as the other, so I headed toward where the "good" series was located, *Tokyo Mew Mew*, and found book #2, *Tokyo Mew Mew a La Mode*. Mom looked it over, after joining me, and started to walk off with it.

I told her to put it back and she said no, she was getting it for me. I told her Robert said she couldn't and she just said he won't know the difference and he doesn't look at her receipts, so it won't matter. So, she bought it for me and here we are, back at home, after a little more mall browsing.

Sometimes I can't help but give in. She's my mom and I really do want to like her, but it's hard not to think about the times she's just an idiot. Robert doesn't like having me here because I guess I haven't been nice to him over the years, but as I explained to my mom, I am to him what he is to me. The times he's a jerk, so am I.

Mom always said Robert never tried to take my dad's place, he just wanted to goof around with me like he does my siblings now, but I always felt he did want to take his place and I didn't like to goof around. And the time my mom and him tried getting me to go along with Robert officially adopting me sort of ruined their whole "he's not trying to be your dad" thing.

I just started the South Beach Diet. Not officially, I don't use their meal planner or buy their food, but I'm going to try the two weeks without carbs and then eat only good carbs after that. My friend tried it once and it worked well for her and I really want to lose weight. My weight for my height should be 95 - 128 pounds, and I still weigh 154 from the kids. We were weighed in P.E. yesterday, it was depressing.

I'm excited for Friday and break with Shawn and happy I started on my rag today so I have a few less days on it while with him. I know it's sort of a poor reason to want to see him, but it's been a while since we've fooled around and I sort of would like to again. I was worried that I'd start while there and then, because of only being with him about five or six days, not getting to at all. And I'm even more excited for next Thursday. I'm glad everyone is in agreement for this. Now I have to call my dad to see if he'll be a witness.

December 24

Shawn and I didn't do anything overly special for the holiday as of yet. Spent time together, fooled around, that's about all. Tomorrow we might be going to his grandma's house, depends if he's awake after working all night.

Yesterday I cleaned his room for him while he was working and that was a treat. I promised him I would do it, but when I got here I didn't expect it to be worse than last time I was here. Luckily it was mainly clothing, so once that was picked up and sorted, there was a whole other layer of flooring made from clothing and army stuff; it was pretty decent.

The more I spend time in the apartment, the better I feel about it. It is messy, due to two guys living here and not giving a crap about what it's looking like, but it's not completely trashed, so I can deal. As soon as we get a vacuum I think we'll be much better off. I think my dad's getting us one.

Mark, the roommate, and I have talked quite a bit now in person as opposed to online and I really like and get along with him now. I originally didn't like his girlfriend, Lila, a very pretty girl. She gave me a bad vibe, but since she's been over a couple times in the past couple days, I really like her. She was really nice to me.

On to a bigger subject: Pot. Lila was here and offered me pot both last night and Friday night, but I turned her down. I told Shawn I want to do my first time with just him and I told Mark the same and he told Lila. Everyone understood. Today when Shawn and I had nothing to do, I tried it a little, obviously not a lot, because I didn't feel that weird or anything. It really burned my throat and made me a little "off."

As I told Shawn, looking at the floor made it seem slightly higher and slightly lower than it really is at the same time. I may try more when everyone's doing it; I just wanted to see my tolerance. I don't mind doing it and having tried it makes me feel better about Shawn doing it because it really doesn't feel like a big deal. I know he and his friends are responsible. I'll write more on this whole issue later when I've done more and gotten higher. I will leave my mind open for change.

December 27

As of now, Mark is still going to live with us after I move in. He and Lila go at it a lot, but I don't really mind. It's funny to listen to sometimes and I'm sure they can hear Shawn and I at times, too, so it's sort of a mutual understanding thing. As long as they're audible, they can't say anything if Shawn and I are audible.

When Mark is here, he's nice to talk to. It was funny because the other day he was getting dressed to go to Lila's for the holiday and he asked me if his outfit looked okay. I like how being the female of the house, I automatically get to have a say in what the roomy wears.

I do get bored a lot being here when Shawn is working. Mark has his own life and isn't always around, so I have nothing to do. We got the PS2 hooked up last night, so I finally have that to mess around with. I really like the "daily living" with Shawn, though. I like when we can sit down and have a meal together or go grocery shopping, the simple things. He agrees it's nice to do that sort of thing together.

Tomorrow is still when we're getting married. I'm really excited! I'm hoping Shawn will be okay with such little sleep, though. He only got seven hours last night or will have gotten since he's in bed and I'm waking him up at 1:00 because he works at 2:00, its 12:30 now. And if he goes to bed right at 11 tonight when he gets home, he'll only get about six hours of sleep because we're leaving at 5:00 a.m. But he can always nap tomorrow afternoon when he gets home.

I don't know why he didn't come to bed until 5 a.m., but he didn't. I went at like 2 or 3. We were watching movies. Then he came to bed and we fooled around for an hour and then went to bed.

All I know is, being here Shawn and I get more "us" time and I will admit I'm concerned that a time will come that it gets old. We're very active individuals, so I do fear that one day we'll get bored with sex and then will be like, "Why are we more than friends?" I guess everyone worries they'll lose the spark, I just hope we don't!

December 28

We went to the courthouse and got the papers all filled out. It took longer than expected which would've been okay if we got there sooner, but Shawn got sick from an energy drink that was in the cooler at work with an expired date on it and I had to drive and pull over a few times.

So we didn't get the three day wait waived or the license signed yet, but Wednesday I hope to set up a way to get it signed and make it official. So we're in marriage purgatory. I am wearing the wedding band, though, and will still go by Shawn's last name instead of mine. Shawn told me its close enough, that's why I get the ring now.

Mom moved my blankets to the basement and everything else into the garage. I feel really sad that I'm home now for a couple more weeks before being with Shawn full time. It was hard telling him goodbye. I know he and I both enjoyed living together, and I really hope that enjoyment lasts. I'm tired now, slept an hour this morning and then napped briefly twice.

December 29

I have to call a magistrate to sign the paper. Wednesday is when the three day wait is over because Saturday and Sunday don't count. I can pick up the license then and just have to have a magistrate scheduled to sign it. I tried calling the three people they gave me numbers for, but only one showed a sign of hope; I have to call back in 20 minutes. The first one wasn't there and I didn't get info on when he'd be there, the second one wouldn't answer. We'll see how it goes.

I don't think Shawn can be here for the signing, so I have to see if that's okay or if we'll have to really work to get him here. Worse comes to worse, Nora said Shawn's old priest can do it.

I know it'll be different being married and it's up to us to talk things through and make compromises. I'm really excited and willing to make it all work out and as far as I can tell, so is Shawn. I was in a "mood" the other day and got sort of ticked and walked off to our room to lie down and think and he came in and talked to me.

I got sad, it was Wednesday night before the marriage stuff Thursday, and I cried and we talked it out, and now we're fine. Then we had a great night, he showed me his old yearbooks and told me about friends and was just a complete goof, making me laugh and smile the whole time.

Finally found a magistrate! He can see us at 9:00 a.m. on Wednesday. We'll have to pick up the certificate and license right away in the morning, probably 8:00 a.m. and then get over there. I like to be early. He originally said 9:00 and then 9:30, so I'm going with 9:00. That's what I'm telling Shawn, too, so he's on time. I figure it being in the morning he can be here and then go home for work afterward.

December 30

Well, this past year was crazy. There are plenty of words to describe different parts of the year, but overall "crazy" is the best for the year as a whole.

Beginning of January I was still "normal," not dating Shawn and still in a crummy relationship with someone else. Of course when that ended, Shawn picked up the pieces and made it all better, really made it all better. Until I found out I was pregnant, then you really have to question things, don't you? Was it fate that made him rush in to save me from depression, fate that made the condom tear and the morning after pill fail and pregnancy test lie to me? And was it fate that made me have twins?

There are actually a few good things about having the twins. For one, the time I was carrying them, after saying I was going to keep them, I got along with my mother. That's something that probably won't happen again and I know sure as hell didn't happen before, so it was a nice experience.

Another good thing is that it really did bring me closer to Shawn's family and in reality closer to him. Having him stay in the hospital to help me out, that meant a lot to me and stuff like that really shows something about our relationship, I think. And also, finally, it helped out another family. They now have the joy of two children instead of only one.

And now, things are settled and as the year closes and a new year begins, I'm getting married and moving out. With all the stress and fights and whatever else you want to call the things that happened, I still say I don't regret any of it. I don't really regret getting pregnant, carrying the twins, giving them away, none of it. Everything happens for a reason and I've survived it, so I really can't complain. Now I get to relax a little bit until I get a job when I move in with Shawn and then start college in the fall.

Now that it's all said and done or almost done, like the marriage thing, I can just sit back, sigh, and think to myself: "I managed, I'm alive, and that wasn't so bad." I do think certain things in life make you stronger. And I can tell I've changed as a person, but for the better, not for the worse.

January 1

At least my life makes a good book. Someone today said I should write a book and I laughed because in a way I am. Last night I found out that Saturday night Shawn slept with another girl, a very *nasty* girl that he used to work with. I know who she is because Shawn and I ran into her at the mall while I was staying with him. He agreed she's icky. He claims he was drinking and I know with his meds he's not supposed to drink, so I figure he either forgot to take his pill and then drank or drank on top of the pill and that's why he's been so weird and did such a thing.

He called last night and claims he "can't do this" and he can't see us getting old together, only lasting maybe five or six years. I told him to worry about getting married and that "five or six years," not worry about getting elderly yet, but he wants a "sure thing." It doesn't make much sense because he came up, filled out papers, told me he wants me to wear the wedding band even though it's not final and I read a message on my MySpace page from him from earlier Saturday and he said "love you babe" at the end of it. I talked to him before that message and he was perfectly fine. So something's fishy.

I don't like that he had sex with another girl, especially someone like that, but I can deal with a mistake. I don't think a life together is worth throwing away for that one time and I told him that. I'm supposed to talk to him today, but have yet to get hold of him.

I don't know what more to say now. I talked to a few mutual friends, like Mark the roommate and his girlfriend Lila, on the phone last night and some others and they all say Shawn is an idiot and to call everything off, but I refuse. We're engaged, not just dating, so it's a bit different. You can't just say "I'm done" and truly be done. I know we'll always be friends and no matter what I'm moving into that apartment because I signed the lease, but I still don't want to say things are over.

I FUCKING HATE SURPRISES!

I don't want to change Shawn, he's perfect. He made a mistake; I can deal with that. I still think the alcohol or pills were involved. I had my friend, Cynthia, try his cell because I thought maybe he was ignoring my calls, but she got voicemail as well, so I know he's just not answering to anyone. The meds he takes are for depression, not bad meds. He's supposed to take one a day, but may have forgotten with such a busy work schedule. I know that's all not an excuse, but I know he has never cheated before, so I find this to be a bit weird for him. I really think there's more to it. I still want to talk to him and get the "low-down" more before I jump to conclusions.

I'm not just marrying him to escape from my mom. Sure, it's a good bonus, but I really do love him and feel ready. Hell, after all the "growing up" I had to do and all the shit I've been through, I feel ready to have it all settled and be with Shawn. I want to talk to him and just keep hoping when I do it'll make it all better. I really haven't a clue what to do or think or how to fix this.

I want to cry so bad, but hate to in front of my mother, so I won't. I haven't eaten in 24 hours; I can't bring myself to do it. I don't feel hungry and feel *if* I did eat, I'd get sick. I just wish I could talk to him; or one better, see him. I tried talking my dad into going, but he wouldn't, he said he didn't want to see him right now, and I have no other vehicle to use.

I talked to Nora on AIM a little while ago, so that's helpful. She thinks he's just scared to be married. I told her I'll move out, no matter what, in 10 days. Screw mom, it's my life and if I have to wait to be married, that's perfectly fine with me. So long as I don't lose him.

Nora said a lot of other stuff, some I don't agree with and some I do. She's trying to push him into going full-time military and I'm all for that. She's also trying to push me into stepping away from him and working on my own life without any thought of him being a part of it. I'm not in the least interested in that and told her so.

The more we talked the more it seemed she was trying to force us apart and that's not an option. I just need to talk to him to get things right between us. I really can't help but pay attention to her final opinions, how she thinks he does love me "as best he knows how" and how she thinks he's just scared. It makes me feel that it'll work, but I hate getting my hopes up.

I guess I'm not supposed to move in with him, but now I have the "balls" to say I don't care and do it anyway. I mean, what's stopping me? If I get my stuff moved out then there's nothing that mom can do about it, right?

Well, as I keep saying, I want to talk to him. We'll see what happens from there. Love hurts, love stinks, there's a billion songs about it, I know.

January 2

Nora and I talked online again later on last night. I cried through most of our conversation but she didn't help much with her "Figure out what you want to do with *your* life" and "You have to have a life and not plan around Shawn."

Shawn *is* my life! I need to talk with him!

Maybe Nora is right that I don't have control over another person, in this case Shawn, but I'm not going to just walk away. I am still moving into the apartment. I need to know what's going on with Shawn because I don't care what my mom says or Nora says, I am staking my claim to that apartment, my name is on the lease, and I want to know what's going on.

Nora said she would try to talk to Shawn and she'd be honest and tell me what he said. I wasn't feeling good while we talked, I haven't had anything to eat, I've barely slept, and I can't stop crying. I'm afraid of what he'll say. Nora told me to get mad, really mad, at Shawn for treating me this way, for sleeping with someone else and then telling me about it on the phone. But I can't. I'm scared because he hasn't called me. I know there's something horribly wrong. She said she thinks he really does love me the best he can but that he wants to live a life with no ties.

After talking with her, I went to bed and actually did get a little bit of sleep. When I got up this morning I finally caught Shawn on MSN Messenger which isn't as good as talking face-to-face or on the phone but it was better than not talking at all. I apologized for sending him so many emails and said I had calmed down and asked if he read any of my messages. He said he had but that he hadn't changed his mind – he didn't love me, he didn't even want to date me. I told him I didn't want to get married now, I just didn't want to lose him, and all he kept saying was "I'm sorry."

I begged him to call me so we could talk but he wouldn't. I asked him if he was afraid to get married and he said a little but he mostly just didn't want to date right now, not me, not anyone. I asked if he would be okay with me moving in and he said he supposed he could deal with it. When I asked if it meant no sex, too, he paused and then said "That's a good question." I told him I'd still like to do it but would feel bad if he was going with a bunch of other girls, too, and he said I shouldn't think about it, him being with other girls.

He said he thought I was "a great person, fun to be with" just not for him, that he didn't have any feelings for me any more. How could that be when just a few days before he said how he loved how I could "play wife" and live with him, fetch his things, and loved doing "us" stuff? His whole thing is that he says marriage should be a lifetime commitment and he doesn't see us lasting more than five or six years. Then he said he didn't think I was "the one" and he needs time to think about his life, not to do any dating, just have a little space.

Then, he threw another bombshell: he said he had just gotten fired from his job. It seems that he'd been partying the night before, had an accident and was passed out in a ditch, bleeding from a cut on his head. His boss didn't believe him and fired him. I *knew* something bad had happened that kept him from calling! He said he tried to get someone to cover for him but they wouldn't and now he didn't know how he was going to pay his rent. I told him not to worry about that because I had several people interested in my game stuff and, since I was moving into the apartment in ten days, I'd be able to help with the rent. That at least got a positive reaction out of him.

I told him that his mom thought he should be responsible for paying for the magistrate since he was the one who cancelled the wedding. He didn't like that idea. I asked why he had me wear the wedding band and he said because it made me happy, that he didn't like to see people unhappy but if he didn't change he was going to go insane. He said he put my happiness in front of his and it was driving him insane.

We talked about sex and stuff for a while and then he asked "So are we good then? Friends?" and I told him "Yes, we're friends. I still love you and want more but I can handle it so long as you're not running out and a sleeping with a bunch of people."

He said he wouldn't make any promises and I said I didn't expect a promise then asked if I had to sleep on the couch or could I still use the bed. He said, "I think I can allow you in the bed" but when I asked if I could sleep nude he said he didn't know.

He wanted to know what I'd do if he brought someone home and I said I'd have to approve her before letting her in his bed but I wanted to be the special one. He said I'd always have a special place in his heart and in his bed. I tried to explain that I won't have sex with anyone else because unless it means something to me it's meaningless and he said he'd have to hook me up with someone.

He said he wanted me to move in mainly because he thought it was better for me to be living in the apartment than at home with my mother and he thought it'd be fun with me there. We talked about my rings, whether I should wear them on my right hand or what and he asked if he could have them back.

I told him it hurt for him to want them back and he said he'd meant to say (type, actually) that I can have them but that he really wanted the money from them to pay the rent. I reminded him that I will pay the rent and asked if I could keep the rings on my left hand but he insisted I wear them on my right even though they're too tight on that hand. He finally said I could keep them on my left hand.

When I asked him if he'd cheated on me other than the one time, he said he hadn't. And then we finally talked about how we should have been more honest with each other when the discussion of abortion came up because I wasn't into being a mom but wanted to have the kids because I knew he liked kids. He said he would have been happier without them being born and that there would have been a lot less stress on both of us.

The more we talked the worse I felt because Shawn wasn't giving me any hope that there was any type of future for us. Without Shawn, life just really seems pointless and when I said that he said "You make it sound like you want to kill yourself." I told him I felt that being dead would be better than feeling this way but that I wasn't going to kill myself which is why I was talking about it. He couldn't understand how much I needed to have him tell me he loved me and that he would give me a chance to make things right between us. That being "Just Friends" wasn't good enough even when he called me his best friend.

A lot was said. And it seems that's it for the two of us. I pretty much voiced how I feel and what I think. Now I don't know. I want to talk to people about it, yet at the same time I want nothing to do with the world.

Afterwards I talked to Mark's girlfriend Lila. She said she thinks that no title is the best thing because nobody's tied down. I told her that it's good for him because he can sleep around (although I can't see him jumping into that, especially if he's bringing the girl over to the bed I sleep in, too), but I don't want to sleep around so it doesn't help me any. She said Shawn is still 14 on the inside, like most guys his age, and he just wants to "be a kid." She didn't use those terms, but that's what she meant, I believe.

I still love him and still think this sucks, but I'm glad we talked and are friends and I can move in. I don't really care if anyone has things to say about me sharing a bed with him and sleeping with him. I don't really care. Sex and love aren't always connected; you can have meaningless sex (I think). I hate the thought of being meaningless, but at the same time I don't give a frack.

Life is pointless. You waste time setting yourself up for disappointment later on. No wonder people "live it to the fullest" and go out and have "fun" all the time. No disappointment if you don't have situations to cause it.

I took a hot shower and thought more and I think I'm doing much better. Then I talked to Shawn on the phone for a couple minutes and was able to laugh and joke around with him. I told him about trying to reach Alan and how I think fate doesn't want me to talk to him because something always seems to be going on that I can't talk to him and Shawn was like, "You have a crush on Alan!" I told him sort of, but didn't know if I could see myself being physical with Alan and still wanted to be physical with him (Shawn). He said he'd call later because he had to go, didn't say what he's up to, but I guess it's none of my business anymore. Next week I'll be moving in, no matter what mom says, and that's that.

I had another conversation on MSN Messenger with Nora. Fuck, I hate life. That's about it. Nora talked with Shawn and knew I was moving in next week and that I was hoping to talk to Shawn's friend Alan. She thought it was good that I was "looking at other guys." I told her there's no way I'm jumping from Shawn to Alan! He's someone I can talk to but I love Shawn. I told her we'd still be sharing the same bed and she told me not to "be hopping into bed with him whenever he wants," that it isn't fair to me especially when there was some other girl spending time with him.

What?!! He said he didn't want to date – not me, not anybody – and now Nora was talking like he's got another girlfriend. My mind was on overload and when I asked was there another girl already she said she figured it was probably Victoria, the girl he'd had sex with, since they had gone grocery shopping earlier in the day.

I guess Nora didn't realize I didn't know because she said maybe they were just friends and all that and then that there will be other girls if we're broken up and there'll be other guys for me. She kept pushing for me to think about myself and stop thinking about Shawn, to figure out what I'm doing with my life and not plan it around him but that's pretty impossible because without him I don't *have* a life! *How do I get people to understand?!* I don't *want* anyone else!

Nora got on my nerves trying to force me to move on, not move in with Shawn, get my stuff back, tell him goodbye and "start a new chapter" in my life without him. She said now I could go back to "being 17, being a kid, have fun, enjoy, and dream big." She can't understand that I've been through a lot in a short time and being with Shawn makes me happy. Being with him *is* my big dream, my future. I don't want anyone else. And now, in less than two days, he's already got another girl thinking they're in a "relationship."

After talking with Nora, I called Shawn, and he did just what I thought he'd do, got pissy and hung up. I don't know what to think. I'm going to try not to call him if he doesn't call me tonight. Tomorrow is school, so I'm sure I'll be in the guidance office for the whole day. I'm moving in next week. I hope something's figured out by then at least.

What'd I do to make karma come back this strong? I don't know that I hurt anybody, but it had to be bad for three-fold to be this bad on me. I just haven't a clue. When I was with Shawn, things were perfect. If I hoped for things to go a certain way, they did. We both seemed happy and enjoyed each other and connected. Then it blew up. Maybe this is balancing me out for being so happy. Something seems wrong with the world, things are unbalanced. I want it to fix itself.

January 3

I tried talking to my dad last night. I am not one that wants a lot of relationships; I like to have good ones that last a while, not a bunch of ones that don't go anywhere. I don't know.

I just hope Shawn's careful and thinks things through before acting too rashly. I love him as a friend and still as more, of course, and he is my best friend, even if he's an idiot, and I'll never completely let him go. He'll always be my friend and I have a scar on my abdomen to remind me of him. I just don't want him getting more hurt or hurting more people. I wish he'd slow down and think about his life for a while before doing anything anywhere with anyone. But I can't make him do anything. I'm half-asleep and thinking clearer than when I'm awake. I do hope as time goes on we can work it out, but at the same time right now I just want to not think about it.

I talked to my guidance counselor today about the whole thing. He said he thinks moving in, sharing a bed with him every night, will make things better, not worse. He said the fact Shawn wants me to move in, or is allowing it, and is okay with me being in his bed, means that there is still something there. He may say we're just friends, but there's more to it than that. He said it's all about timing and he thinks me living there will make timing better.

I think later I'm going to meditate to try and clear my mind, then try and think about things. If it is karma doing this, I have to figure out what I did to unbalance my life and fix it, or do something that will balance it out. I'm not saying I don't hurt, but being "numb" is better for me than feeling bad because if I have feelings of my own to think about, then I tend to make them worse. Emotional masochism.

Technically it's still "our" bed; it was given to "us." I'm sleeping in it and will go to bed at an earlier hour than he does if that's what it takes to keep other girls out because I'm not sleeping in a bed he has sex with other girls in.

As far as sex, I still don't know if I will with him or not. I want to and my counselor said that if I do, it's really not bad. I'm sleeping with someone I love, not bringing home a stranger just for that. Either way it's consensual so it's not like it's that wrong in the first place. I know some people say we shouldn't, but him and I agreed that if Shawn and I are sleeping in the same bed every night, it'll happen. And, I don't think that Shawn would ever turn violent toward me. He's not like that, but then again he's weird lately.

I sent one final email to him. He hasn't replied to any of my messages lately, so I have no idea what is happening.

> *Sighs* Well, I doubt I'll be seeing you tomorrow, right? And I doubt you'll even call. I wanted to be friends, and then you freak when I ask you questions. I mean, when you tell me one thing and

do another, that's just not like you really. You're normally not a jerk.

I still love you, as a friend (and more, but let's not talk about that right now), and will be moving in regardless in 10 days. I do hope we straighten something out before then. You did say I could share the bed, which I still plan to, but as far as sex goes I don't think I want to... Not right now... maybe later.

The whole Victoria thing is a bit scary for me, considering how fast you seem to be going with all that for not wanting a relationship and for just getting out of an engagement. If that's what you want, I can't stop it.

You are my best friend and even though I'm a bit shocked and confused, that won't change. I still love you (AS A FRIEND, only talking about that right now) and hope you don't get hurt or do something stupid.

Be safe, think clearly, and be sure you're taking your Prozac. I'm going to try my hardest to "back off" for a little bit. If you're online, I'll say "hey." If you call, I'll talk. But I'm going to really try not to go out of my way to reach you. I do hope you reply to this and keep a little contact, but if nothing else I guess I'll see you next week.

Please think about everything. I understand we need a break, whatever, we're friends. I understand that moving in won't win you back (that's not why I'm doing it). I understand all of that. So don't rush into other things, you are vulnerable yet too (believe it or not). As much as I don't like Victoria, don't hurt her or yourself any more. I do want you happy, even though right now I want it to be with me or with nobody. Maybe eventually I'll let go or you'll come back or something, but either way, just be careful.

I hope you have a good evening, either way, and I will talk to you later.

I signed it "Your friend" instead of "Love you" or something more.

I talked to my dad and he doesn't want to go to Shawn's to get my stuff that's there. Then I called Shawn and he got online. We talked about me moving in and he was still okay with it and I asked him about this girl, were they dating, and he said they were. That it started when they slept together even though he was still technically with me. That he left me for her, not because he needed to be alone.

Of course with them supposedly in a relationship that changed us being in the same bed and I asked if I could still use the bed, that I'd keep my clothes on, and he said he'd planned on sleeping at her place or on the floor instead of in the bed with me. That he'd feel bad if I didn't sleep in the bed. And, no, we wouldn't be having sex.

He wouldn't answer my questions about what made him stop loving me or having feelings for me and started getting irritated. I told him most of my game stuff was sold so I'd be able to spot him the rent money until he gets a job. And then I made the mistake of asking what he'd done during the day. It seems he helped Victoria clean her apartment but he did nothing about the mess in his (our) apartment. It'd be nice to move into a decent place but it seems that he's preoccupied with Victoria at the moment.

I handled it well, I think. I'm still not crying. I'll just be a friend and go from there later, if necessary. I'm surprised how well I am being a friend and only that, but it still hurts and I still want more deep down. I want him happy, but I really can't see this going into something good. And I still don't understand a lot and am impatient to talk to him next weekend to find out more.

And now, I want to cry. I was fine through that, but now I'm not. I just don't know, I want to talk about it now, but he won't until I'm up there and in person which is a better way to talk about it I guess. I don't like that he cheated, but the part that bugs me more is it lead into something.

I hurt. I want to know what to do. Obviously I'm not going to like what I hear, though, because I'm going to be told to move on and give up and he doesn't love me anymore and there's no hope at all in getting him back. Seriously, what the fuck did I do in a past life or this one that's *so bad* it comes back as this?

I just posted this on my MySpace page:

"HE is the one that messed up, NOT YOU!" My friend told me that... And now I know there is no hope. There really isn't. Something went wrong and it can't be fixed. I suck. That's all there is to it. I'm glad to know the truth, but I really hate the thought of losing it all.

Fiancé... He was my fiancé... HE asked ME to marry him and HE was the one more excited than I was. HE wanted me to move in so bad; HE came with me to fill out the marriage application... HE is with HER.

I may not have messed up at all, but if I did I could fix it. I can't control other people. As much as I'd like to, I just can't. Like my counselor told me, it's all about timing and our timing was not right and I guess theirs was. Being three hours away does not help me any. When I get up there in 10 days, I can find out more... He'll tell me more in person; tell me whatever he thinks he can't online or over the phone.

Ridiculous, it's just plain ridiculous. How can someone do everything right and still be so wrong? I used to think being engaged meant something. Thought it was a step higher than being a girlfriend, making it harder to lose that one you love... But the reality is, it's no different, just a title. It's just as easy to break off an engagement as it is to ruin anything below that title. Marriage makes you safe, but if mistakes are bound to happen, then I guess really it just makes you trapped.

Karma. Friggin' karma. I must've messed up bad in this life or one of my past lives because this hurts more than I thought my heart could. Sure, I've been heartbroken before and I thought it'd get easier, but it seems I just fall harder and harder.

My life is unbalanced. I need to balance it out... I take that back, I CAN'T balance it out; it has to do it naturally. Just like I can't fix my karma, that'll come naturally, too. Meditate, clear my head... Reevaluate what's going on, make myself think clearer. That I can do.

Maybe I just suck at being natural. If things have to go according to how they're meant to go and would naturally, and they continue to fail, then what do I do? I know I'm not the most active person as is, but now I feel even more lethargic. I don't feel I have the will to do anything... I should pack a few more things, do my laundry, do the little bit of homework I have, eat... Yeah, I should eat... But I just don't want to. I don't feel the need. I don't feel like it'd help me now, so I eat about one meal a day right now. I guess love is the best diet after all. So there's a note to you all, if you want to lose weight, get your heart smashed. Works every time. Hell, I'm sure with some people it could help them gain weight if they wanted.

Part of me wants to move on and find someone new, but at the same time it's hard to let go. I guess if I want to sleep with more guys, since I never have with anyone but him, now's the time. Hell, if I wanna experiment with a girl, now's the time.

In closing, this is what I've learned... Don't make plans, live life as it is. If things are good, be happy. If they're bad, wade through the sorrow and deal with it. That's all there is.

Now, for me to take my own advice and live my life.

One of my friends is bi and she's surprisingly helping me a lot. And since I'm free, I'm a bit tempted. She actually is helping me smile and forget "him." Is that bad? I'm not sure, but as I put in my thing, if I'm going to try it, now's the time. I won't deny I have feelings for Shawn, but I'm trying my best to move on.

I called and told him I might like someone else. He asked who and I told him. He was all happy for me and will call later to talk more about it.

Friends is good. Maybe later I can have more, we'll see. Right now I sort of like the freedom, I feel okay with flirting instead of guilty and who knows what'll happen, right? I hope it all turns out okay, no matter what happens. Part of me is still pulling for Shawn, but part says just to lay low for a while. That second part is a bit stronger right now.

I talked to Mark online and he said I can always talk to him, so that's good. And I know I can talk to Lila. Mark told me that life goes on no matter what, which is true and really I never thought of it that simply and in those exact terms. He reassured me that Victoria is scary, and, it was my time, so I had the right to be upset, and said he was surprised and doesn't know what Shawn is thinking, but doesn't know him well enough to know and said he thinks I was good with Shawn and better than Victoria is. Right now I feel like a little girl with a crush on him, giggling with my friends about him as he does his own thing.

I told Shawn I'd be his friend and pretend nothing happened around him, but I reserve the right to get upset on my time. I talked to him on the phone and he was really nice. I even asked if he had any friends he could hook me up with and he mentioned one that I've met before. But he had to cut me short because he was getting head while talking to me. I can guarantee that Victoria only did it because it was me on the line. Shawn said he'll talk to me on MSN video chat to make up for it, so we can talk and see each other. He said when I get up there and we're not around Victoria he'll explain more to me.

The friend Shawn mentioned is a guy we ran into at the mall the same day that we ran into Victoria. I told Shawn he seemed nice and was sort of like our friend Alan. If his friend was interested in going out, I'd try it. I still like Shawn, but I'm willing to try others in the meantime. Obviously I just don't want to hurt anyone else.

I talked to Nora and she knows Shawn's friend and said he seems nice. She told me to move forward, find some guys to go out with. She said she told Shawn to figure out what he's doing and I guess she's mad at his immaturity and hygiene. Lately she says he's gross, but he showered when I was there. She said she doesn't talk to him too much on the phone or anything and I know she won't step foot in the apartment.

As for the moving, mom didn't want me to move before I was 18. Well, I mentioned to her I still plan on moving at semester end because I might go to college right away, which I know I won't, but it's a good excuse. She asked when I planned on telling her, and I said when I know more, or I guess right now works. She didn't say no or anything, so I'm still moving out next weekend. I don't really care what she says anyway, she can't stop me and I now have "balls" to just tell her I don't care if she complains. My dad said he'd talk to child support and my mom will, too. Dad said if I go to school, he'll help me out and still give me a little something which will pay rent, probably.

January 4

I talked to Shawn today. I called at about 9:00 a.m. to get him on MSN Messenger. We did video chat all day until about 2:30. There were a couple breaks in there when my computer got effed up, but for the most part we talked and laughed all day. His new "girlfriend" is more "country" and likes that type of music and everything. Shawn doesn't and thinks he can break her of it, whereas I bet she's hoping the same damn thing about breaking him of his habits and likes. Also, I guess she's "jealous of me" still, that's what he said, but I didn't ask why. I didn't really want to talk about her.

Mark was around a bit, so I got to talk and "hang out" with them via the webcam and microphone. It was nice. Considering we spent five hours together today, in a sense, that made me feel good. I know I'm still attached more than I should be. But at the same time, I'm still being a friend.

Shawn was a bit concerned that I only eat one meal a day. I told him I get hungry, but don't have the will to eat. It's like something's telling me I just don't want to. He told me not to get stupid and become anorexic and I reassured him I eat that one meal so I don't, because otherwise I probably wouldn't eat at all.

I don't want to say one thing and then read too much into it or "infer" anything. Shawn taught me that word today, along with "insinuate." He was afraid to say some things thinking I'd do that. He slipped and called me "babe" and "sweetheart." I asked him about both and he acted like he meant to do it, just let it go. Don't want to ruin my good mood by having it all evaluated and brought into real perspective, because I'm sure it all means nothing. Let the little girl have her crush, it's not hurting me at the moment.

I talked to my dad on the phone and he said, "I thought he was all wrapped up with that other girl" because I told him we spent five hours in video chat. I told him we goofed and talked and just hung out and had fun. I told about him wanting to change her and how I bet she thinks the same of him. Well, dad and I agreed and I made this comment to Shawn, although I don't know if he knew what I meant by it: *"Changing people is just as complicated as time travel."*

He gave me a look when I said that, like how did I come to that? Time travel can create problems, but also fix things. But overall, it changes the course of events, messes with people. That can cause problems to everyone else. I could go on, but I'll go on forever about time travel, so I try not to think about it. If you try and change a person, you may get what you want if they change. But then they're not them. So basically it's like saying you don't want them.

I told Shawn that if you could change people it'd be neat so I could change him and make things work, but at the same time it'd make him not him and I'd rather have him be himself than I get what I want so easily. If that makes sense!

I don't know, obviously I read a lot into things and want to believe and Shawn keeps saying I have to watch *Kimi Ga Nozomu Eien* and it'll all make sense. I gues I'm kind of like Haruka, and he's just like Takayuki. He said he hopes I watch it before he has a talk with me about everything. That way I understand and maybe go, "Oh, okay..." instead of getting upset, because he said our talk will probably make me upset. If it's involving him and Victoria, it can't make me feel good, but I don't know. The anime doesn't load well on my computer, I can get a few episodes on *Yahoo!* so I've only seen the first two.

I pointed out that Takayuki does whatever he can to make everyone happy and Shawn made a face like "Really?" and I said how Takayuki went out with Haruka because she cried and sort of guilted him into it, but then Takayuki began to really like and care for Haruka and he did that "Really?" face/thing again. Then I said to him how the girls in the anime, both Haruka and Mitsuki have this "it's better to stick with your feelings" thing, where if they really like one person, they'll hold out and wait for it to happen. I asked him about that and he said, "Just watch the anime, it'll make sense."

I guess I have too much time to think and not enough stuff to keep me busy. I'll consider that excuse enough for the MySpace message I posted today to Victoria's page which actually was a reply to her reply to my frist message to her from a couple days ago. It probably makes more sense to include all the messages in order.

Two days ago I posted to her MySpace page:

You know, on any other terms, we could've been friends, but the fact you insisted on ruining my life and taking over where I once was comfortable is NOT okay. What were you thinking? I hope you like the thought of ruining someone's life, taking away their everything, and being hated. When I die, I will haunt you. If it weren't illegal, I'd do more now. I hope the same happens to you as happened to me. -- Katie

Earlier today, she posted this on my page:

Thing is I understand how you feel. I am sorry for the way this all happened. But Shawn and I were hanging out and I told him how I had felt about him since the moment we met. That was all I did and I let him make the choice from there. This was his choice and I supported him in whatever his decision was. I'm sorry he chose me over you. But in my opinion a marriage shouldn't happen if it feels just like an obligation. I'm really sorry. I hope we can come to terms with this. - Victoria

Okay, so I posted this to her page:

I just told Shawn today that I will try hard to get along with you. I mean, I'm glad you understand and all... And I have liked Shawn for as long as I've known him, too (although was pretty stupid about it for a while 'cause of ANOTHER boy). I'm not going to say I wish you luck or I hope it fails, I'll keep my opinions to myself, but I do hope to get along. If I'm living in his apartment, we're gonna see each other. I'd like to get to know you and I think that'll make me more comfortable. I do agree about being obligated and marriage (I felt a bit pressured/rushed as well), but I do wish he would've spoke up. I still find it hard to believe he has no feelings for me "like that," but again I don't really want to discuss it and I'll keep that to myself. If you have AIM or MSN, I have both and will be cool talking any time.

Again, sorry to seem rude, I had to get htat out of my system. I do want to try and get along, so long as you understand I'm still not perfectly happy or anything like that.

Hope to hear from you soon, otherwise I'm moving up on the 13th and I'll see you around then. -- Katie

Another of Shawn's friends subscribes to my MySpace blog. She posted, in response to what's going on, a lot of not nice things about this girl. I will try and get along and get to know her, but nobody gives me a good impression.

Earlier, I was kidding with Shawn and he turned off the microphone on his end, so I said "I'll show you titties if you turn it back on" which I wouldn't have anyway, especially with the roommate around and he gave me a "Really?" kind of face and turned the volume back on and I was like, "You really want to see them?" and he kept the face and waited a minute, then muted again and eventually took the mute off and said he didn't want to or he better not. Strange boy.

I also know he thinks I'm a "very pretty girl" and he thinks I'm "sexually attractive." It's really hard to explain stuff without someone being there to see/hear/read it for themselves. I will admit I had to dig for the attractive stuff, pretty/sexual. Other than that I didn't act as more than a friend. I'm not saying it's easy, though.

I understand that if Victoria is around, Shawn will act more like a jerk; he claims she's still jealous of me. But when it's him and I, he's great. He's still confusing. I sort of get where he's going with the anime stuff, but at the same time I think he's asking me to compare closer than I need to, so it's really not that great to use anyway.

My bi friend (I officially decided I like penis/men/masculine/etc., so not into dating her) asked me if I think it'd be easier if Shawn didn't have Victoria. I think she meant as far as if I'd be able to get him back. I told her that I could sleep with him then, so maybe. But that's really shallow to think about.

He and I were very sexual, but I don't know if that's a good thought or a bad one. I've always said that if you don't do physical stuff with someone, they're just your friend. That's how I am and how I think of it, I'm just really physical, as is he. So that's why I think it'd be good, but I don't know. I don't like to be wrong, thinking or speaking. Overall I still feel that today went well, the conversations and actions between us went well, everything.

I can't stress enough that I am trying hard to be a friend, but still want more. When things go well, I have some hope. But then he says it wouldn't work and its like, do I pay attention to the actions or what he says? Actions speak louder than words, right? Then I'll just watch him.

For my English class I have to do a "people watching paper." It basically gives us permission to stalk someone because we're supposed to watch someone, without them knowing, and write a paper about what we see. I told Shawn about it, in conversation, but I think I might use him. He still didn't realize I could be watching him. I think if I use him for the paper I might understand things more. Or I'll read too deep for my own good. I just thought it'd help me pay attention to actions.

January 5

I finally got to view the *Rumbling Hearts* CD, or at least the first three episodes. I can't find the next few episodes, so I found a synopsis and a bunch of reviews. In the end, Takayuki goes with Mitsuki. I guess he felt guilty/obligated/responsible to be with Haruka, but grew feelings elsewhere as well, so he went with that instead. It's long and I guess there's more to it, but even though I can see comparing Shawn to Takayuki, comparing me or Victoria to the girls or our situation to the anime's just doesn't work.

There are a lot of differences in character between Haruka and I and Victoria and Mitsuki. The situation is way different. Haruka goes in a coma for three years while Takayuki and Mitsuki get together, whereas in real life it all happened at the same time, one relationship over another. And also, the ending, from what I read, was leading you to believe that he went with Mitsuki, but I guess really was "uncertain." Things aren't always as they seem. So, it feels like it could have gone either way. Like my counselor said, timing.

In a way, I want to take this to heart because Shawn stressed watching/learning about it. But at the same time, it's so different. I messaged him and told him I'll talk to him more about it when I get up there. I asked him again if I get to keep my rings and he said he might need the money. I told him I did want to keep them and he said he knows, he'll try to work it out so that I can keep them because he "wants" me to have them. "A gift from a friend" is how he put it.

In the anime, Mitsuki is given a ring from Takayuki before the whole coma deal with Haruka and it's just a "gift from a friend" and she wears it on her left hand, She held on to hope until the moment was right to get in there, so I really have to wonder about everything.

What I got out of this anime is, life is not like a cartoon, it won't play out the same way every time. I shouldn't hang on to hope and not do anything with any other guys or try elsewhere, but I shouldn't give up and let it all go either if I really feel that I'm in love and it's possible. It's a "hold on loosely, but don't let go" sort of thing.

I talked to my other counselor today since Mr. B was busy. She basically agreed with what I've been saying and backed up what Mr. B said. We agreed about how fast those two are moving and how it's all heading in a bad direction.

There's a lot to talk to Shawn about and I have told him I think we shouldn't compare our lives to an Anime. I don't know how much I'll actually say to him. I think I'll let him say what he wants and go from there, maybe only say the simplest things possible. I'm at school, so I can't think that straight right now.

When I got home from school, I talked to Nora on Instant Messenger for a couple minutes, long enough for her again to tell me that life isn't fair, that if it was, she wouldn't have stayed in a marriage that "should never have happened" with Shawn's dad.

In a way, I guess that over-analyzing is what I'm hoping/doing. But at the same time I am trying to cope without him. I cope by writing out my thoughts which is what I did and posted to *MySpace*.

Title: Over-Analyzing

I think too hard about everything. Ever since I was told that "things are never as they appear," I want to read into things... Find out what they are if they're not what I'm seeing.

Infer, insinuate... I was told not to do it. He himself told me not to. But I just can't help it. Slip-ups... Sure they are. I can't stop myself from imagining they were meant to be said and that there's meaning behind such a habit. Babe, sweetheart... I love you. Okay, so maybe not "I love you." But you know that's where my mind went. If he can have habits, so can I, and mine is to immediately think that's what he's going to tell me.

He used to tell me all the time. On the phone, the 'net, in person. I was always the skeptical one, asking if he really meant it. As soon as I got that hug and that special tone full of "of course I do!" along with a kiss on the cheek or forehead... Or lips... Then I believed him.

Liar. I believed that liar. Or ~was~ he lying? Maybe now is the lie. It's hard to tell with that boy. I've heard opposites so many times, I'm lucky to know which way is up.

"Actions speak louder than words." That's so cliché isn't it? It can't possibly be true, can it? If it is, then when he smiles softly as if to say, "You're so adorable," or maybe even, "I love how you do

that," should I believe him? I can't help but think there's so much more to it than what I hear... But at the same time, I feel maybe he really is someone that has everything on the surface, speaks what he feels. Then again, he didn't speak how he felt many times. So maybe, again, he's lying now.

He's cute when he talks to me. He tries so hard to be so negative. I can tell he doesn't mean all of it. Right? I mean, nobody can mean such things spoken after all that happened. It's impossible.

Three hours away, we are now. And we have been for a long time. It was farther when we started dating, he was in college, but three hours is still far when it comes to these things. It's not fair... Not having a proper chance to develop a relationship is just not fair. If given the right opportunities, the same ones given to the current hen, I could have made it.

I know I'm thinking too much about it all... But wouldn't you, too? I know for some it's hard to imagine this even happening, let alone how you'd react X number of days after the fact. I was told I'm resilient, handling things better and overcoming them faster than anyone known to the person who confessed this information to me. I guess that's a good thing.

I can only imagine how hard it would be if I didn't have the strength I supposedly possess. I want to believe and have hope, yet I feel there is none and no point to trying. I want to get along and not perform the silent cat fights women so often have, but I know I don't like the new hen. I want to see him happy and be able to smile when he tells me about her, but I also want to be the one he talks about and is pleased with.

Understanding does help ease the pain, but it also makes you look at both sides of things. It suckers you into thinking maybe they're right—maybe they make the good point and you haven't got a clue.

Well, I was told to understand, yet support my own thoughts... So that's what I'll do.

I think this is all bullshit.

January 7

I just got home from being with my dad. I talked to Shawn very briefly on the phone yesterday, but he was at drill. First time he just said he was at drill; second time he answered with a "hello" but then told me he's still at drill, so I asked him not to answer so I could leave a message on his voicemail. Obviously I still like him, I will for a while, maybe for a really long time, but I do feel better than I did. When I get there, that could be different.

Mom called me at my dad's yesterday, complaining about my grades. I have to hand in some stuff for my civics class and take a few tests in another class, so civics is at an F and the other is at a D. I told her once I turn in everything it'll be fine. I was missing the past couple civics classes from being at the counselors, so I have three things to write. She kept going on and on, but I know it'll be fine.

I went shopping, bought some clothes and some makeup; that made me feel a little better. Trying to be nice I also replied to Victoria's latest MySpace messeage. She wrote:

I completely understand everything you are going through. I've been there. I know it is weird to talk about him to me, it's ok. I know it is hard to have a long distance relationship with me it most generally doesn't work. I used to date a guy over in your area and it obviously didn't work. I know this might be a little weird but do you need any help moving? I can help if you need it just let me know. Also know that I know you are moving in with him because your name is on the lease but understand I am a little uncomfortable with it. I guess I don't know what else to say. I hope you and I can get past this and good luck with everything. But let me know if you need help moving. – Victoria

My message back is less chatty:

Well, my dad is bringing the rest of my stuff in a van and Shawn said he'd help me get it up the steps and all that, so I think I'll be okay. Thanks for asking, though. – Katie

It's not easy, but, I'm trying to keep my "enemy" closer. And, while I am so into journaling and texting everyone, I put still another blog/note on MySpace which pretty much explains my thoughts to this point:

Play the Game

Is it wrong to refer to life as a game? No matter who I talk to, it all comes down to the same generic statement: "You just have to play the game."

Now, I know people refer to the game of life or the game of love, but it's all in good fun... right? I mean, I don't think such a complex category, life, or even the only-slightly-less complex sub-category, love, is as simple to maintain by playing it like a game.

If it were, then we've solved a huge mystery a long time ago, but everyone was too stupid to realize it. Maybe I'm really making a huge step by noticing such a discovery. It only takes one person to bring the world into perspective, at least that's how it seems to have gone so far with the Earth's history. Be it by mistake, coincidence, chance, luck, fate, intention... There's always some sucker who manages to become a star by pointing out the obvious.

Well, I'll step forward and be that sucker. I'll take the risk, take advantage of opportunity, and conduct the first real test-run of such a marvelous idea. Assuming nobody else tried, of course... I have yet to find recordings if they have.

Arranged things at the courthouse: My move.

Followed through and bragged to friends: His move.

Bragged to friends and scheduled a magistrate: My move.

Cheated: His move.

Pursued discussion: My move.

Reluctantly answered questions: His move.

Sank into the role of friend: My move.

If you break it down, it can be simplified as moves/turns in a game. Of course there is some overlap, making it more complicated than the board game, Life. But, all in all, it's the same concept. Everyone just wants to come out on top.

Now, with any game, there are ties. In such a case, do both people win or lose? Or is everyone neutral and we call that good enough?

Also, opponents, competitors. Who am I playing against? Do I have allies? Are there people on teams?

Lucky for me, life and love are games that you can learn as you go along; you don't have to know the rules up front. You can also play them at the same time. There are advantages and disadvantages to the parallel play, but it's all dependent on the people involved. Deciding upon separation is, unfortunately, based on a guess. Different points of the game may require it one way over the other.

If you think about it, it really is like another generic phrase, "All's fair in love and war." It really is like a war. Alliances, enemies, battle... Yes, battle. Quarrel and conquest.

So, war is all a game. That makes plenty of sense. You use tactics, pawns, and strategies. And if love and war are comparable by the statement "All's fair in love and war," then love must be a game, too. And because love, in my case anyway, is life, Life is just a game.

Now, to await his move.

January 9

Well, today I was in a great mood. Of course, coming home to talk to Shawn, I feared something bad would happen, but so far we're chatting and fine. I'm even #1 on his MySpace page again.

I found out I will *not* be failing any classes (my mom was worried) and will be moving. So I'm in a great mood, for the most part. **knocks on wood** I don't doubt something will happen to make me upset again, but I'm enjoying what I have now.

Shawn and I aren't "fixed," but at the moment I'm okay with how things are. He's been friendly and allowing me to be semi-affectionate online, so that's good. I still hope it improves over more time. We're getting along and I feel great. I do hope it continues down a good path, but have a feeling my luck will run out. All I know is I'm taking advantage of our getting along and enjoying it while I can. Live life to the fullest, right?

My mom gave me a lecture about Shawn. A recruiter called for Army Reserves and asked me about joining. Mom picked up the phone, I guess thinking it was Shawn, and listened the whole time as we chatted and I kindly told him I'm not interested. She came down and asked me who it was, like she couldn't tell, and I told her it was a recruiter and I heard her on the phone. She said she was hoping it was Shawn so she could yell at him. She started to go on about me going to school up there and moving, and I told her flat out I didn't want to have that conversation with her. She started again and I repeated, "I don't want to have this conversation with you." She asked why and I told her, bluntly, because she does nothing but yell, so I don't want to. Then she had her "last word" which I forget what it even was and walked away.

January 10

I thought the good was to balance out the terrible feelings I had before it, and now it seems to feel bad again. I don't understand the world's idea of balance, that's for sure. Shawn and I were perfectly fine. We got into a video chat, all was still well, and then he mentioned bringing another girl over, hypothetically, and I crashed. Now I feel terrible all over again. I want to have our talk; I want it to be Saturday!

Moving, Shawn, my mother; I need to be locked in a padded room pretty quick. I'm impatient, we all know this. It's not hard to pick out. It is hard to wait for Saturday so Shawn and I can really talk instead of me getting half-ass answers to hold me over.

I do know something I didn't, Shawn thinks he's a failure, that's what he said, and thinks he will ruin my life and I am better off without him. Whether that means anything or not, I don't know, but I know the very first time he pulled the leaving me crap was for all of that, because he felt I can do better, etc. That time I told him he's wrong, he's not ruining my life, and we fixed it. I'm not saying this means anything; I just see a fishy pattern that bugs me. Hell, I don't know.

I've been thinking about school and I might go to community college for my general credits and then to regular college for my majoring, whatever I decide to go for. I'm not sure yet, I haven't gotten a letter from regular college yet, but I figure it'd save me some money. A friend told me about FAFSA financial aid for college. I don't know if I qualify, but I might look into it. That would help, too, along with grants and scholarships, if I get any. My dad pays child support, which pays rent/utilities. I may pick up a job. I also have the money from selling my game stuff to hold me over a bit. My grades aren't bad, other than two this year, really. I will look into FAFSA, otherwise I'll get loans.

On Saturday, I don't know what Shawn'll say. I expect him to explain more than he can now. He's very particular about it being *in person*. I asked him if I'd not like the talk and he said he didn't know, so it's not a definite bad talk I guess; just a talk.

I *will* be moving in with him on Saturday, permanently. I've asked a few times if he's okay with me moving in and he always says yes. We've even talked about building an igloo next winter if there's enough snow. I guess the only thing that bothers me is the fact he could possibly bring home another girl.

January 12

Yesterday was my last day with school and it was nice to be done. People were sad that I was leaving, which made me feel loved. I packed everything up but my computer and printer, so I have to do that in the next hour or so. My dad's picking me up and I'm staying with him tonight, packing it in the van tonight, and then I'm moving tomorrow morning early.

Shawn I guess called in a "booty call" (that's a stupid term) with Victoria. I found out she knows she's being used, yet she insists on getting rid of me. She's trying to sound nice, but likes to bring up certain things, like drinking with Shawn since she's older, to tick me off. I've been playing dumb and acting oblivious.

Tomorrow's the "big talk." I already got a warm-up for "the talk." Shawn said after a while he "didn't feel it" being with me anymore and it was mainly because we were so far apart. He said he doesn't want to try it again with me, "not yet." He said it like that. He said he wants me to try dating other guys and if after a while it doesn't work or I still feel I like him, he'll try again. That was our "compromise." He's "serious" and means it, I asked a lot, so hopefully it's the truth.

I guess there's more to talk about tomorrow. I thought maybe that was most of it, just how he felt and such, but it's not all. I do have more questions, like about the ruining my life thing. I asked him if he's using me because we're not dating and having sex with someone you're not with always made me feel that's what's going on. He said no because he wants me around for friendship, too, not just sex, whereas Victoria was just for sex, like yesterday. I still feel sex does not make a relationship, although you can make it mean something if you're in one.

So, it begins. I have to pack up my computer now, hoping to get things situated before my mom gets here. There may still be hope, later on. I told him I don't want to be with him right now anyway, because honestly, feeling how I do, I don't think it's wise. I want to be in it for the right reasons, too, *not* just because I feel I'm lacking without him, so I feel time *would* be a good idea; even though I do still feel love for him.

January 13

I just got boxes moved in and yes we've had sex. I don't know what's going on and now that we're comfortable, kissing, and he's ignoring calls from Victoria I am trying to put off the talk. I don't want things ruined right now. I guess we'll see how it goes. I've only been here an hour.

January 14

So, Shawn and I sort of had a talk. I went in the bedroom to get something and he came down the hall and we hugged and I started to get sad and we went in the bedroom and lay down. I just hugged him a bunch and was upset and it turned into him saying that I can do better and I'm "too good for him" and he made himself sound like crap and said he's hurting me.

I told him that I love him, flaws and all, and understand I have to take the bad with the good and that there's more good than bad. He hugged me and said he loves me and apologized and said he realizes it now, all that good stuff, and so we're dating — just dating. I didn't even expect it. He asked about marriage and said we don't have to now, right? I was like, uh, no we don't, I just wanted to move out and now I'm out anyway, so it doesn't matter.

We ended up going over to his friend's house and hung out with a few people, playing video games and having a good old time. Things went *really* well and I expected the worst.

January 17

Life is lazy.

Considering my funds saved plus the child support I'll be getting from my dad each month, I currently do not need to work. I still have stuff to unpack, but Shawn and I have been sick the past couple days.

The cats are adjusting well to the apartment, better than I expected. Anaki, the younger of the two, cries because she does not have my dad's kitten to play with and gets bored. Mark says his cat is at his sister's, so Shawn and I most likely will find another cat/kitten for Anaki to play with. Shawn wants one that's his own. Dad sent two large bags of food and four things of litter, so they're stocked for a while and I plan to always buy in bulk.

As for Shawn and I, we're doing good. The most fighting we do is over Monster Rancher for PS2, we've been playing it addictively the past two days. That's what he's doing right now next to me while I journal, then it's my turn again. We actually got in a big argument about a battle that he won and he was like, "Oh my gawd, our first fight," seeing as we never have before, like, ever. And I laughed and said, "Yeah... and it was over Monster Rancher." He said we have to start somewhere and that fighting is normal and healthy. I still think it's funny.

And as for *me*, I'm good. I feel so much less depressed since being here even though I feel sick (stomach feels icky, headache, and my nose is messed up making me sneeze a bunch). I haven't talked to my mom at all since I left, but I've called dad each night. In all honesty, I've called for his sake and not my own. He says he appreciates me calling, so I think it's still a bit hard for him.

Yesterday I shipped out my game stuff and the guy who bought it seems quite excited. In a way it's sad to see all that go, but at the same time I do feel that Shawn and this apartment and the cats, and school and work, other life in general, seems more important right now.

I talked to my dad about the fact I want breast implants this X-mas, figuring I'll have a couple weeks off for recovery, and he said his insurance might cover dependents, so I may be able to get them this summer more or less for free.

Since I'm not 18, dad said he'll sign consent if necessary. He asked if it really bugs me that I am not "well-endowed" and I told him yes, because it does. If his insurance does cover such cosmetic work then I also hope to get other stuff done eventually, but this is my main concern. Otherwise my dad said he may still help around December. I guess we'll see.

January 18

I'm moved out of my mom's house, I have Shawn, and I'm comfortable. Only way it could be better is this darned cold could be gone. My glands are swollen and my nose is effed up. But, I can live with that. I will eventually have to email my mom to ask about my college letter. I don't know that I even got one. If not, then worse case scenario I'll be going to community college. Either way I'll be going to school.

My cold has gotten worse, just like Shawn's did a couple nights ago. I was cold, yet my head was hot, so I had to be under a bunch of blankets with a cold wash cloth on my head, same as he had gone through. I laid out in the living room on the couch for a while, but with the TV on and Shawn and the roommate smoking, it was too much action for me. So I got up and carried my stuff to bed and the instant I stood up from the couch and was uncovered from the blankets I began to shiver. I was achy everywhere and just wanted it to be done. All this plus still having my nose messed up and the swollen glands and then my stomach decided to get gassy and rumble.

January 19

I "sweat it out" last night, waking up when Shawn came to bed at 2:30 a.m. (I went to bed around midnight) and talking to him a bit about it. He said this may be the worst of it and he helped me out a lot. He got me the washcloth and helped keep me tucked in. Even when I got hot he kept telling me I have to sweat it out. I woke up this morning feeling a bit better. My nose is still weird and my glands are still swollen, but not as bad. I took a shower already, so I feel cleaner. Hopefully as the day progresses, I get better and not worse again. All that and on top of it, I'm on my rag.

I have two cats; Anaki, a 6-month-old kitten, and Whisper, an unknown-aged cat that tends to have PMS and growl a lot. We're looking into getting another kitten so Anaki has a friend. We found one through a pet finder website. Shawn wants to call him Poindexter, since we're dorks like that and it'll be his cat. He's a month or two younger than Anaki and fixed. Anaki has been running around all morning, trying to play with everything, and now has stopped by my side to paw at me to be petted. She's used to having my dad's kitten, poor thing.

Yesterday evening Shawn got mad at Whisper because she was being herself. She was growling at him as he was walking by her. She growls a lot, but if she wants attention she'll climb up in your lap and purr and be the cuddliest little thing ever. So he took her in the bathroom for some "tough love." He put on a glove and held her while she got pissed off and hissed and when he got really mad that she wouldn't calm down and give in to him trying to love her, he stuck her in the closet and stood there.

I got mad at him and told him she's not like a dog, you can't be mean to her, she's a cat and they're much more sensitive. So now I guess we're not giving Whisper attention so that she learns to be nice. I personally think we should let her be herself, but I'll humor him.

January 20

Today I got high. I've only done it twice now because the first time Shawn had me try it, I didn't get enough to feel anything, so I don't count that. Lila's brother, Adam, got a new bong that's like 2-1/2 feet tall that we all tried. Adam lit it for me, I just had to suck. I guess what he gave me was a *big* hit, so I got really high. Everyone was sort of yelling at him for it because I coughed a lot and considering my low experience with it all. He said he thought I told him he could do a big one, but what I told him is he could light it.

Long story short, getting high isn't *that* great. Its okay, but I don't really think I like feeling like that and even if I were to do it on occasion, I don't feel the need to get high all the time. I don't understand the thrill I guess. Shawn does it sometimes, but still not much compared to the roommate and his girlfriend. They go places, to peoples' houses, and do it besides doing it here. I think as far as my future experiences with weed, they'll be slim.

January 21

My cold is getter better, other than a headache and the slightest possible feeling of swollen glands, along with a couple sensitive taste buds on my tongue. I took some Tylenol, so I should be okay. I'm getting through it a lot faster than Shawn, so he's a bit jealous of that.

As for him and me, we're fine. We are "back to normal" other than we have a different label on it, but things are great. I made him call Victoria Friday night because she calls all the time and texts, but even after a very vague conversation, he had it on speaker so I could hear. She called yesterday during the day and he ignored it. He has *no* interest in dealing with her, especially because she's being a bit obsessive.

My mom replied to my email asking about my college letter. She said she didn't get anything as of yet, so now I get to figure out what I'm doing as far as that goes. She also said that DHS (Department of Human Services) called asking about me and moving, and she gave them Shawn's number. She called him an idiot in the email and I told her not to do that. I talked to DHS before she told me, so I didn't bother calling them back. Obviously I talked to them after she did since they called me on Shawn's phone.

January 23

Shawn and I stayed up until about 4 a.m. I'm over my cold now and Shawn is for the most part, too. Just a few coughs now and then. Pot isn't that grand and I told Shawn that. He said I didn't have to do it all the time, he won't make me, but I didn't expect he would.

This morning, waking up to Shawn *not* wanting to "play" was a bit surprising. He said that now that I'm here all the time, he doesn't feel like going at it all the time. Unfortunately, I want more than he can provide because I'm in the mood more. I suppose it's something to work through.

January 24

Lately I've been talking to Victoria on MySpace via our messages. I think she only talks to me to find out about Shawn, but I am good at playing along. I try to be nice, as I tell Shawn–friends close, enemies closer–but it's getting hard to do. I guess she's hung up on everything because she told him she loved him and he told her it back, but, as I figured, it was only to make her happy and hush her up, not because he meant it. Which of course brought me to asking him about telling me that, but he reassured me he really means it with me. That boy likes to dig a lot of holes.

I basically told her in my last message that I'm trying to be honest, which I was, telling her probably more than I should about what I know from Shawn, but also trying to be nice, which caused me to stop "spilling" when I got to the point of replying about their sex life. I told her it's hard to do both and I'll try and answer questions she may have, but if she asks too much I can easily see myself getting snotty and mean because I know myself well enough to warn her that. I still don't want to be flat out mean, even though I don't like her.

My mom emailed me. She said she got it switched so that child support goes into my account at her bank as soon as it goes to her, immediate transfer I guess. Unfortunately, there is no branch up here, so I have to see if she can get it to go to the bank where I set up the account yesterday for my debit card. At least she's working on it, that's nice. I think her emails of notification on this stuff are just her way of talking to me, though. That's my opinion.

Shawn had to get on the checking account with me, but he won't have a card. It was only because of the fact I'm not yet 18. I trust that he won't do anything with my money, but at the same time as soon as he can get off the account I may be making him get off.

Last night, as well as a couple nights ago, I had a really bad dream about Shawn leaving me. The first time I had one, I woke up crying and Shawn was too tired to do more than give me a hug and roll over. Today I didn't cry, but I still had a wave of "OMG-ness" and tried to cling to him, but he was again too tired.

It's obvious I have a big fear of losing him, again and forever. I just don't think I need to be reminded at night while I'm trying to sleep. Death is my biggest fear; I don't even want to talk about it. I am possibly to the point of phobia with it. I am slowly trying to do the day-by-day thing.

With Victoria I am getting more tempted to be honest with her than nice. In her recent message she said she is "over Shawn" and "just wants to be friends." I told her that's great but I still don't want her alone with him.

I just bought Shawn a GameCube on eBay. Tomorrow we'll have been together a year. He knows I got it for him. I don't know that he'll get me anything. I know he'd buy me something if he could afford it, but having no job right now, he can't. I don't need anything but it'd be nice to get something. I said he doesn't need to buy me anything, he can do something else. I don't know if he will or not.

January 25

We are on a terrible sleeping schedule right now. We went to be at 3:30 a.m. and I just woke up. Now he's still in bed; 11:35 a.m. is what the laptop tells me. I don't sleep as much as he does, he'll probably be in bed a while yet. He's excited about his GameCube and I'm excited about my new Tamagotchis. It'll be like a holiday on the days the stuff arrives.

I've been so caught up in living here with Shawn the past few days I haven't called my dad. I intended to tonight when Shawn's minutes are free on his phone, but seem to space it off. It'll be a bit after ten and I realize I didn't call. Tonight I hope to call. He always told me I'd grow up and move away and forget about him, so I'm determined to prove him wrong. I can't forget my dad. Especially because of the bond I had with him opposed to my mother. He sort of took the place of both emotionally for me, so I can't ever let that go.

Shawn claims he does not have any job opportunities available at the moment. I think he wants to take online classes this fall because then the reserve will pay for it and if he takes them through the community college he'll actually make money because courses cost less than they'd pay him per class. I still haven't heard from college and still don't have a clue who to contact. One of the reasons I wanted to talk to dad is because he seems to know a lot about this stuff.

As far as the twins, I personally don't get updates but my mom and Shawn's mom do and my dad is supposed to, but I don't think the Clarks email him. Mom claims she gave the family his email address, but she may be lying because she hates dad and feels the fact he never held the twins or had them at his house means he didn't care. But I have no idea what's going on. They're not mine, not my worry. I really am detached. I know Shawn says he cares about them but I don't think he checks up on them either. I know he has tried to be detached, too.

Well, as I was journaling I got a reply from my mother. At the end of my last email I asked her how long she was going to be mad at Shawn and she said probably for the rest of his life and I can stop commenting about him in my emails because she doesn't care about him. Taking my first minor stab at her, still kept it fairly clean since I'm not 18 and don't know what she can legally do as far as bringing me home, I said that it's her choice and I learned a long time ago that she does what she wants, no matter what, other people don't matter. Dane Cook is a stand-up comic who said how women plant bombs in a fight, things that sit and develop and explode later, so that's sort of what that was.

January 26

We just got home from getting Poindexter, our new cat. Shawn named him for the guy in *Revenge of the Nerds* since we are Internet junkies/nerds. We'll probably call him Dex most of the time; hopefully it shouldn't confuse the cat. Last night, Whisper shat on Shawn's coat as he watched. I might see if my dad can take her back because she doesn't get along with the other cats *or* Shawn.

Last night Shawn and I had a talk after sex. He didn't get me off and I felt bad that he couldn't. I don't know how one thing leads to another, but it does and we got to talking about loving each other. He says he does love me, more than the other girls he's dated although he still loves each and every one of them. I understand how that won't fade completely.

He cares about me and wants the best for me, but he's afraid of commitment and doesn't know if he can see us lasting. Again he mentioned "until we're old." He says he wants something that he can see lasting, yet he's afraid to commit. I guess I'm his longest relationship. He said he knows that when I tell him I love him it means *so much* more than when he says it, so now he says he thinks he wants to wait to say it. I understand, but it still feels too much like going backwards. Yes, I cried, but I'm trying to cope.

He said he will still tell me he loves me. I told him I know what it means from him, that it's not as much as when I say it, but I still like to hear it if that's how he feels. Also, I told him I don't want him to love me as much as I love him because then all we'd do is sit around, stare at each other, tell each other we love the other, and have sex. That's boring. He does treat me right and we have a great time together, we are doing great, so I think I just won't bring it up unless there's a problem which I can't see us having, we don't have many problems really.

I talked to my dad last night, so that was good. He said he'd let me go three times, but kept talking. In the end he said he missed our weekend runs together and finally said goodbye.

January 28

Shawn is playing with his GameCube. His stomach has been bugging him, but he can miraculously recover long enough to play with it. Mark and his Lila were looking at an apartment today. I guess sometime between now and the beginning of summer they want to get an apartment, so it'll be just Shawn and I. I may have to get a job, but with his tax money he's getting and the reserve money, plus me getting child support, I still might not have to for a while. We'll see how things go.

The extra room might be nice, give the cats more space because then I might see if my dad will build them a tower instead of me buying one. Now we must go check the mail, hopefully my PIN number arrived for my debit card.

January 29

Yesterday into last night, Shawn was feeling sick. His lower abdominals, or as he keeps saying, his intestines, hurt. We went to bed at about midnight and I told him if he needs anything to wake me up. Around 1:00 a.m. he got me up and asked me to go get the blue bowl we just got recently, because it's large, and bring it in because he feels like he's going to throw up. I did and went back to sleep. I woke up quite a few times because he was whining, literally whining and almost crying, about the pains and throwing up occasionally.

Finally about 4:30 a.m. he had me call his mom. He said he thought he needed to go to the hospital/ER because there were specks of blood in his vomit. That and he couldn't sleep, he rolled around a lot and cussed and hit pillows out of pain. I called his mother and she wasn't thrilled, she talked to him, but he handed me the phone back so he could throw up again. After a little discussion she came and took us to her house so she could go back to bed and we could use the van. I didn't have my glasses on, thinking she was driving us, so considering

Shawn was unable to drive I had a real fun time with that one. Luckily nobody was on the roads so early.

We made it to the ER in one piece, he went in and they asked him questions after getting him seated on a bed; took his blood pressure, temperature, all that stuff. Shawn does not have insurance, I do through my dad, thankfully for me, and so I'm a bit uneasy about how this'll turn out when a bill arrives. They ended up giving him an IV in his arm and took some blood for lab work. A doctor came in and felt his stomach/abdominals and he is tender on his right side more so than the other side, but is really just sore all over; dull pains, he says.

Blood work came back fine and the drugs they also put in the IV seemed to help. They gave me a bottle of red cherry drink (Magnesium Citrate Oral Solution, according to the label) and he was to take half a bottle when we got home, which he did, and the other half four hours later if he was still feeling terrible. The nurse pushed Shawn in a wheelchair to the van and he seemed okay, but as soon as he got in the van, he went back to feeling shitty.

He did drink the stuff when we got home, but threw it all up, which the nurse said he shouldn't throw up anymore with the drugs. The drink was supposed to give him diarrhea to flush him out about an hour after he drank it because the doctor said he could have something backed up, but it didn't stay down. So in about 45 minutes I have to make him drink the rest. He finally got to sleep, after his grandma called offering to bring us milk and some other groceries. Hopefully he sleeps for the next 45 minutes and is okay when I go in there.

January 31

Oh boy, where to begin. Well, we went to the doctor again yesterday. He didn't improve and was screaming, crying, whining, hitting things, and throwing stuff. He went through a wide range of emotions because of his pain. He got a CT scan and they poked his rectum and decided he wasn't constipated and maybe it was his appendix. They sent us over to the hospital since we were at the clinic and they were going to remove the appendix, but the surgeon said he thought it was something else. There was fluid built up and an inflamed part of the small intestine. He didn't know for sure what was wrong but decided upon "exploratory surgery" as primitive as it sounds. *Surgery!*

So, they went in and removed the appendix anyway and turns out he had a rare hernia that was sucking part of his intestines into a sack and bruising them. He was most likely born with it. He's had problems before, but they just called it constipation, and it was a serious situation. This time could have killed him.

Now he has a tube through his nose so that his stomach stays empty and he's in the hospital through the weekend. I'm home tonight to take care of the cats, while he's out of it, and will go back in the morning. I talked to him a little, although he was a bit drugged, and he said he loved me and all that and told me to give Dex love. It was a long day and, as with most shocking experiences in my life, I can't think as straight now as I will be able to tomorrow. The doctor even said he could've died. It was so scary!

When the surgeon left after saying he wants to do surgery, but not because of the appendix, I went over to Shawn and tried talking to him, but his grandma, who gave us a ride around the countryside to all the doctors, was still in there. I think she picked up on the fact I wanted to talk to him, so she excused herself to the restroom. I sort of teared up and asked him if he'll be okay and of course he was all, "I'll be fine, don't worry," yadda, yadda, yadda.

I think he's filling out papers for financial aid. His grandma said she can cover the expenses, she sold some property and is now technically rich, but if there's aid to help, that'd be nice. So I don't know if he'll have to pay for it at all anyway.

I sure hope once he comes home Mark is nice enough to *not* invite over a ton of people. If Lila is here, fine, as long as we're just chilling watching a movie.

At the hospital, Shawn isn't allowed to smoke anywhere and he can't right now anyway. But his mom and grandmother and the nurse are all going to try and get him to quit since he'll have five days or so to start with. If he quits that'd be nice, save money and his health, but if he doesn't that's his choice. I learned a while ago, last time he had his head up his ass before this more recent time, that if he's going to do it, he's going to do it and I'll take him as is.

A lady came in and helped him fill out the paperwork for financial aid/Medicaid; asked him questions and wrote it out for him, and she did not include me on it. I don't think she technically can anyway. We asked about the checking account we share, but she said she won't put it because then they'll look at my finances, too. So it's all him.

February 1

He's doing better today than we all thought. He still has to ask the doctor about his drill in a month and he's going to ask about his sexual activity, when it's safe to "get back on the horse" I guess you could say. This morning he managed to pee on his own, so no need for a catheter, which is good. Now they want him to pass gas so he can start eating. Gas means that things are moving through his intestines okay. He's got the tube in his nose to his stomach until then.

I'm staying the night. Left a note for Mark so he knows, hopefully he'll do dishes and wash towels and then when I go home sometime tomorrow I hope to clean the apartment more and get it organized to surprise Shawn when he comes home. Shawn said as long as I want to be here he wants me here, so I may come back tomorrow night as well. I know that having someone to talk to does help. I stay in his room as he is in a private room.

February 2

Shawn is lucky to be alone in his room. I'll probably go home to take care of the cats today and then be back again tonight. We just went for a walk. He's doing really well, the nurse said; we just need him to fart so he can get the tube out of him and eat some food. Then he'll be doing really well. In his procedure, they actually pulled out his small intestines, which is amazing because his two little incisions aren't very big, and did their thing, then put them back. Nora told him that yesterday and he wasn't thrilled to hear it.

He just got his tube hooked up again about twenty minutes ago, so about one o'clock or so they'll check to see how much it's sucking out and if it's less than it was before (it was 80 – 90 cc) then he can leave the tube out. He wanted me to help him put his leg pumps (the things that are to help keep circulation going in your legs, they wrap around the legs and fill with air) back on after a walk and I didn't understand what he was asking me to do. Something about moving some blankets before hooking him up and he sort of yelled at me and I cowered down, being terrible at handling yelling (thanks, Mom). And he moved things around, I hooked him up, and then he called me over and sort of hugged me. He did what he could, considering the tenderness of his tummy.

He actually cried, let out a few tears, and said he was sorry for getting mad at me and he just held me. I have no idea what it was all about, I told him I understand. If he hurts, he's irritable, I get it. But he just had a moment of apology like he was saying sorry for more than just that. I have no idea, but I didn't ask questions and just let him do his thing.

February 3

I'm home with the cats tonight. Have to shower and clean up the apartment. Mark didn't do what I asked him to, so I have more to do than I hoped for. He cleans some, more than Shawn. But he lets it get fairly bad before he does so. He takes care of the garbage more than anything, but again, he lets it pile up a lot first. I picked up a few things and the dishes are washing in the dishwasher. I used dish soap, not dish *washer* soap, so it decided to bubble onto the floor. I put a towel down and am letting it finish. We don't have other soap, we ran out, so it'll have to work.

Rent is due today, but Mark isn't around to pay his half and my half (Shawn's and mine, but I'm covering it for him this month) is on its way from PayPal to my account as of today. Shawn called the landlord to say he's in the hospital, so I think we have a few days leeway.

The cats act like they haven't had love in ages.

Shawn got off of morphine and on something else, a synthetic morphine, because he gets hives with morphine. Now that he has painkillers in his system again (he was trying not to use the morphine), he seems to be better than he was when he woke up. They're giving him milk products and "full liquids" this afternoon instead of clear liquids, so maybe tomorrow he can go home.

February 4

Shawn's been in the hospital a lot longer than I though he'd be. Seems his problem was much more serious than a bottle of pink stuff could cure, and then some! His problem was definitely a big one. I'm still mad at the ER where we went for just blowing it off as a virus. He might come home tomorrow, but he wants to stay until he's "sure he's ready." I told him he'll still be hurting when he comes home, he won't be one hundred percent, but I guess I'll let him whine. When they kick him out of the hospital, then he'll know.

Mom emailed me again. I asked her about my savings bonds and she said I can "suck rocks" and I won't get them until she feels I'm mature enough to have them. I told her it doesn't matter, they're not worth their full potential yet anyway, and then I said she's not one to be telling me about maturity. She wants a fight, then fine, but so far she's already on fire and I'm just sort of like, "Okay, sure."

February 5

Shawn's grandma has church this morning, so I can't give her a shout to ask about visiting Shawn. Hopefully he can come home today. She is my only ride at this point. No idea when he'll have a car again. We both need jobs and I think we're both going to go to community college this fall. The regular college still hasn't sent my letter, supposedly. It's cheaper anyway.

Shawn applied for Medicaid, most likely he'll get it, I don't know for sure. His grandma will pay otherwise, but I still like to have extra cash just in case, part of the reason of wanting to make money on the other game stuff I'm trying to sell, that and rent and the need for a car.

I know he's going to need some waiting on when he gets home but I already wait on him, and don't really mind. I'm sure he'll get on my nerves a bit when he comes home, though, because it's going to be so much worse. But at the same time, I like to take care of him.

I've been thinking a lot about my breast implants lately. I won't know more about getting them for a couple months yet, my dad has to talk to his insurance rep. The more I think about it, I think I want to get the implants, a tummy tuck to fix the stretched places from the kids, and liposuction on my thighs and butt, again due to stretching and swelling from pregnancy, at the same time. Seeing Shawn in the hospital reminds me how sucky surgery is and I really don't want to go through it multiple times if I don't have to. If I have to pay for it myself then it'll be just boobs for now.

February 6

Shawn came home yesterday evening!

I'm getting annoyed with Mark and Lila. Mark hasn't paid his half of the rent yet and doesn't seem in a hurry to do it. He leaves lights on, "forgets" to flush the toilet, leaves stuff lying around, and eats Shawn's and my food. Luckily he's moving out within the next month or two.

I have to talk to my old bank about them sending child support to my new bank account. I was going to call, but don't seem to have the right paperwork and account number with me. I have two accounts, one with my dad and one that my mom set me up with and I only have the stuff from my dad. So they'll want my ID and such and it's easier in person to straighten it out than over the phone.

If that works out okay and Shawn is up to paying half the rent, so far it's just sort of whoever has the money pays for things, then maybe I can keep my game stuff a bit longer. I really do want to keep some of it, no doubt about that, just a matter of affording it.

February 7

Well, within a couple months Mark should be gone. I tell Shawn about my feelings and he agrees on some of it. His unopened soda was taken yesterday, so when he asked me to get it and I told him, I think that's what helped him agree with me. I think Grandma Margaret will help us with rent because Mark said he's broke until Thursday.

Shawn is getting his car back *plus* he's getting a free car because someone was giving it away. It was owned by a mechanic, well up-kept (although it has 100,000 miles on it) and has a new engine. That car will be for me to use if need be. Also, Shawn found a job that's sort of like Mark's, four days a week, 12 hours a day, and it pays *great* ($16.50 an hour) plus benefits. So that's good.

Shawn's job would be during the day. It'd be 6 to 6 or something like that. Shawn said he's getting me an application for a job at the same place. Assuming I don't have to be 18 to work there, it sounds like a good idea. It's factory work.

I honestly don't know about being a Suicide Girl anymore. I sort of want to, but it sounds very complicated and I know a couple people that are doing it and I don't like the idea of "going with the crowd." Shawn was okay with the idea if I were to follow through, though.

February 11

Today is Shawn's doctor's appointment to get checked, make sure everything's healing okay. Near the incision his tummy is swollen still, but it doesn't bother him more than he thinks it should. He has been playing with the GameCube. I tell him to take it easy, but he still tries to move around a bit more than he probably should. He's good about not lifting anything over 10 pounds, though.

We are both a bit "restless" from being in the apartment all day. I find myself acting over-dramatic to create a bit more excitement in our days, but that tends to get annoying. He has the urge to clean to stay busy which isn't annoying until he wants to straighten cords on the TV while I'm watching it. He has to unhook them and fix them, then rehook them, then do it again. Our living room and kitchen looks fairly decent now. Our bedroom will improve once Mark leaves and we have the other room for my computer and other stuff.

The cats, at least the two younger ones, run around crazy a lot in the mornings and then again in the evenings. They're restless, too. I had a leash for Anaki, who is really skittish, but it was a rabbit harness, so if she got scared she'd be in tight so I could walk her in the halls or outside. Not now that it's cold, but at least take her out a bit, but I left it at my dad's. So, everyone is fidgety and it sucks.

Mark and Lila just got home and it makes me think how happy I'll be when they're not here daily. I got up this morning, anxious to eat my favorite PopTarts and I find an empty box in there. My last pack that I was saving for this morning was gone. I even had my name on the box in two places, although hard to read. I am not happy with them. It seems so simple, but it was really the "last straw" so to speak.

Shawn moved the laptop into the bedroom while cleaning yesterday. He said that way we can spend time together in the living room instead of on the computer all the time. I thought it was sweet.

This summer we plan to go camping, bowling, mini golfing, and he's planning a trip for just us to go to Disney World. Seems to me he has no plans of leaving me for at least the length of the summer. Where he thinks he's getting money, though, I'm not entirely sure!

We rented video games today after his doctor's appointment, grocery shopping, and supper with his grandmother. We also watched some of my anime series I have on DVD called *Chobits*. There are seven discs; we did two and a half today and we'll do two and a half more tomorrow.

Together time is good. Normally then we take a moment out of the day where he'll go check his email, etc., and then I will and we get that bit to ourselves. And we don't spend so much time on the computer and don't run off to it so much. I do think it's working out well. The only reason I'm journaling now is because I just woke up and he's still "working on it" and playing with his kitty. Not being clingy is hard, but I am trying. We're good about talking to each other.

Last night we were joking around and I kept giving him a hard time. He laughed a lot of the time, so I thought he was having a good time, too, but then he got mad and turned away. It was while lying in bed, it was really dark, we were going to be going to sleep, but I always seem not tired when my head hits the pillow. I asked him what's wrong because at first I thought he was pretending to be mad.

He yelled and said he's tired of people having a good time at his expense and he's had that all his life and he's an adult now and shouldn't have to deal with it. I apologized and asked him what that was all about since he laughed, too, and he said sometimes it was funny how

I was kidding with him, but he didn't like what I was kidding about. I mentioned this one morning when we woke up and he was laying on his side, outside the covers, in just boxers and the pant leg was flipped just right he was "exposed" and he didn't realize it until I pointed it out. I cried, and he apologized after I said I wouldn't kid about that stuff again and he said he won't leave me over something so stupid, not to worry. It was interesting.

February 12

Nora and I get along okay. She *really* hates Shawn smoking and I am a bit indifferent, so we don't get along on that topic, but otherwise we're fine.

I'm still a bit PO'd at Mark and Lila and came home from the witchy vet to see those two *and* another one of their mutual girl friends all here, plus Shawn being here with them, all of them high, and the oven on. I shut it off, and I'm in the bedroom with all the cats right now, sipping my strawberry soda, just trying to ignore them.

Shawn started getting high before I left, but I didn't know how high he had gotten, but obviously high enough since I had to shut off the oven. That scared me a little bit, I'll admit. I told him I don't like pot, not for me at all. I don't like how it makes me feel and I turn it down all the time around here. I don't really like him doing it either, but I admitted that I know if I told him not to and he did it anyway, which he would, then I'd just get really mad, so why bother? He said once Mark's gone he won't do it anymore since he won't get it for free.

Shawn is doing much better; he even took out the garbage today which I asked him to do while I got the laundry going. Last night we got to have sex, even though he's not really supposed to for a couple weeks. I wasn't expecting it, so it was a nice surprise in a way. Lucky for him I'm getting close to "my time of the month," so he won't have to over-strain himself anymore until that's over with.

Victoria is coming over today. Shawn and I are bored and she asked if she, Shawn, and I could hang out. I'm sure I was only included because I've told her Shawn and her will not be alone together again. She told me way back when that she is over him and I told Shawn if she comes over with a "revealing" shirt then we know she lies. Shawn and I debated about hanging out with her, but, we're bored, so we're going to try and make peace for something to do. Pathetic.

February 13

Mark still hasn't paid this month's part of the rent, last month's part of the electric bill, or this month's part of the electric bill. I've very frustrated. My hand cream has "disappeared" and when I went looking for the long mirror this morning, it was in Mark's room. Shawn went in while he was out; it is *our* apartment after all. He still is on my nerves. He was just here and then left, I don't think he said a word to Shawn and I know he didn't say anything to me. Whenever he gets home I'll be asking, or making Shawn ask him, for the rent again.

Tomorrow being Valentine's Day, Shawn and I plan to go out. His car hasn't come around yet. He's supposed to get a call when one of the two cars he gets is ready, so I think he may borrow his grandmother's. We plan to go for Chinese, our favorite, and to a movie.

It didn't go bad with Victoria, but it didn't go well either. I tried to be nice and talked to her and acted like we were cool, but she barely said anything to me and had no interest in being nice. It was long, silent, boring. Then she left.

February 14

Mark claims his mom won't pay rent so now he will be doing it next Thursday. But that's what he said last time before he said his mother would do it.

Shawn and I did get to go out; we used his grandmother's car. We had a nice time, although he strained himself a bit earlier today. He said he thought he was ready to have sex and was fine after, but that plus walking around a lot today and him not being able to take pain killers so he could drive made him sore. Other than all that, he's good and I'm good and it was a nice, simple Valentine's Day.

Shawn is returning my rings finally so we have a few extra bucks on hand and because we're not ready for them anyway. He did say that one day maybe I'll get rings again. He said I can wear the "promise ring" he gave me, the original ring that was his mother's. I told him I want to get married when I'm 20, or later, so I told him not to run off and then we can talk about marriage and he said okay. We still have camping plans and all sorts of stuff planned for this summer, so I think he plans to stick around a while, just not *commit*, which is fine by me. I like what we have right now.

I'm not ready for "lifetime" yet, but I do see it being highly possible that it turns into that. I still feel I love Shawn more than anything and that I'd be very content spending my life with him, but there are things we should work on or work out before we take such a plunge of commitment.

Both he and I have stuff we need to improve on. I see my life going as us working at it together, I don't really see a whole lot that I feel I need to go at alone or on my own.

It's nice to have someone to be supportive. And, the fact he said he doesn't plan on running away the next few years is nice to know. No pressure on figuring it all out today or tomorrow whereas before I had the feeling it was "now or never."

February 15

Shawn is figuring out his taxes and his financial aid for his doctor bills, at least he's supposed to be. I mean, he's doing it, but he's doing it slowly. Unfortunately we both like to procrastinate.

Something I didn't know, when Victoria was here the other day, Mark had asked Shawn what was going on(it was while he asked about the rent again, the TV was on so Victoria and I couldn't hear what they were saying in Mark's room) and Shawn told him it was my idea for Victoria to come over, which is half true. Then Shawn mentioned to Mark that I wasn't very happy lately with the lack of rent payment and everything and Mark told him he understood.

Today Mark picked up an employment application for himself and brought two extra home, one for me and one for Shawn, although looking at it, I have to be at least 18 to apply. I thought it was kind of sweet so when I asked Shawn about it he said he told Mark I wasn't happy. It was a nice gesture, I think. And next week he said he'll have all that he owes us.

Lila mentioned a place I could apply where you only have to be 16. It's working with mentally challenged people and I think she said you make $9 an hour. My dad has worked with handicapped, so having been around it and gone to work with him, I thought, hey, that sounds like an idea right there. I mean, it's not hard to do and that's good pay for someone my age. I'll definitely have to look into it.

I talked to my dad about taxes so I can apply for FAFSA for school and I asked about his insurance paying for plastic surgery. He says right now he's not sure but he's still checking. So by the time I'm 18 and can legally get the surgery I think he may have what I need to cover it.

February 19

Today Shawn should be dropping off his job application. I went through it with him to be sure he filled it out and we had two copies, so he did one and I rewrote it onto the other so it was slightly more legible. Him having an "insider," he insists he'll get the job, but of course I still am concerned. We're still waiting on him to get a reply from the convenience store on getting his pay stubs so he can get financial aid on his medical stuff since he had automatic payment/direct deposit and didn't get pay stubs. Whenever we go to the video store again I will pick up an application.

We have to pay the landlady for having the cats (deposit + monthly fee) and Shawn and I are going to ask her what the rule is about skunks as we want to get an albino one. We know of a breeder and we know they are legal; it's just up to the apartment rules. They are similar to cats, but remind me more of ferrets in how they act. They can be litter trained, so it's not any extra headache. It would be an interesting pet.

Dad picks up his tax stuff Tuesday and he is having the college forward my mail here instead of my mom's, but I still may just go to the community college. I'm waiting to get FAFSA figured out before I do more. Luckily with the community college I don't feel as rushed to "get in." And I have to call the bank.

I guess the landlord/landlady is checking apartments. If they smell smoke, we're in trouble. Also have to pay the cat stuff before they come around. If they do come before we've paid, we decided to say we *just recently* got the cats. I guess they smelled smoke in Mark's friend's apartment and he got reprimanded, so I don't know that we'd lose the apartment if they checked ours. I told Shawn that now it's getting warmer he should smoke outside and Mark already has been taking it outside without me asking. We burn incense to cover up the smell a lot and if they ask about smell we can just say it's the incense.

Money will be a stressor for a bit, at least until Shawn's job gets going. We won't add another pet to the mix unless the landlady okays it and we can really afford it. Skunks need veggies and meats, which wouldn't be cheap, so we may not get one until late next year.

After our lease is up we plan to renew it once and then Shawn said we can buy a trailer. It's not quite a house, but a bit more our own. It gives us time to save up to buy the plot and the trailer, and the skunk.

February 20

Shawn turned in his application and the papers he needs for financial aid. I have to talk to my dad tonight about switching child support to go to my new bank account instead of the current bank because they said it'd be through Child Support Recovery. Hopefully my dad can get it all figured out, but I'm not sure. My biggest fear is I'd have to talk to my mother and I haven't talked to her in a long while.

February 21

The jewelers called this morning with a pre-recorded message telling Shawn to call them. He's returning the rings, so if he does call it'll just be to notify them. He lets me wear the original ring that was his mother's; it's sort of like a promise ring. The other night I was sitting next to him when he was online and someone asked him about him having a fiancée and he said, "More or less."

Last night I watched a show called America's Next Top Model. I love modeling shows; mainly because I always wanted to be a model and I know it never would happen. A little girlie factoid that *nobody* knows about me other than Shawn and I told him not to tell.

After I took over the computer we started doing this thing called Hot or Not on the Internet where you rate pictures from 1 (not) to 10 (hot) and I asked him my rating and he said 9 and he ended up explaining my face is a 10, body is a 7. I asked him what happens when a 10 comes along and he said he loves *me*. I said that I don't mean to bring up the past since I haven't in so long, but I told him I can't forget that conversation about how he loves me, but not as much as I love him. He was, "But I love you tons more now," and I asked when that happened and said if that's the case then I'm not so insecure.

And besides with getting surgery/ies I'll fix the flaws from getting pregnant, that stretched/squishy junk, and fix the flaws of nature, small boobles. So I guess I'm really not that worried. It is my face I take the most pride in anyway and that's already a 10.

Shawn is healing and I swear he's almost back to normal. I can lay on him and his stomach as long as I don't just flop down violently. He's been going against doctor's orders and we've had "relations" at least once the past few days or so. Today he's been capable of going twice without hurting after, so that's good. It's a good workout for him.

He is thinking of getting a membership at the local gym and he said he'd get it so I could come with. I told him I'd work out with him, but more for the social aspect of it than the getting in shape part. I'd like to tone up naturally, too, but other than what I plan to fix with surgery I'm not too insecure about the rest. That'll be nice, but with getting jobs and me going to school and possibly him, too, not sure how much time we'll have for a gym. I guess we'll see!

February 22

Mark's supposed to pay us our money today. He owes $353 total. We saw him earlier today, but he was fixing his car in the parking lot. He just left. We were out and just got home. So hopefully he's bringing stuff back with him.

Shawn tried to return the rings, but can't without the original receipt and it's been more than 90 days, I think. Assuming he gets the job, he'll be okay, but right now his credit is getting messed up because we're broke. (*Thanks, Mark.*)

I have to email my mom about the bank and child support, so hopefully she's not a complete idiot about that.

I was supposed to get my hair cut today, but only Shawn got his cut since he has to for drill this weekend (*again, thanks, Mark*). Today sucks and I'm in such a bad mood.

February 23

Mom emailed me and said she'll call when she gets to it which she said could be a month and she accused me of not trying to call the bank at all, which I did. So, I most likely will have to do something about going there soon. Shawn has drill tomorrow and Sunday, so hopefully next week.

Mark came home this evening and moved all his stuff out and is gone, gone, gone. He did not pay Shawn and me back and he didn't really say anything about it when Shawn asked him. Also, because of him and Lila and how hard they "go at it," there's a good-sized hole in the wall from the bed. He didn't tell us about that, we found out when we looked. Tomorrow I plan to move stuff into the room while Shawn is gone.

February 24

Shawn just left for drill. The weather is really bad, there's rain and ice and snow to come, so Shawn might not get far and come home or he may get there and be stuck there overnight and maybe tomorrow night, too, which would suck, because he plans to come home tonight to sleep and then go back and he's done Sunday afternoon. So I guess we'll see, just as long as he doesn't get hurt.

Shawn said Mark might come back today, but then after he said it a little while later we both agreed he probably wouldn't. Shawn thinks he's running without paying us, but that won't happen. I won't let it. My dad's a big guy, we'll hunt him down. He left behind his drinking glasses, and the couch and chair. Other than the garbage and the hole in the wall, that's all he has left here, so I can't see him coming back. I don't want him to have a key any more and I don't think he left it around here anywhere. I feel like I'm finally free to do what I want in *my* apartment, but then I remember he has a key.

I knew Mark was leaving because he picked up the living room, something we normally have to do for him and the towel supply went down. I guess one of the towels I used when I shower was Mark's because it was gone. He didn't notify us he was going; we just sort of figured it out. He barely said anything when he left.

I still have to talk to dad more about the bank stuff. Shawn has the phone, so I am without a means to call him and all that needs to get sorted. I have money for next month's rent, just a matter of getting it to where I can use it.

Well, Shawn is home early from drill on account of the bad weather. He got home a little before 3 p.m. And drill is cancelled for tomorrow. I took the garbage out and there was an inch of ice over *everything*, trees, rocks, grass, sidewalk, etc. And now there's a whiteout of snow. It's a doozy out there.

Mark left someone's coat behind; I think it was his friend's. And I found his house key in his room, so he shouldn't be back. In the coat I found a watch that Shawn and I are guessing is worth around $40. We looked on the website it says on the back and this particular watch isn't listed, it's similar to the $40 and $50 ones. So I gained a watch.

Shawn left Mark a message and my dad said if he needed to talk to Mark or come up here he would. Hopefully in hearing that, Mark will pay. Dad said he'd fix the hole in the wall when the weather gets nicer, so that's good.

Money is sort of a problem, but if/when I get my bank stuff situated we'll be okay for a little longer and Shawn's job will help *tons*.

I'd still like to get some surgery done. Mainly I just want to smooth out my butt and thighs and get rid of the stretched part on my belly. I don't mind having some meat to me. I always have, but was a lot smaller, so it seems anyway, before the kids. I just want to be smooth again. I plan to work out if/when Shawn gets a gym membership for us. That way it'll be social and I can stay toned a bit and I won't feel pressured to work out if I'm going with Shawn.

February 26

Tomorrow Shawn and I are going to my old bank so I can at least withdraw my money from my account, since my mom plans to take her sweet time to get things switched around. That way I can pay rent and electricity and maybe even pay back Grandma Margaret (depends on how much I have) since she helped out a bit when Mark skimped us. The money in that bank account should hold us over another month, at least until Shawn gets his job, so I think we're okay.

February 28

Yesterday Shawn and I went to the bank and to visit dad. We took Anaki and Dex, who had a terrible time in the car and at dad's house. Dad's cat, Eli, forgot who Anaki was since the removal of his coconuts and didn't like Dex, but it was good to see Eli again either way.

Dad took us out to lunch and to a movie and then I finally got to the bank to withdraw what I had in there. There's still $260 that needs to transfer, but my dad said they just took it out this past Friday. I only had $404 and took out $400. Shawn talked to his grandma when we got home and she gave him a check for rent, so I can pay electricity and the cat stuff and hopefully get my hair cut!

Mark still owes us, but Shawn called yesterday and left a voicemail for him and Mark texted back. He wasn't thrilled and was saying it was stupid how he was the only one with a job when he was here and said that Shawn and I planned to have the place to ourselves anyway, so why do we need his money so bad, yadda, yadda, yadda. Shawn told him what I said, which was to the effect of even though we don't have jobs, we still managed to find a way to pay our share *and* his. We may have planned to "go it alone" on the apartment, but having him there changed our plans and considering he used up our electricity and ate our food, he can't expect us to cover him.

Shawn said we still want to be his friend, but we do need the money and Mark said he'll get it when he can; times are hard for him right now. Shawn told him they are for us too; he's not the only one. Mark stopped by to pick up his "male enhancement" pills after we got home and while Shawn was returning his grandma's car, so I was the only one that had to talk to him face-to-face which didn't consist of much more than a "hi" and a "bye." So, as Shawn's Grandma Margaret said, we probably won't see that money. But at least she's willing to help us out until Shawn's job pulls through or mine, although mine won't pay nearly as much and without having a car, it wouldn't matter right now if I did get the job. Although the money thing still sort of sucks, I got to see my dad and Eli, which was nice. I got to see the movie *Eurotrip*, which was a good movie. And, my dad got me a cell phone, finally. It's a new phone and it has a camera and all, so that's cool.

We're squeaking by, but we're not failing, so I guess we can't complain yet. Unfortunately I think Mark is a lost cause, but I sure hope not. I'm still not happy with that whole situation. I don't really like using my money for everything, but I'm the one that seems to have it, not a lot, but some.

I told Shawn that after I pay electricity tomorrow and pay for the cat down payment (landlord does not know about the cats until I pay) then I'll help him pay off my rings. He owes $55 a month for them, but can't pay this month due to the lack of job, so I said I'd put my last $125 down so they'll stop calling for a while. I'm doing it because I love him and also because right now I live with him and am dating him and if he looks bad so do I. I'm not saying we will get married someday, although he says we will, but there's always the chance that his credit will affect me. In a way, I'm covering my own ass.

Times may get worse before they get better. But I hope we can handle it. My dad will help when/however he can, but I know he has his own problems to deal with so there'll be times when he just can't. It was funny what he put in an email the other day, "You can be anything you want to be (except a man, it's too expensive)." That made me laugh out loud.

Dad and Shawn are getting along fine. Dad said he does not like what Shawn did to me, but he still thinks it's my choice to be with him and is okay with him so long as I'm not hurting. I guess dad's girlfriend is unhappy with what Shawn did and my decision to move in with him and the fact we both are unemployed, but I didn't see her much when I was there, so I'm not too concerned.

Cable was out a bit this evening, it just got back up (right before I go to bed, of course), and so we only had basic TV and no Internet. Shawn was watching his stuff in the living room and as soon as cable came back I ran in the bedroom to watch *America's Next Top Model* and

Will & Grace. It was nice having time doing our own thing. I'm sure Shawn likes it, too although when he went to drill the other day he came home telling me he missed me and hugged me like crazy. And he was worried about me when the Saturday siren went off, which it does every Saturday at noon, because he thought I'd freak out thinking it was a storm warning.

I'm tired and drank too much pop, so to bed with me now.

March 2

Shawn and I are on a terrible sleep schedule. Last night I slept the longest I think I ever have. We went to bed at about midnight; I woke up at 7:00 a.m. to use the restroom then zonked out again until 11:00.

This storm we have going on right now makes it *freezing* in the house. I try to keep the heat turned down, but there's a draft that comes in the sliding glass door, third floor makes the wind so much worse, too. Not sure how to close it up more than it already is. Needless to say, it makes the heat we do use seem like nothing. I think I'll be in bed on the computer a lot today so that I don't have to leave the covers.

Prom is the end of April; I need to be getting a dress, but am thinking it's not worth the money. I may just reuse the one from last year; it should fit better now than when I was pregnant.

March 3

I have yet to look outside at the snow this morning; I'm sort of afraid to. Shawn and I got up at about 9 a.m. today, which is a bit better of a schedule, although he insists we don't need a schedule until we have stuff to do. He says right now he's still "flexible" so he can go either way, depending if the job he gets is day shift or night shift.

Dad's mailing me a copy of his tax information so I can fill out FAFSA. I sort of want to take classes online, but all the general education courses you have to go to the school, at least that's how it appears for community college.

Dad wants me to go to regular college if I can get it covered by FAFSA which makes sense, but if it's not covered, then community college it is. I looked at the community college website, looking at what courses are considered general education and it scared me to realize all the stuff I have to take. I don't really want to go to college, but I don't know what I want to do with my life and it's better to go and make it look good on some application than not. Plus I get paid child support if I go to school.

You pay money to go to school so you can get a job and make money. I think we should cut out the middle man and just live. But that's fairly uncivilized, isn't it? I understand that I need a good job to make money and that whole bit. College is good, I know, but what about apprenticeships? In Europe that's much more popular than it seems here in the U.S. But I wonder what sort of careers I could look into that support that style of learning. That's the way I'd rather do it. You go to college and learn a lot of extra stuff that you'll never need and has nothing to do with the career you go into, it just looks good.

I'll research and see what I can do that's a bit more straight forward than doing this, that, and the other thing that has nothing to do with any job I'd ever want. I really am a believer of doing what makes you happy instead of doing what you should and being miserable, so now's the time to find a happy medium until I can afford to be happy.

March 4

I've noticed that Shawn and I have "tiffs" a lot more now that we're living together. I was a bit worried that was a bad thing, but he told me it's normal to disagree and annoy each other and get in little fights and he told me it's okay to "let him have it" if I get mad. He said that's just part of a healthy relationship and at the end of the day we still want to live together, so we're fine.

I told him not long ago that I hate how he always has to be right. For example, I'm holding the cat and he meows, so Shawn tells me to let him go and freaks until I do. Shawn holds the cat and he meows, he continues to hold him and it's "okay" for him to do it. Then last night he pointed out the thing about me that bothers him. He told me I whine too much. So we're both compromising. I understand I need to relax and it's good to hear him say we're normal for disagreeing and annoying each other, it's not going to end our relationship if we have a fight.

I signed on Instant Messenger, but my mother was on so I quickly signed off. Still not feeling I want to talk to her about anything. My dad ran into her at a basketball game a few weeks ago and mom said that she never hears from me except when I want something and the mail I send is "hate mail." Which I guess is true, I say the bare minimum to that woman and when she calls Shawn an idiot or makes me sound stupid then I am going to say something in return. I tell her he's not an idiot and I tell her that she shouldn't talk when she calls me immature.

I wonder how long until we can get along, if we ever can. I honestly don't care if we don't. I feel bad sometimes not having attachment to people, but as far as my mom goes, I have none. And with the babies, I still don't feel I made a bad choice. The only time I feel bad is when I realize that I don't feel bad about them. I think that made sense.

I bought Shawn a CAC reader so he can do his online military stuff. I guess he needs to change stuff and a week ago they said, "Hey, you need this." His birthday is coming up, so I told him that was it. If I could afford more, I would buy him more, but I can't.

He still plays with the Game Boy every day even though we only have one game and I shouldn't have even spent money on that. I told him he's an expensive boy to keep around. I was kidding, but was serious at the same time. I hope he gets that job soon so I can stop paying for everything. Grandma Margaret helps a lot where I can't. He's going to call about his car again today. Hopefully he can find out more about the job, too.

This turned out a lot longer than I thought it would. I guess there's a lot on my mind. A lot of it is more feelings than something I can say. Like, obviously I know money's tight and Shawn is expensive, but it's hard to express how I feel about it. I'm sort of mad that I pay for so much, but at the same time I don't have a job either. I also don't have a car and don't have a way to buy one without a job, so I'm relying on that freebie he's supposedly getting. I also can't stop thinking about the surgeries I'm to get assuming dad's stuff works out for me.

It is hard to think I may never get along with my own mother but at least I have my father and that's a good thing. I always felt, even though I lived with my mother, my father covered both roles. I'd always take my dad shopping even for bras and underwear and homecoming dresses and even took him when I found out I was pregnant.

I really hate to remember the pregnancy thing. That was such a hard moment when that lady told me so bluntly it came back positive. I still wish the whole thing never happened.

Mom and her mother didn't get along when she was living at home either, that's what my dad said, and then the same for my mom and I. I always got along with my dad and I'm more like my dad, which is why my dad and I think my mom dislikes me.

I tend to feel the lonely child inside more than I probably should. Hopefully that eases with time. I don't think my mom would go to very high lengths to try and make me unhappy because it may in turn get around and make her look bad. She's very much about image, sadly.

Dad used to ask why he paid child support if mom refused to buy me clothing or anything. Mom's excuse for not school shopping is "I just bought you clothes last year." I would tell my dad and he'd agree with me that kids grow every year.

And it drives me crazy to think how much the other kids get. Mom insists that I'd get more if I was nicer to my step-dad, but she also claims he never tried to replace my dad. In reality, when I was nine years old, my mom and him tried talking me into letting him adopt me, which I sure as hell didn't want. I knew even back then that was unwise. I know I never had it as bad as my own father, who attempted suicide at age 10, but still.

Emotional lacking sucks no matter how strong the loss. Maybe that's why I worry so much about losing Shawn. Finally got me some loving and don't want to lose it. And now I feel all teary eyed. Dammit.

March 6

Today Shawn and I talked to the case worker and his medical things are all handled and we applied for food assistance. I picked up my application for the video store and yesterday his sergeant told Shawn about a possible job through the reserve that pays $32,000 - $41,000 annually. His sergeant is going to help him fill out the forms for it and maybe that'll come through if the other job doesn't. Hopefully he gets a job soon since we have more options now. The pay for that job sounds grand and there are benefits, which is good, too.

Shawn and I have still been discussing my boobs increasing. We took a moment to examine them, nothing sexual, literally just seeing if they seem bigger, and they do seem like they're growing. They don't feel like they're gaining milk or anything weird, they just leak a miniscule amount. I thought they stopped, but Shawn squeezed and got them to do it again. They leak barely anything yet they still are growing and it's not a full "with milk" growth.

Hell, maybe I'll get lucky and I won't need implants in the end. I was told girls finish developing between ages 19 and 21 or something like that. The doctor said I was done growing, but I guess he just meant height-wise. I'm really hoping they go somewhere, save me the worst part of the surgery, but I have my doubts. My family is full of petites.

March 7

Shawn got a call today saying that his car will be towed/impounded soon if he doesn't figure out what he's doing with it. His sergeant told him it was getting fixed and he explained that to the guy, but the guy insisted he call around and talk to different people about it. Shawn tried calling both of his sergeants but no word from either. So, hopefully he gets it sorted soon.

He has an appointment Monday with the doctor to make sure he's healed up okay. I hope so since he hasn't been following the rules exactly for a little while now. He lifts over 10 pounds sometimes, not often, and we do sleep together which we're not supposed to yet. Then after the appointment we're to go to Nora's for Shawn's birthday dinner since he turns 20.

Friday, his sergeant is taking him to get the freebie car, so I guess that's good. But Shawn has stuff in his regular car and he was hoping to sell it or the freebie for a little extra cash. He'd hate to have to pay into it. So now he's moping a bit, watching TV.

I filled out my job application for the video store and will take it in whenever Shawn's car is back. Grandma Margaret dropped off ground beef and some eggs a little bit ago, so we should be able to make a nice supper tonight.

Things are still iffy and I'm ready for some good news/luck to come our way. Not saying we're unlucky, we're getting by, but I do hope to eventually be more than "just getting by."

March 9

The car thing turned out okay. The sergeant had her car there, too, and they thought it was Shawn's. It wasn't even his car the guy was freaking out about.

I've been thinking about what sort of job I want, something I'd like to do the rest of my life and I really think about how much I love my cats and animals in general. I don't want to be a veterinarian because I wouldn't be able to handle cutting open an animal, nor being near that happening. And I don't want to work at a zoo; especially since there's not one around here. Those are the two big things you find in a search for animal jobs.

The only other things I saw listed were things like pet groomer or trainer. Pet groomer pay of $30,000 isn't bad and it'd be something I like to do, dealing with pets all day. I may have to go to *Petco* and ask the groomers what it takes to be a groomer. I feel sort of silly saying I may want to groom dogs and cats for a living, but at the same time, it's something I know I could do and be happy with.

March 13

Today feels like a good day. I didn't realize the schooling involved for grooming and then I realized that some purebreds have special hairstyles for show. Shawn and I looked on the community college website and they don't have courses for animal grooming. I'll have to see if the regular college does, otherwise I think there's a trade school nearby. Somebody around here has to have some classes. And maybe I can take a few online courses, too. I think I'd learn a bunch at school, it sounds like something I could comprehend and do.

I like that it's a more dedicated area of study, like hair dressing. And I think it's something I'd be interested in and could enjoy for an extended period of time although I still need a job now. I know I can't just jump into grooming, which I wouldn't want to; there may be some angry customers if I did!

I've listed most of my game stuff and Tamagotchis on eBay but there are tons of similar things listed. I just want the stuff to sell. I'm finding next month's rent to be a harder and harder thing to come up with.

Shawn informed me recently that next year he'll have to be deployed; it's a 95% chance. He'll be with his battalion and they're saying he may go to Bosnia. He says it'd only be for eight months because some people volunteered and aren't going to be happy still having to be deployed; something about restarting the deployment clock. So there's a good chance he'll be gone for a bit. In a way, it'll be good so I can focus on studying more and the money he makes will get sent back home, so rent will be covered while he's gone. But I will miss him.

Nora saw a psychic when she was on a trip recently and she told us at supper last night that the psychic said Shawn would lose his car and then get it back and that he would have a few run-ins with the law. What I found out today is that, while I was using the restroom, Nora told Shawn that the psychic also said that I would leave Shawn. And Nora told the psychic "you're right" because as everyone knows, that's very unlikely and the psychic said that either way we won't last more than a year. So I don't know.

Shawn said he's a little worried and Nora told him not to tell me. I was freaked, too. I don't know how well I trust the psychic. I mean, those things can be really hit and miss. And Shawn already lost his car and is getting it back, so we were kidding that maybe she's behind the times since we already broke up a few weeks before the one year anniversary, but then got back together. I don't know what to think of it all.

I mentioned to Shawn about Suicide Girls. I watch *America's Next Top Model* as well as the Australian version sometimes, but know that with my height, etc., Suicide Girls would be the way to take it for a part-time thing, money on the side. He said he supports it, so maybe after surgeries it'd be a way to calm that modeling urge a bit and it'd be a neat experience.

I told my dad yesterday about pet grooming and he didn't say much one way or the other, so not sure what he thinks of it.

March 14

Last night Shawn and I had a big heart-to-heart. He ended up rolling over and wouldn't talk to me for the longest time. Through most of his silence I thought he was just kidding around and then finally I noticed his eyes getting red and a bit moist, more like anger than sorrow and I finally got him to talk.

He said I don't listen. Turns out he still thinks I get pissy because I'm such high energy and we got down to where he said something along the lines of: "If I'm not in the mood to play or goof around then I'm just not in the mood. I still love you; I just don't feel like it at the time." I told him okay, I thought he was just kidding around earlier and a lot of times he seems to be joking with me and okay with me being so bouncy.

We're fine now and I'm glad he got my attention. I understand it is hard being in an apartment with someone for so long. He told me he needs time to himself so he really wants his car back and a job and he told me he'd be fine staying home if I went out with a girlfriend. He kept saying he still loves me and isn't going to run away or anything; he just wants to be able to have his time. Again, I understand, I am pretty high-energy.

We also talked about a fallout plan in case we do ever split. He kept saying *"hypothetically"* so that I knew it was just in case, not because he's plotting. It's still iffy, but we know that whoever breaks up with the other, if it ever happens, sleeps on the couch. He said I still will have a place to stay and he still wants Anaki and Dex to be able to play together. And he told me I'm his best friend. He seemed to even put me above his bestest best friend who's away at college. So we had a mature moment and we are good. Working through problems is good.

Today Shawn will be going on another bike ride, as he did yesterday. He's trying to "get back in shape." He's not fat, but he feels he lacks muscle and toning. I wish I had a bike to go with, I like to bike ride. Shawn said we'd do crunches and push-ups together here at home, though, so that's cool. The doctor told him he's free to do whatever in the reserve, but they won't let him do PT tests or anything too terrible for six more weeks. He has that time to prep, as he's doing. The doctor said Shawn wouldn't be fully back to normal for a year, though, which sort of sucks.

My dad has a bike, a crappy one I can take if I get the means to bring it back next time I visit. I had a bike, but it's at my mom's and she pretty much adopted it for my brother to have although it was a birthday gift for me years ago. That would be a nice healthy quality activity for Shawn and me.

Shawn said sometimes he raises his voice and blames it on the bipolar/depression thing. He says he doesn't mean to, he just can't help it. If this is surprising then I wonder how it'll be once he has space and gets new happy pills; when he gets a job he wants to get more Prozac.

I have time to decide on the Suicide Girls thing. I don't have to have surgeries to be one, but I know I lack the confidence it takes right now. That'll be the deciding factor after the surgeries, if I feel confident enough then. I still know I won't be stick-skinny with huge boobs like most modeling girls, like a lot of the Suicide Girls even, but that's okay with me. I just want to feel okay with my body. I guess I'll just wait and see what happens. I'm confident about who I am, for the most part, although I do have my weak moments. But physically I'm not; just trying to tie it all together.

Self-fulfilling prophecy is what I think about the whole psychic thing. They say it'll happen, so you in turn make it happen, by choice or not. I don't think I'm too big into the psychic thing. If someone were really psychic, why the hell would they be performing for a living?

March 16

I've been researching the schooling for pet grooming and realized that the closest school is a little over two hours away. I found one online that offers courses and emailed them asking if their online courses are all I'd need to get started as a pet groomer since I would think I'd have to do something on-site with actual dogs.

They only offer dog grooming, so if I wanted to learn about cat grooming, which I don't think I do, I'd have to take classes elsewhere. I also emailed the college to ask if they had courses on pet grooming just in case I was wrong and overlooked it while searching their website.

I talked to dad about taking the stuff online and he thinks that's fine, but said I should still go to the regular college and take computer classes or something to get a degree and have a backup plan, so I told him I would take a few classes there, although I really don't want to, but I know it's the smart thing to do.

Shawn and I have been talking and we did want a skunk, but he was concerned about being able to keep track of it and take care of it since they get into so much so we decided we'd get a dog instead. I've never had my own dog before, and it's exciting to think about. I can't wait until late next year when we can move out and get one; assuming things go all right until then. I want to get a French Bulldog, preferably a cream/blonde colored one. Shawn really wants a Siberian Husky, so if finances are in order I can easily see us ending up with two dogs.

Shawn said that he's going to finish his time with the reserve and then he wants to go to school for culinary arts. I guess the community college has a really good program for it.

Michelle, Shawn's ex-girlfriend, who is now sort of my friend and pregnant, showed up with her brother and asked me if I was doing anything tonight. I said no and Shawn said, "No! She's not doing anything!" She said that's good and to be ready to go out by 8 p.m., it's a girl's night out. Shawn's more excited than I am because, although I have friends, I never really went out and wasn't the one that everyone wanted to invite over. I've never "partied" or had a girl's night before, really. Shawn was saying how we're stuck in the apartment together all the time and he feels like he needs some "him time," so it was perfect timing. I don't know where we're going tonight, she just asked if I'm 17 and if I have an ID.

March 17

I think Michelle wanted someone to talk to and that's why I was invited to go last night, which is fine. We saw Secret Window. You have to be 17 to get into R-rated movies, but that one wasn't R-rated. We had fun.

Oddly enough, I got home and Shawn told me how bored he was without me. He said me lying next to him on the couch or while he's on the computer makes things less boring. So he missed me. It was sweet and I told him now I want to get out more so that he misses me more. He was a little thrown off, though, when I told him that she told me that I shouldn't really trust him when he tells me he loves me. Right now she's a "man-hater" because of her baby's daddy being a jerk, so I don't know how seriously she was implying that. Shawn talked online with his other friend, Cheri, when I got home and she plans to "steal" me sometime, too.

March 18

The online grooming place actually called me and it sounds great. They're mailing a pack with all the information we discussed and they have a program where I can do half online and then half in person and if I did the schooling full-time I could get it done in like three and a half months. It'd be a full load, but it'd be quick and painless. Now to tell Shawn. I'm all worked up and excited!

I've talked to Shawn and my dad about what was discussed with the woman from the grooming academy. I really want to do it and looking at the price guide this may be the only thing I do since it's between $8-9,000. After I complete the courses and get my diploma/certificate then I have the opportunity to go to Japan with the exchange program; schooling's free, but trip and stay isn't.

I want to go to Japan so bad and this would be the perfect excuse! The only bad thing is they don't take FAFSA, but they're mailing papers and included information on the loans they work with. I emailed questions about Japan and the six week part of the courses where I'd be living away, and told them about Shawn and the reserve, so I was a bit concerned about my cats as well.

I also asked if piercings are accepted during the on-site portion of the courses. I said how much I enjoy mine and would hate to remove them, but said I also understand how they'd be a hazard. I can see a dog ripping my lip ring out. Hopefully I can keep them. The thing that made me think of it is when looking over the fees I noticed "uniform - $50" and realized that piercings aren't very "uniform."

I think Shawn thought the reserve was a safe way to get money for school, but now even they are getting sent places. But he's "owned by the government" so he can't do much about it. I don't think he can say his religion is against war or something.

I got an email in response to mine when I asked about my piercings, Japan, and about pets, just in case Shawn ends up going overseas around the time I'm gone somewhere. They said my piercings shouldn't be a problem if they're small and that instead of loops I might think about using studs or barbells while I'm in school.

They also said students can't bring pets with them because if everyone brought their pets, some of the pets might not get along, plus some pets might damage stuff in the apartments. They also gave me a website to check for the Japan program. And, they're mailing me some stuff, too. Luckily I just need to get a stud for my lip then, so it's smaller. The eyebrow already has a barbell. I wouldn't be in Japan *too* overly long, either, so I wouldn't feel as bad about going. I'm still really excited about this!

To my knowledge, the Japanese program is guaranteed. I don't know costs of living right now; they'll inform me when time gets closer. It's good that they're anxious to have me join, I'm anxious to join! The home study would only be for two months, I think I can handle that. I know Shawn will push me to get through it. Next time I get a response from them I'll ask about previous takers of the courses as references.

March 20

Shawn was a bit icky today; he needed "space" again, so I tried hard to give it to him. It's hard to waste time in the living room so he can talk to friends online, his "only means to get in touch with other people."

I'm hoping to get my hair cut and colored soon, either bleached white or a really light blue. Just have to have the cash.

Shawn's grandma said that she'll help us with rent for a while if we need it, but she can't forever, so we should be set next month if we can't get it ourselves. Shawn has drill this weekend and is getting his car back, plus should be finding out about jobs. Also, we got a scratch thing in the mail and won $4,000 towards a used car from some place in the next town over. So that's neat. It was so unexpected!

March 22

The more Shawn reassures me that we're gonna be together "forever and ever" and he "loves me with all his heart," that helps me be able to give him his "space."

Shawn's cat, Dex, I think is in love with me. In the morning he meows and whines very loudly wanting in and when he gets in he runs to me, not Shawn. Last night we let him in for a while before bed. I guess he hissed at Shawn in the living room, so Shawn locked him out when we went to sleep. Dex likes to "beat up" my stuffed dog I sleep with and I gave it to Shawn for a bit to try and get Dex over there, which he did go, but Shawn said he put his face in the dog and took in my scent and when Shawn put his hand in front of Dex's nose he stopped and stepped over the hand and kept going, like he was avoiding Shawn.

Dex also lay up by my head for a bit and "cleaned" me. I was always afraid he'd eat my hair, but I decided to give it a shot and let Dex get it out of his system, so he did his best to groom me. I read somewhere that's a sign of affection, like accepting me into the "pack." Poor Shawn, though! I don't know why Dex likes me. I kid Shawn and say he just wants his momma. I'm "momma" and Shawn is "daddy" to the cats. We're crazy pet people.

Last night we went to visit Wayne and Naomi, Shawn's friends from high school who have a 3-year-old son. Shawn used to be over there a lot at one point and it annoyed me. Now I think they're not half bad and we just hung out and watched TV; she likes the model shows like I do. She's pregnant, seven months along I think. Their apartment is in the fixed income section.

I do not want a life like them!! I don't necessarily feel we need to be extremely wealthy or anything, but I would like to be able to get by and have some spending money on the side. We don't need a perfect life, that would make us into snobs, but I can't help but want to have a fairly easy and happy life. When they offered that we could stay the night, I said no and used the excuse it was too warm. But I really didn't want to be around them that long, especially with the little boy.

March 23

Shawn is going to get rechecked to possibly get on his Prozac again, which I think is smart. I feel he needs it again. But he also said he'd ask the doctor about another problem. Lately he seems to have little to no sex drive. I told him I love him, even if we never had sex again, which is true, but at the same time it would be nice to not have to fight with him to get him to want to do it.

Sometimes his penis says yes (quite often his penis says yes), but he just doesn't want to. He physically wants to, just not mentally. He says it's not me, but at the same time it still makes me feel bad. He used to tell me to "go play," but my "toy" broke two days ago, so I can't even entertain myself now. It's silly this is a "big dilemma" in our lives.

Mom emailed me, telling me about my bank account and child support, switching it from my old bank to my new one, and she said her name has to be on the account and some stuff about we most likely will have to be in person, together, at the bank in order for them to switch stuff around. So I had to tell her that next week Shawn and I will be going to see my dad and withdraw money from my account, so if she has time we can go to the bank together and maybe eat lunch so I can tell her about my college plans since she still hasn't a clue.

I don't really want to try and be her friend, but at the same time maybe it's not all that bad of an idea. Shawn tried saying if I call this place and that and do something-or-other I can make it work without seeing my mom, but I told him I'll just do it this way.

March 24

My natural hair color is dishwater blonde, a darker blonde. It's not a bad color, just gets sort of boring to look at. I'm still thinking that white tips would be cool, though, or black with light blue tips. I've considered dying it back to normal or maybe slightly darker since roots don't seem to show as bad for a while that way and getting tips. I could always go back to normal and get bleached tips or streaks underneath.

That way when it grows out it won't matter. I don't get my hair cut often and the tips will slowly disappear with each hair cut. We'll see.

I know what I have in mind for education; it's Shawn that's still sorting things out. Just last night he said he may want to study theology instead of going to school for culinary arts; after the military is up, I assume. I told him he better realize that culinary arts is sort of like what I'm doing, it's specialized and not a lot of extra classes on the side, but theology you have to learn everything that you don't want in order to get a degree in what you do want. He said he understood, but I can't see him sticking with that, he's sort of like me. That's why I thought the culinary arts would be good for him. I have no idea what he'd do with theology. He can do more with culinary arts. And, I think with his attention span he's better off with the food stuff.

I told him I'm sorry I take away the hunt as far as sex. I said it a few days ago, and he said it's okay and he doesn't mind, he is sort of lazy that way. Yesterday we did it in the morning and evening and I told him that I'm good with that or one or the other, at least it's something. But I'm worried he's doing it when he physically wants to and not because he mentally wants to, that's not fair to him. And I told him that last night when he started, but he asked me if I want it. I was going to sleep nude, but I don't if we have sex before bed. So I don't know.

At least sex isn't everything and if we both wanted sex at the same time all the time, we'd never get anything done. I have a feeling the reason I want it so much is because there's nothing else to do right now. Add in jobs and schooling and I'm sure it'll be even less often that we will have and want to have sex. Boredom does make a person want sex; it passes the time, even if it doesn't last *that* long, 10–30 minutes, depending on Shawn's stamina at the time. And it feels good.

March 25

I'll try to play nice with my mom. I don't plan to spend the whole time with her, just enough for the bank stuff and possibly lunch if she wants to do that. I hope to see my dad the rest of the time. I'll have to tell Shawn (repeatedly) not to say anything mean to my mother. I'm sure those two won't get along at all. I guess I'll figure it out.

Shawn hooked up the Internet to my computer now. He's taking his laptop with him to drill so they can figure out his CAC stuff. Erica should be over soon. I have my game stuff out right now while I check my email while I wait. She's also into manga and anime and she's bringing anime for us to watch. Shawn said we can "ni-ni-ni" when he gets back; I don't call it sex or having sex.

March 26

This morning it stormed and then Erica's car battery was dead. She just left, it's 2:10 p.m., and she originally was going to leave early this morning. We had a blast hanging out and the first two hours or so she was here we just talked about everything.

A comment she made, that I agree with, is even though we've never hung out before in person and have only talked online, it's like we've known each other a long time. We were just really comfortable and relaxed. She said she may have to come over more often now that she knows how short the drive is. I told her that'd be good because not only do I need a friend to hang out with, Shawn has been depressed about how his friends don't really call or write to him much anymore.

Shawn will be home from drill Sunday evening. I texted with him a little bit during the car dilemma and he told me to get hold of Grandma Margaret, which I did, and Shawn's cousin came over to fix the car. He couldn't text for long, though, because he'd get in trouble. He was nice enough to call last night to see how things were going.

My mom emailed and said she's open Wednesday, but then emailed again in response to mine and said that she's "eating lunch with Lisa and Jeffrey at school" on Wednesday. So I replied asking if she can still go to the bank that afternoon and we can skip having lunch. You'd think that since this is one of the very few times I'll be around there *and* willing to see her, that she'd want to go to lunch and could make it work, but it didn't seem that way at all.

I have a few female friends, Andrea and Kimberlee and Sharon and now Erica. I talked to Andrea and Kimberlee on the phone last night, actually, because Kimberlee wants to go out with a guy in school I dated once. She thought I had some "insight" into the situation, but I wasn't much help. I didn't date him long because he was *really* clingy from the start, which was weird because we were friends for the longest time. Then when I dumped him I called the next day to see if he was okay, and he called back an hour later saying he loved me and he has for a while. I still feel bad about being mean, but I told him I don't feel the same and hung up the phone. We haven't talked a lot since.

Erica can easily turn into a best buddy, which is nice. I still feel a bit awkward at times because we are just starting to hang out in real life instead of just online, but I think I'll manage.

March 27

Mom was on AIM, so I talked to her, and we're going to meet right after she's done eating with the kids. She said to be at the bank by noon, and I told her Shawn would be there and asked if she'd be okay with him there and she said she doesn't have a choice so she guesses she'll manage. The thing that bothered me throughout the whole conversation is this kid that's two weeks younger than me, so I can actually call him a kid, who's been hanging out with my brother (who just turned 8), playing video games and stuff with him. Mom said he's a nice kid and she's "considering adopting him so that Jeffrey has a big brother." I don't think she'd seriously adopt him, that'd just be weird, but I remember being around Jeffrey's age and mom getting pregnant with him and I told my mom I wanted an older brother, not a younger one. So glad my half-brother can live out what I always wanted.

The other feeling I got from that is having an oldest daughter isn't enough, or Jeffrey having a big sister isn't enough, he needs a big brother, instead. Mom emailed me a picture of him, it was really weird. I told her I though he looked creepy but she just kept saying he's a really nice kid. I don't even want to talk about that part anymore.

I talked to Shawn about two seconds last night. I called at about 10:30 p.m. and it was really noisy and he said he was going to call when he got out of where he was. I said just call back when you can and it got to be 11:30 p.m. and I got tired of waiting. So I called him and he said he just got back, he was getting ready to call. I guess he and some of his buds from drill went to a sports club, and he had to be the designated driver for three drunk guys. I heard some chick ask where they're taking some guy and Shawn told her he didn't know and said he'd call back after he got the guy into bed. So I thought, all right, just call me back in a few minutes then.

Twenty-five minutes later I didn't hear anything so I called him and he said that one of the guys he was with got in trouble, so he didn't feel like talking now.

Did I get upset? Yes I did, but I didn't say it, he could just hear that I was getting watery-eyed. He said he loves me and it's not that he doesn't want to talk to *me*, he just doesn't want to talk right now and he misses me and he'll see me tomorrow (today now) and so on. I stayed up until midnight waiting for him to get his head out of his butt and I didn't even get to talk to him and ask about the job stuff or about his car *or* tell him all the stuff that's gone on while he's gone.

March 28

Shawn came home yesterday and had a short fuse. He didn't have a Hepatitis A shot on record, so they had to give him one, and it made him feel icky. Plus, he was supposed to get his car last night, but his sergeant never called. Also, he didn't get a lot of sleep during drill because of going out and he said he wouldn't have slept well anyway because people were coming in at all hours of the night; one guy came in at 3:00 a.m.

So, with his short fuse, he yelled at me a lot, not meaning to be mean to me, he just was testy, and he made me cry a few times. When we went to bed he threw a fit because the bed wasn't made. I had most of the covers at the bottom of the bed and the comforter is one of the lighter weight ones, so that was pulled up because it was so friggin' hot. I told him I had it set up because I thought he'd be warm, but he went on about how he wants to know exactly where his blankets are if he gets cold at night.

When I got upset from being yelled at so much he ended up comforting me and cooled down and said this was the last time he'd tell me to stop getting upset over stupid things before he will get mad at me and yell at me for real. It's just hard not to get upset when you didn't do anything and you're getting yelled at. This morning I made him pancakes (surprised him) and he was happy. Then he asked me to do the dishes and I reluctantly did, so he's in a good mood now.

Today I was hoping to go outside on Shawn's bike. He was going to jog and I said I'd ride the bike so we can go about the same speed. I'd be faster, but it's more evenly matched than if I were the one jogging. Then we'd go to the post office to mail my package and maybe to the grocery store for some food and to the bank so he can get money out for his car insurance. He decided it would be faster if he just took the bike, so here I am in the house waiting for his return. I just got done talking to my dad and he said I can take the mountain bike he has so I have a bike, too. Shawn still doesn't know about his car, so we may have to ask Nora for her van. But considering we're bringing back a kitchen table, however small, and a mountain bike, we may want to ask her either way.

Hopefully tomorrow I can get the bank stuff straightened out, see my dad, see Andrea, maybe see my great grandma in the nursing home. I have a lot to do! And it will probably all come down to how nice Shawn's mom wants to be.

I hope to lose five pounds for prom, which is in a month. I brought home some weights and my elastic band, and my "thigh master." Between that, push-ups, and sit-ups, Shawn and I can work out some and I think I can lose at least five pounds. I still don't plan to cut back a whole lot with my diet. I will eat the stuff I like, when I'm hungry, but try not to eat out of boredom at all. This will be a good start and then later if I still feel I want to lose more, then I'll work on the food part.

When I got money out yesterday I had more than I thought I would have, which was surprising, but that just means I can pay more bills, a lot of which are Shawn's, like his car insurance and his phone bill, without having to borrow from his grandma. We'll still need her help, but not as much as we thought.

March 29

When I saw mom she criticized Shawn, saying he smells like smoke, which is odd she'd complain since her very own husband smokes as well. While we were there, Shawn and I got some groceries with our food stamps. Before we met mom, as we were driving around trying to find her and I was talking with her on my cell phone, I told her I'd write the number down for her, but she said it's probably long distance. I told her the area code and she's like, "Yeah, long distance." She never did take the number or show any interest, so she must not want to call.

We had time so I went to my high school to pick up art stuff I forgot on my last day, but the teacher said she wanted to keep it for the art show and I could have it at graduation. A bunch of people said "hey" and were "excited" to see me. I felt awkward, though, and just wanted to get out of there.

We went to Applebee's for supper. Andrea met us there and ate with us and it was fun. Dad let me borrow some GameCube games and some DVDs. We got home and unpacked, Shawn got mad at one point at all the stuff, but when he came back from returning Nora's van he apologized and hugged me and told me not to be scared because I was freaked out. We watched a movie and went to bed.

It was a simple day and went fairly smooth, which was good.

March 30

Today we got to see Shawn's friends Steve and Juanita. We had a "picnic" at the trailer that Steve is selling and then went to his girlfriend Juanita's new apartment so we could see their rabbits. Then out to eat and to the mall to bum around.

Erica came over later to visit. It was a busy day, but it was good for Shawn to get out and see people. Last night I dyed my hair black and tomorrow we're supposed to see Wayne and Naomi. The fun never stops!

March 31

We just got home from Wayne and Naomi's. I really like Wayne and Naomi is all right, too. She wants me to go to her baby shower next weekend. She has a 3-year-old and another on the way, she's seven months along. I can only handle being there so long.

Shawn plans to look into a landscaping job, but with being gone this afternoon until now, he never did call. He played *Rogue Leader* on the GameCube until we left. That boy needs me to push him.

April 2

I survived meeting with my mom, it could've been better but I guess it could've been worse. The end of this month I may have to make another trip, depending on how long it takes for everything to get switched around, but after that it should all be in order.

My dad is still pushing for me to go to college for a backup degree in something, but I told him I don't want to. I forgot to take the packet of stuff with me yesterday, Shawn moved it, so out of sight, out of mind, and it made discussing it harder. I need to talk to him more so I can fill out the enrollment stuff and the loan application.

I'm not sure about the loan application, having never taken out a loan, so I have to talk to dad while I fill it out probably. And as far as I know, I get child support while I go to school, period. But, at the same time, this schooling isn't that long, so I won't be getting child support until I'm 21, only until I finish whenever that is.

Shawn and I have been exercising with some weights lately and we'll go for a walk whenever I can convince him to get out. He's playing Super Monkey Ball now. He beat Rogue Leader as of yesterday. I think he enjoyed his day of socialization, he hasn't whined about needing "space" since. And he just tried calling regarding a job, but no answer, so I told him to call again later.

I haven't heard about the twins lately. I'll get pictures when the Clarks send them out to everyone again. They said I can get them more often if I want, but I told them they can just send me what everyone else gets. I don't really like to think about that whole thing, honestly, so it's easier not to if I don't get pictures. Not because I regret giving them up, just because I still regret getting pregnant.

Tomorrow Shawn has to go out of town. A relative of his died and he's a pall bearer. I told him while he's gone I'm going to exercise a bunch, as if a few days will make a drastic difference, but it could help get me on a better track for when he comes home. Last night I took some initiative and was on top during sex. Normally I'm "chicken" and don't like that much attention on my performance, but I tried for a while and man is that a lot of work! I told Shawn that he has a hard job and I'm sure that's part of the reason he stays in good shape although he does nothing else really for exercise. So maybe that's another, more enjoyable, way to exercise.

I really want to turn 18 because I want to get my tattoos; still getting the mini wings on my back and recently decided *against* the barcode and *for* cherry blossoms, *and* so I can get my surgery/ies. The cherry blossom branch tattoo will be on my hip, creeping onto my stomach. Sort of a way to show off a better stomach after I get that all taken care of and to make me feel more confident to show it off instead of hiding a lot of myself.

April 4

Shawn will be home tomorrow around 4:00 p.m. and I was hoping to clean the apartment while he was gone, but, wind seems to come in every window and the sliding glass door, which does not lock, the past two mornings has been cracked open by the wind. I can literally see my breath this morning and am wearing a ton of stuff to stay warm, including my hobo-gloves which are stretch gloves with the fingers cut off. It's all I have because mom kept all my "bundle" stuff. I cranked the heat in all the rooms and am still not feeling it. I can see my breath still. I hope to heat this place up, and then turn the heat down to save electricity. I tried not to use it at all, but it's to the point I may lose a finger if I don't turn the heat up.

MySpace is amazing. I had a friend in 5th grade that was my *best* friend, but moved away at the end of 6th grade. I didn't have an address or phone number or *anything* and this morning I got a message on MySpace from him saying, "Hey, hope you remember me..." and so on. For a while after he moved I tried to "hunt him down" but didn't have much luck, and now out of nowhere I get a message.

While Shawn is away we don't have a whole lot of food options and I need to do the dishes to eat anything anyway, but again, it's freezing and I'm avoiding water until it warms up. So I've been eating a lot of Wheat Thins and granola bars. I told Shawn I'd starve against my will. He told me to call Grandma Margaret and I said I can make noodles when I do the dishes.

I talked to my dad yesterday and he mentioned college and FAFSA again. I told him I really don't want to go and explained I know that if I'm working somewhere doing dog grooming, even if I'm just starting out, I'm going to favor that over school. I can tell right now which one will get more attention and I told him I know I won't give the focus to college that I should for the price. He said he can't make me go, but he'd really like me to, but in the end it's my choice. So I think finally I'm getting somewhere with that.

My friend Kimberlee has been turning to me lately for relationship advice. I have been through a lot in her eyes although I haven't had serious relationships with more than two guys and although our friends Andrea and Lori try to help her, Lori never has had a boyfriend and Andrea is currently in Europe with her family on vacation.

The guy Kimberlee likes is someone I dated once, and it last like, three days. We were great friends for a year and then when we dated he was clingly right away and I couldn't handle it. I called the day aftger to make sure he was okay and he said yeah but called back an hour later and told me he loved me which was really weird. I had never seen him so sensitive and it creeped me out and I told him I'm sorry and hung up.

She knows all this stuff and I told her he wouldn't be bad if you're prepared for that and it's her choice. I am trying to give her advice but she asks over and over, "What should I do?" and I have no clue. I told her that her situation is different than what I've been through and he is a hard one to judge, but she still thinks I'm her "hero" to talk to about it. I never understood why people like me, but I guess it's a good thing.

Then, in the afternoon, my mom and I had a conversation on AIM and she now officially knows my plans for college and pet grooming. Another letter came from the college and she wanted to know if she should open it. I said I didn't care, I wouldn't be going there, and then told her about the online grooming place and going to school in Japan for a month. She wanted to know if it was a real college and I told her yes that I'd talked to the woman in charge on the phone a few times.

I still don't understand why she made fun of Shawn for smelling like smoke, she pretty much avoided that. All she said about schooling is that I won't make a lot of money doing dog grooming. I just want to scream at her sometimes.

April 5

Today it's not as cold and last night I opened up Shawn's sleeping bag and slept in that under all the other blankets. I actually got to the point I got out of the sleeping bag but I was glad to get too warm instead of freezing.

I went over to Grandma Margaret's house to play with her dog. I played with her yesterday a bit after grocery shopping with Margaret and then today after noon. I got home from there a little bit ago; we played and hung out for about two hours. Dolly doesn't get a ton of attention. She gets outside, but isn't free to roam the whole house. She's kenneled a lot, and she barks a lot, but I got her to understand that I'll pet her if she sits, but not if she jumps up and barks. By the time I left she was doing pretty well with that concept.

It was nice to hear from Russ, my friend from *MySpace*, and we did talk on MSN Messenger for a while last night, but I don't really want to "meet" with him anywhere. It's good to find an old friend, especially since he was my best friend "back in the day," but I know Shawn probably wouldn't like the idea a whole lot and I wouldn't like it if he did that with an old girlfriend of his although he is friends with a lot of his exes. I was surprised to hear from him and sort of happy because I did try to find his new address right after he moved but as a sixth grader, I wasn't that on top of things. At the same time we haven't talked in a while and it's just like making a new friend all over again because of how long it's been.

April 7

Today I get to go to Naomi's baby shower. I'm still iffy about the whole idea, especially because I'm feeling sick and have been since yesterday, but I'll go so Shawn has "alone time" with his video game.

This is sort of a cleaning day. We got the garbage taken out and I swept the kitchen, as well as straightened the litter box, and I'm doing the laundry. There are a couple spots on the floor from where the litter box was and from the cat food getting soggy that Shawn is going to clean up while I'm gone today, or at least he's supposed to.

When everything's cleaned then Shawn wants to invite Nora over. I'm not looking forward to that, but at the same time he's going to make chili when she comes and I love chili.

This baby shower, I think, will be awkward. I don't know anyone other than Naomi and Shawn's grandmother. And I don't like babies. Spending an afternoon celebrating someone that's going to have a baby with people I don't know just doesn't appeal to me. I hope Shawn appreciates this.

April 8

Last night they forgot me for the baby shower, at least I think they did. Wayne called and asked about us coming over, but we were making chicken and rice for supper and couldn't.

Today we went over to Nora's for Easter. It was good eats and Nora was nice to me, so maybe I was wrong about her not liking me, I don't know. She told me where I should apply for a job, a cafe, which doesn't appeal to me since I hate coffee, but I guess I'll humor her and apply. But if they don't allow piercings then forget it, I refuse to remove mine. She gave a few suggestions for Shawn as well and so did his uncle and a couple other relatives. Tomorrow we'll borrow Grandma Margaret's car to go get job applications everywhere and I'm going to apply at the mall for sure.

Shawn text messaged Mark to ask about the money that he owes and Mark said he's jobless, although Lila has a job, and that they are scraping for funds and he just got "jacked" which I assume means he was robbed, but I don't know what was taken. I think he said his apartment was jacked, so maybe furniture? Hope he realizes I won't let him go without paying up. I waited two years for a kid to pay me $5 he owed me on a bet, so for $353 I'll be pestering him for a while!

April 9

We went to the mall today. I got an application for the video store in the mall, as did Shawn, and he's going online to apply for some army thing. We met up with his sergeant today, finally, but no luck with the car yet although it's almost ready.

I got my hair cut and now I need to wash it because here they don't do a wash and style as part of the hair cut deal so I said I'd do it myself. I also got studs for my lip, including a clear one; it came in the package, in case I need it for a job. I had a hell of a time getting the stud in, so my lip is swollen really badly right now.

When we were driving to go talk to his sergeant, Shawn stopped the car to turn into the parking lot outside of the building and a big truck rear-ended us. The guy said he looked down for a second and when he looked up we were stopped and his brakes are new, so they didn't work like the old ones. Shawn braced himself pretty well because he saw it coming before I did. I was seat-belted, luckily, but went forward and then back, hitting my head on the head of the seat. Although it's padded, it sure can give you a lump and a headache. I ended up crying from being scared and slightly injured.

They sent an ambulance and everything; military people don't mess around! They wanted to check me over, but I said I was fine other than a headache and they had to call my dad to be sure I could say I didn't want to be looked at because I'm not 18 so I couldn't sign the refusal paper. The whole thing took forever to sort out. And Grandma Margaret's car that we were driving is pretty messed up in the back and the trunk doesn't even close, us being stopped and a big truck going at least 25 MPH, which was the speed limit, it was an uneven match. The truck had nothing more than a bent license plate.

The weirdest part of the whole thing is before we left with the car, Grandma Margaret told us she has insurance up to date and we'd be covered since she gave us permission to drive the car.

I thought something was going to happen before all this when a guy pulled in front of Shawn when the guy had a red light and ours was green. We were going fast through the light, the speed limit, and the guy pulled out. Shawn honked and the guy leaned out his window and caught up to us after we passed him, yelling at us, then he got ahead of us, into the middle of the lanes and slowed down to spit on our car. It was sort of funny that the guy had an angel on his dashboard.

My dad told me next time to get checked, no matter what.

April 11

Tonight Shawn was going to do his taxes. He's missing one W2, but they're mailing it to him. But, although he put the W2s he has in a safe place, we can't seem to find them, and he just realized it this evening. I looked harder than he did, high, low, under, over, and in everything, but I can't find the damned things. He stopped looking before I did saying he'd just get pissed if he looked any more tonight. And he told his mom he'll find them tomorrow. Needless to say, I'm pissed at him, although he doesn't realize it, for not continuing to look, even after a break. He better find them, that is all I have to say.

We talked about it, and have somewhat of an idea where they are. We knew where we last saw them, so that may help. We had them in a small USPS Priority box to carry with us when we applied for food stamps. I remember I took them out and gave them to Shawn (or set them down? I won't rule that out) because I needed the box and wanted to save it. The box was in the room with the computer and is now gone. But as for the papers within, I don't know. I don't think we threw them out, I can't see that happening, but Shawn won't talk about it any more tonight. I really hope we find them!

April 12

We found them this morning! I told him what I knew, that they were in that box and when we cleaned the bedroom I gave them to him so I could have the box and I know we had a "save papers" box somewhere and then he found it on the dresser. I didn't even know that's the box he put them in and sifted through and there they were. I'm really excited because that means I get a GameCube. I don't have to do taxes until next year, so I don't understand that stuff completely.

Tonight we're doing taxes. My dad said Shawn may get $300 or more, but he can't tell without doing the taxes himself. I also found out that my dad's insurance won't cover my surgeries, so I feel a bit depressed trying to figure out how I'll pay for them. I don't really want to talk about it, but at the same time I feel like crap.

April 13

Last night before bed, Shawn and I had another "heart-to-heart." We went back and forth saying something that bothered us about the other person and then talking about it to try and find a solution or compromise. It wasn't perfect and neither of us came out completely satisfied, but it did give us ideas of how to improve ourselves and the relationship. Shawn spread his out more, picking out little things that were all part of one problem and mine I just came out with as one thing so it sounded like I'm completely screwed up and he's only a little bit. But I let him do it his way.

I told him his problem is that he always has to be right, in charge, and he knows everything, no matter what. A prime example is when we played Super Monkey Ball for the GameCube. We rented it and extended the rental on it an extra turn so that it could get beaten. When we first rented it, he also got Rogue Leader and that was "his game" and Monkey Ball was "my game." After he beat Rogue Leader, which I think is a dumb game, he started to take turns with me on Monkey Ball which turned into he wouldn't let me play and it became "his game," leaving me with none.

He actually didn't go on the Internet for a couple days he took over Monkey Ball so bad and he'd freak out if he went to the restroom and I just wanted to run around. I spent a lot of time sitting next to him. I've played these games before and a lot of things are similar, like some monsters or some clues, and if he got confused or stuck I'd tell him what I thought was the way to do it and 95% of the time I was right, he was wrong, and he doubted me, having to do it his way. He had to have control. He summed it up as the "Napoleon Complex" and said he'd try to stop that if I try to fix my problem.

Mine, we decided after he nitpicked for a while, came down to a trust issue. I have a problem with him going somewhere without me or if we're somewhere together, him being far away. He asked why I cling so much and I told him it's a trust issue. I know he won't be stupid, but I still worry and although I do think I'm mature for my age mentally, emotionally not quite and a lot of times emotion takes over and I worry that he'll do something stupid. I want to let go that he already did something stupid, but it's hard to and it keeps coming into my mind. I know he won't do it again, but then I rethink it.

So he said the big "test" for me will be next month when his friend, Darlene, a girl he dated right before him and I dated, is having an open house. He and she slept together when they were dating and they broke up over a "misunderstanding." She writes on his MySpace and I get the feeling she ignores the fact it says he's in a relationship with me on there because she seems to "come on to him." But I'm supposed to be able to let him go to that and completely trust him, so I told him okay.

The other things he mentioned were how I normally have him talk to people, like ordering at a restaurant, and the fact I'm so self-conscious about my stomach and butt and want those surgeries. He said that he doesn't care about my tummy or whatever, he wouldn't be with me if he did, and just went on and on about how he could care less if I get surgery or not, he loves me anyway. I told him that was my issue. I know he doesn't mind and doesn't care if I get surgery or not, but I do and it's for me.

Anyway, I did a fairly good job of not getting too emotional, nervous laughter helps. So I am going to try trusting him and see how that goes. I told him I'll trust him until he gives me (another) reason to worry. And I told him to never pull that crap where he says he doesn't love me and never did again.

Taxes are done. After fees and stuff Shawn will be getting $850-ish. That's rent and our GameCube stuff.

April 14

I told Shawn I still don't feel comfortable with him going alone to Darlene's open house and I'll trust him with time. I don't want to be tested. I told him, "I have a hard time telling you no since you want to be right, which I can handle, but it's when you get mad about it that makes it hard. I love you, but I don't like that situation and don't want you going alone." I just didn't want to make him mad by saying I'm uncomfortable, but he said okay, we'll go together. He was fine about it, didn't throw a fit. If he's not telling me something, that's his problem, just like it's my problem if I don't speak up.

I know things could be worse. Every time something bad happens I think that, no matter what, which is why when I'm uncomfortable with Shawn doing something, like the "test" and wanting to go alone, I just think how some girls have abusive boyfriends, so at least he's not that. Something extreme that shouldn't even be used in that situation to compare. I need some work.

Assuming makes an ass out of you and me; my dad *always* told me that growing up and still does. I'm glad I said the right thing this time, about not wanting him to go to the open house alone. I feel much better now that I can go. Something tells me if he says I can and acts nice for a while, I may end up saying I don't want to go with him. But that's another assumption; I like to call it a hunch and I won't worry about it.

I also told him that if he shows me that he's insecure sometimes, too, then I won't feel so bad because in the beginning, he was insecure and I was totally, "I got this," so now that he's totally secure, I don't feel as secure. Since I mentioned that, he has been "giving in" a bit with being insecure. If I say, "Are you mad?" instead of just saying no, he's all like, "No!" and hugging me. If it's an act, it's cute, but he shouldn't be acting, I didn't ask him to do that.

I want to feel comfortable wearing what I like, wearing my old clothing, putting on a swimsuit. I hate water and swimming, but Shawn likes it and I'll go if I feel okay doing it and if we go to Florida, I'm going to go in the ocean. If I can even get back to how I was before, that'd be fine with me. Smooth it out, tighten the tummy, I'll be set. Then I can wear my old clothing. Then I don't have to feel like I have a constant reminder of part of my life I wish never happened.

I already wish I would've had an abortion; I don't want to look down and think that all the time because I really don't want to even think about the whole thing. It's such a horror in my mind that it all happened, how uncomfortable I was with doctor's appointments and knowing I was carrying children. I really don't like them or pregnancy or the feeling I get of the whole idea of that.

Prom is coming up soon. I don't know if I'm going or not, depends on if dad can come and get me since Shawn has drill. I need to get hold of Andrea to see if I can go with her, otherwise I don't know. Hopefully I'll find out later today what my dad's schedule is.

Last night Shawn told me that my boobs no longer are exciting. He didn't mean it in a mean way, he still likes them, he just was saying that they're not how they used to be because when we first were together I never wanted him to see any part of me and now I'm comfortable with him. Or at least as long as I don't really think about it, because if I do then I'm self-conscious all over again. So he sees them "too much" for there to be as much excitement.

I told him he can't see them or have sex with me until he wants it enough that they're exciting because he's making me self-conscious about them all over again. It doesn't feel nice to hear your boobs aren't exciting.

I don't think he meant anything bad when he made the comment about my boobs, he just told me that he sees them so much that I can't persuade him with them like I used to be able to. But I know if I say something about his penis he freaks out, going into a story about how he was laughed at all his life and yadda, yadda, and then it's not a huge deal to say that to me.

Maybe that's why the past never worked well for him. He never seemed to have long relationships; he broke up with people a lot. I do admit that I never play "hard to get," so maybe it's time I start. I just feel that there's that chance I play too hard to get and he stops trying. It's hard to explain.

April 16

Shawn and I had a bit of a problem yesterday after solving the boob thing. Lately he's been spending a ton of time online, ever since we got the wireless box so he can use the laptop in the living room, and yesterday I tried getting him off of it to spend quality time with me. I don't mind being by him while he's on the computer, but I would like some attention, too. He got off once, but then got on the GameCube and didn't let me play with him, then got back online.

When he "paused" and made supper, the computer was still on, he just told the people he was talking to he'd be right back. I talked to him more about it and he said that he likes to be on all the time with new friends because they're on all the time and he doesn't want them to think he doesn't like them.

I told him he'd better worry about me liking him and leaving him before he worries about some 15-year-old girls. There are a couple girls he's in a forum with that he also talks to on MSN Messenger, they're 15 and live in the UK. Last night when it got to be 10:00 p.m., I told him to get offline and tell the main one to go to bed because it's 3:00 a.m. there. Whether she has school or not, she can go to bed, she's effin' 15-years-old, she doesn't need to be talking to 20-year-olds online and I told Shawn he doesn't need to be talking to 15-year-olds.

I don't care if he's their friend, but when he spends all friggin' day online with them, I get pissed off. I also understand he doesn't want to spend time with me all the time, fine, but he can put the computer down now and then or do something online other than talk to them.

I think he can be online as long as he doesn't throw a fit about me "reading over his shoulder." I don't try to, but when I'm out there, it does happen and he knows it. He went through a day or two where he wouldn't let me and sat so that I couldn't see the screen. I told him I didn't like that, not because I can't see, but because I can't sit next to him and cuddle up to him at all.

How do you tell your boyfriend that he needs to put the computer down or else some bad stuff is going to happen? He didn't seem to quite get it. I mean, I love being online, too, but I love being with him more. And it's not a great message he's sending when he tells me no and says he wants to be online.

I talked to him more about how I feel with him being online constantly and I think we worked it out. He's being a lot better about me being next to him when he's online and he said he won't spend all day online, either.

I talked to Cynthia on MSN and she said she understands how I feel and she told me she wouldn't be offended if he isn't on all the time to talk to them. I told him that, but now there's backup.

I guess the part that bothered me most is that they're young girls he's talking to, but at the same time there's other friends of his that are young or are girls even some that are single that I have no problem with. Anyway, the point is, I think we're good.

April 17

I don't know if this is part of some "plan," but the past few nights and this morning Shawn has been "laying down his best moves" and doing a damn good job in bed. I know there are some nights that even though I get off, I still want him to go again and a couple nights ago, he actually did. I didn't mention it, he just asked if I wanted to; there was about an hour in between, but I didn't notice because we were watching the late night shows.

Last night he didn't make me wait until after the shows were over and this morning when I told him to wake up he sprung from what I thought was a daze. I don't know what's up. His drive's either back, or he's trying to "prove a point" that he's not going to do anything elsewhere so I feel safe and secure.

April 18

Shawn and I met online. Maybe that's another reason I'm so particular about him being online with people, but after talking to Stephanie and the others a bit more, I feel safer. I joined the forum they are all in, but am now leaving it and I only really talk to Stephanie outside of it and will continue that since I think she's pretty cool, too. After finding out both the girls have boyfriends, too, I felt pretty stupid. I really don't think Shawn will do anything.

Last night he was "active" again. I asked him why he was so nice lately and he said no matter what, I think he's up to something. During the day I whine that I want him to pay attention to me and then after we go to bed and cuddle I say he's so great. I didn't realize I was doing it, if that's how it's really going.

He always makes himself the victim but says I do it to me and his mom warned me about that, but I'm not going to point it out or anything stupid, I'll just go with it until it passes. He said that he wants me to trust him and says that because I still see him as a cheater and tell people what he did, they all think he's a no good cheater, too. I never thought about that really. I do trust him the more I talk to him. He's trying really hard lately to prove to me I'm his "one and only" and I feel stupid about worrying over Cynthia and the others.

I asked him if he didn't want me to go to the open house, I still want to go, but I thought he'd tell me he didn't want me there to prove my trust, and he said that's up to me. If I want to go I can because he knows I don't trust her, although he doesn't see what she could do around everyone.

All in all it was another touchy-feely conversation, but I'm glad we talk about things, even though sometimes it's uncomfortable. This morning I asked him if he remembered our talk last night since he was getting tired at the end and he said yes. I told him I do trust him, I just sometimes don't trust other people and reserve that right.

I don't think he's having sex chats online. Even if he is, I've been a part of them before, back when we were far apart, and they're not a whole hell of a lot to worry about. He knows better anyway and knows I wouldn't approve and is actually really good about that. But either way, if he is doing that online, as long as I don't have to see it and he's taking his excitement out on me, that's what matters.

When he was out of town at his uncle's funeral he didn't look at other girls and his mom got "mad." I guess she told him, "You can look, y'know," and he told her no he can't because he knows I wouldn't approve. I wasn't even there and he wouldn't look, so really he is a "good boy." When he got back and I heard this I told him he can look as long as it's not obvious and I can tell he's gawking and he can flirt as long as I don't have to hear it. He knows right from wrong.

I think I can trust him and maybe I should start doing it before he really gets fed up. Other than that one mishap he's always been loyal to the fullest. And considering the pressure of marriage and hurting me, plus being worked over by a whore telling him it was the right thing to do, besides, ever since he cheated, he and I have been better, I think. I mean, I moved in, too, which helps. But I really think things are better since. I do trust Shawn, my gut tells me that. But it also tells me to be there around Darlene since she gives me bad vibes and I'm all about vibes.

My dad always told/tells me not to trust anybody. I will let go of the past and reassured Shawn again that he's a good boyfriend and I was being "stupid" before. I should be at his side for social events; I would like to attend and be shown off as his girlfriend.

He started talking to another female from the UK today. They met in some chat that I'm going to go to now. I kidded around about her typing (wuu2 = what you up to) and that's about it. I told him it's silly he needs to find teen girls to talk to, but I guess they're the same maturity level and he laughed and agreed. I told him to find some immature 20-something-year-olds, but I doubt that'll happen. As long as they're overseas he can't really do anything anyway. I'll try this trust thing.

April 19

We spent some time today with Wayne and Naomi. Naomi filled me in on all the "wonderful" things that Nora says about me. I guess she was complaining about the time I answered Shawn's phone while he was playing his GameCube, going on about how he could have a job if it weren't for me. And then she continued by saying she doesn't understand why I answer his phone anyway.

I told Naomi I rarely do unless he tells me to, same with I tell him to answer my phone if he's closer so that it's answered instead of the call being missed by the time I get to it. Besides that, we're dating, what's the big deal if I answer the phone sometimes?

As Naomi was saying, she doesn't know why Nora went on about how I'm so dependent on Shawn. Naomi said Nora made it sound like I am "up Shawn's ass," her words not mine. And she said she understands I don't know my way around or know many people, plus we're together all the time anyway, so it's not like I have other options right now anyway.

When we got home I told Shawn that if his mother asks about me or anything concerning me, not to tell her. And I don't plan to talk to her online. She normally asks me about Shawn anyway, that way she's not pestering him and can technically say she's not asking him about his business.

My mom said the child support is straightened out, so this month's check should go into my bank account here but last month's is there. After telling me that, she wouldn't talk to me, or chat with me on AIM. I tried saying hello yesterday, but she ignored me as well or was away from the computer, but her "away" wasn't on. I tried being nice to Nora then, too, because she was on, but she wouldn't respond either.

For some reason, mothers don't like me. I told Shawn I'm sorry about answering the phone that time and he said its okay, he didn't want to work at the other place anyway, assuming that's who it was that called. And I said sorry for "ruining his life" and he said he doesn't care if I make his mom mad, he won't choose her over me because he makes her mad all the time anyway. We both find it funny that according to my mom, Shawn ruined my life and according to his, I ruined his life.

April 20

I guess the tax money is in, so tonight Shawn is going to bug his mom about getting it. I think he can go over on his own, I don't really feel "ready" to see her again.

I keep having these dreams with Shawn being a jerk or leaving me. Last night we were with a group of friends, all girls, traveling somewhere in Shawn's car, but he wasn't driving, one of the girls was. We stopped at a place like a train station, and Shawn started talking to various people desperately trying to make friends and started chatting to this one guy a lot. I tried following him to get him to come back to the group, but he ignored me and I think we left without him. It was weird.

April 21

Shawn got his federal taxes and is waiting on the state tax return. We set aside what we need for rent and he bought me a Nintendo and took me to eat. Sunday the new Pokemon games come out, I still want more despite all I have, so he's going to get me one. When the state taxes come, another $300, we'll divvy that up for the other bills and then I get to spend my child support money on a second GameCube if I still want it and Shawn said if we have money he'll get more games.

The night we went out to eat with Nora, Grandma Margaret mentioned something to me in the car about the pimples on my chin. She said she noticed I took out my lip ring and I said I did because it swelled up sometimes and I got tired of it being puffy, and then she proceeded to say it was probably because I was breaking out on my chin. I told Shawn when we got home that before we left I was looking in the mirror and thought they looked better that day. I clean my face with a "system" daily, and then she pointed them out like they were horrible.

Then yesterday we borrowed her car to go out to eat and she just needed us to drop her off at Shawn's brother's soccer game and she started asking what size dress I wear. I said I didn't know and she kept asking what size shirt and pants I wear and I told her I didn't know because I don't fit in my old clothing yet. She started comparing my size to her size and after she got out of the car I felt like I wanted to cry and told Shawn I really don't like her pointing all this stuff out to me. I already feel crappy about certain things with my appearance. I don't think she means to offend.

My dream last night wasn't any better. Something about Shawn would only be with me if I let him continue to talk to girls online and I found out he went on webcam and did sexual things with them and was cheating on me with various girls in person, too. It was scary.

Shawn turned in an application at the grocery store. I guess they're hiring and he knew one of the guys that work there because he came into the convenience store a lot.

I talked to Andrea and she told me all about prom and the drama at school and I kidded with her that I left high school so I should be done with the drama, but people keep sucking me back in. She also told me that some girl in our grade has cancer, but it's the "best kind" because few people die from it.

Via MySpace I was invited to an after prom gathering. Assuming I have a ride to and my dad can pick me up after, I plan to go. I've never been allowed to really go out and do anything; my mom would throw a fit about me going to school stuff most of the time and then complain that I never went outside. So this should be fun, even though I'm not a party kind of person anyway.

I found a site online that shows the steps involved with liposuction in various areas as well as tummy tucks. It is good those cells are gone forever, but there's still the possibility of getting big again though I don't think I would. I'm fairly normal-sized underneath all the "junk" I want to get removed and I eat terribly.

I know after getting all that stuff done I'll automatically be the type of person to eat better because I'd be worried about messing up the work I got done. But it says it doesn't remove cellulite, so I'm confused what cellulite is. I thought it's what makes you lumpy in areas, unless removing fat makes it less noticeable.

I emailed one of the places and didn't get a reply, so I sent another email yesterday and if by the end of the week I don't hear anything then next Monday I'm going to call and ask prices. Healing is a long time, all the more reason to get stuff done at once. And the only thing that bothered me, besides the thought of healing and hurting, is the draining tube things they mention in the tummy tuck, only because they never mentioned removal of them, unless I missed that.

April 22

Grandma Margaret was probably asking so many questions because she had clothing that she was going to offer me, although I can't see myself wearing what she gives and I'd have a really hard time turning her down. I know if I accepted and didn't wear anything she gave me, she'd ask me about it.

Dreams are crazy. I try to think of something I said or thought the day before that may have caused a certain part in the dream because I hear a lot of people say it's just stuff that went on in your day that twists into a dream. I guess you really can take dreams in a variety of ways. Funny part is, last night, the part of my dream that I remember,

I was on the phone with my dad and was in the car with Grandma Margaret and Shawn in the back seat and she kept talking while I was on the phone and I got mad at her.

I've changed a ton since I was 14; I've been through a lot since then. It's hard to imagine being 20 because I know I'll be done with my dog grooming schooling, I'll have a job, be living somewhere else. And I do try to think of Shawn in my life then still, although it can be difficult at times because I worry about what he's going to do with his life and if he'll still want to be around anyway.

April 23

Shawn got a call to come in for an interview about a job this morning. He is supposed to go take a survey and "talk" with someone. Maybe he can get this job and his mom can shut up. I get tired of her saying she's going to stay out of his life, but then do nothing but go on and on when we see her.

April 24

Shawn said when he went for his job interview he took a math test and a survey so they can judge his morality and he'll know in a week or less if he gets hired. He just got a call from his sergeant. He's to expect a call from the other company within the week and Shawn said he'll gladly take the job if it's more hours and more pay than he can get at the place who just interviewed him. Also, tomorrow he's supposed to get a call from his other sergeant and get his car and if he doesn't get that call, then this weekend at drill he'll be getting that free car to use.

I talked to my dad and he said he'll be here Friday around noon to take me to prom and he'll pay for everything for prom for me. I offered to do work for it, but he said he'd cover it. He's still telling me to fill out the financial aid stuff for college and I'm still having a hard time telling him I don't want to go there and have no intent to go.

I plan to take the grooming academy papers to get filled out. I think I'm going to go in January, start the online courses then, and that way, by the time I get a chance to go to Japan, it'll be late spring/early summer. Also, Shawn and his mom are planning a possible trip this winter. His mom planned it and Shawn wants us to go, too, so it'd be better if I hold off. Not that I'm excited to go on a trip involving Nora, but I gotta be friendly sometimes.

Finally got a reply from the surgery place talking about all the things they do and listing their beginning prices for things such as liposuction and tummy tucks. They want $75 for a consultation. I emailed back asking a price of all the things I want together since I can't judge the discount. I originally expected the surgeries to be $15,000. Hopefully they'll be lower.

April 26

Shawn got a call from the first place he interviewed and starts Monday. He'll get some hours Monday and Tuesday and I guess within a week or two he'll have a set schedule and get 30 hours a week at $9 an hour. They just have to train him a bit and get him swapped with whoever is filling in now.

My dad's picking me up for prom this weekend. He hopes to do it tonight, but it depends on his work. I'm going with a group of people to prom, including Andrea. I am also going to "after prom." I was invited to an "after after prom" but I may skip that now that I think about it. They'll probably drink and I don't really like being around drunken people, let alone drunken high schoolers.

The cats are coming with me, Shawn has drill this weekend. Poor things will have to be in carriers for almost three hours.

April 30

Well, I'm back from prom weekend. I wasn't really that thrilled to be at prom. I didn't dance at all, sat and talked to my friend Jimmy the whole time because he doesn't dance either. After prom was fun, we had a hypnotist, and I always enjoy watching that sort of thing. The part about after prom that sucks, though, is that the door prize I got was a gift certificate to a place in town. I'll never use it, so I gave it to Andrea who got the same thing; now she has $20 instead of $10. It was weird seeing everyone and hearing all the "drama." Kimberlee caused most of it and I officially am tired of hearing it.

I went to my old bank and got out what I had there and noticed it was only about half of what it should be. When I got back home and checked my new bank, since things are switched to go there now and this month's payment is only about half as well. I went to my online banking thing to see if maybe mom dipped into it, but it doesn't show that she did. So I wonder if it's set up so she gets half directly. I called my dad and he said they took out what they were supposed to, so I have to find out from mom what's going on.

Back to the prom: After getting to prom, I didn't want to be there. After about one night at my dad's, nothing against him, I didn't want to even be there anymore. I definitely do not miss being there and it just reminds me too much of the reasons I wanted to move away.

I'm really glad to be home, although I'm dreading putting stuff away, since visiting my dad means coming back home with about three times what I went there with. But he got me a floor chair so I can sit easier at the computer.

My high school friends still have the whole drama thing going on, and, although I know I can be pretty darned dramatic at times as well, I also know there's more out there now than just what is presented during high school.

May 1

Shawn's job seems to be working out at least for his first couple days. He worked six and a half hours yesterday and is doing the same today, then has tomorrow and Thursday off. This week is just sort of straightening out the schedule and training. I had to stop by to pick up his state tax refund check from him since he thought he'd get to the bank before work, but didn't, and Grandma Margaret ended up just writing a check and said to pay her back when we cash the check.

He seemed like he already knew what he was doing, not that it seems that complicated of a job working at the meat counter, but even if he doesn't completely know what he's doing, the fact he can make people think he does is still a good asset. Sadly, when it comes to work it's all about looking good and saying the right things, but at least Shawn knows how to do that and he knows how to do the job right.

As for the child support, my mom said that she got a check for half and it was issued three days before the switch and she just put it in the bank Saturday. But she said she won't do anything else to help me find out what's going on and my dad said he can't call, they won't tell him anything. I guess because they take it out directly, they can't give him information on my account or Mom's or anything like that. Dad and I figure that maybe it's a bit slow this month since this is the first "switched" month.

As long as I'm going to school, I get child support. Even though I'll turn 18 before I start school, I'll still get it until I'm done with school, which means around next April or May since it's only four or five months of schooling, including Japan. Considering I'm going to school for something I like, I don't think it'll be hard to get back into the rhythm of studying. If I were going to a four-year college, then I'd have a problem, even if I started this fall. I can't bring myself to take courses on things I don't have interest in and know I won't use. At least the way I'm doing it I'll be making it into a career.

I'll be taking out a loan for the dog grooming courses, Sallie Mae I think it's called. It's actually about $9,000 total. Not sure about the Japan part, may get a loan for that part, too, or maybe I won't go. It all depends on funding. Surgery would be worked around a payment plan. If I got the minimum payments for both the loan plan and the surgery plan, it would be doable, hard, but doable.

I'm sort of looking for work right now, but at the same time am not too serious about it until after grooming school. Then I plan to try working either for a local vet or over at *Petco*, to get experience. After a while I'd like to have my own business. And I am bored being at home when I'm alone, but when Shawn's here I'm all right. There are some times that I wish that he and I could go out, but I still don't have many times that I want to be somewhere other than home or away from him. I'm sure that time will come, though.

May 3

Shawn seems to enjoy his job so far, he even is into eating meat more which is surprising since he's such a carb addict and I normally have to beg for us to have meat in a meal. We talked more about me getting a job and I'm going to apply to be a checker where he works. Even though we'd be working at the same place, he'd be in the back and I'd be in the front of the store, so it wouldn't be us spending time at work together, too, which was a bit of a concern for me.

Another concern was dying my hair. I'm not worried about my eyebrow stud since my bangs, when worn down, can cover it and I have seen people in local places with simple things like that before. But for the hair, I was considering redying it to a bluish-purple blend, more purple than blue. But I'm considering getting it done like I saw on one of the Suicide Girls, with it purplish and pink. To me it's very pretty and I don't normally go for pink.

Shawn's picking me up an application tomorrow when he goes into work. And I plan to call tomorrow afternoon to ask about their policy. I really hate the idea of a job that restricts hair color because in a way it's restricting freedom of speech.

I know it'll happen; I just can't wait for the day of wider acceptance. I don't know who decided it's "unprofessional" to have piercings and dye your hair an unnatural color, but it's just not right. Heck, it's "unnatural" to wear clothing, yet we get in trouble if we don't.

I haven't heard from the Clarks in a while, which actually doesn't bother me at all, but my dad keeps asking to get his email passed along to them so he can receive photos. I have to email Nora because my mom supposedly told them, yet nothing changed. I don't have their email or I'd send it directly. I never saved it.

Some shows on TV are terrible to watch yet I can't stop myself. *Animal Precinct* or whatever it's called, the shows with the abused pets and vets doing emergency stuff. I get so emotional over that. Totally makes me glad I'm going with dog grooming, not being anything vet related.

I plan to ask the policy on hair coloring at the store before putting in an application, although I really hope to get it done at some point. I realize the job comes first right now. I know eventually, in a couple years, when I know what I'm doing with dog grooming, I can open my own business and color my hair if I want then. I think this little town needs someone to be different. Sometimes they remind me of where I used to live, minus the wealth, although it's not a poor town either.

I understand that even with my own business, having my own look will definitely "scare" some people off, but I'm willing to accept that. I think once a few people get their dogs done and see what I can do, assuming I'm good by then, and word gets around, I'll do decent. It's a small town, word travels fast. And the people that go to nearby towns and know people there may even spread the word to them.

May 5

Shawn seems to be all right with his job. Today he works from 8:00 a.m. to 6:00 p.m., so it's a long day. He's supposed to be bringing me an application today, too. I was going to write something else and now I can't remember it for the life of me. I swear, at my young age my memory is already shot. I took a bath today and only remembered to shave my right leg. That's just pathetic.

I was planning on starting the dog grooming classes next spring, a year from now. I understand that waiting may end up causing child support to stop, but with Shawn having a job we can manage without and if I end up getting a job, too, we'll be fine.

My dad used to have a hard time paying child support, so it's automatically taken out now. But I don't mind so much if I don't get child support anymore when I turn 18, so long as my mom doesn't get it. That's my only concern and I know she can't now. She barely used it for me when she did get it.

With Shawn having a job we'll have a couple hundred left over a month. I plan to find work, eventually if not soon, so we'll have even more so that loans are fine. I'm not sure who'll co-sign the loan, maybe my dad will. I don't think Shawn can, otherwise he would. Something we need to discuss yet.

I do know I can't be sure of anything. That's why I hate making plans. I make them and it never fails, something happens. I think there are very few things I've planned that have gone the way I wanted. I think moving in with Shawn is one of them. That's why I try to do minimal and just live, do things last minute. Terrible philosophy, but the fewer plans I have, the better things seem to go. I'm just cursed. Dad said he and I have a "family curse."

I do strive for certain things I really want, but at the same time try to be flexible with planning that stuff. That way I'm not disappointed as badly if it falls through. I tend to be a major pessimist.

Now to get back to Pokemon.

May 7

I cleaned the living room this morning right after Shawn left. I told him I'll clean the apartment a room at a time until I find a job, that way I have something to do each day and it's a nice little surprise for him to come home and see more cleanliness. I really do hope I get a job soon so I can start saving up for school and surgery stuff. Within the next few months, before I turn 18, I could have a good chunk saved up for surgery and can pay that off further and the loan after that.

Shawn makes enough that we have a couple hundred left over, so my paycheck could potentially go directly for school and surgery. I guess I do have a bit of a plan. He's supposed to be bringing an application home today.

May 8

I've been doing a lot of thinking today while Shawn is gone, which is nice to have "me time" so I can do that. He works 3:00 p.m. to 9:30 p.m. closing tonight, so right after he left I cleaned the bedroom, the room he wanted done next, minus the closet because it's full of his military stuff. I need him to tell me how he wants it arranged so he can find stuff for drill.

I think he has off tomorrow and Thursday, so Friday while he's gone I'll do the kitchen and Saturday the bathroom or the other way around since Saturday I'll have more time and the kitchen needs more work than the bathroom.

Playing "wifey" isn't so bad. Once I start picking stuff up, it actually goes really fast. I don't have a TV or anything on while I do it so I focus on the cleaning and it'll be an hour and a half and feel like 20 minutes that way, but that's just how I like to do it. I never thought I'd be into cleaning, but I love looking at the carpet after its vacuumed. And I often find myself saying to Shawn, "What is this you left out on my counter?" I sound like my mother, but I don't mind in this aspect I suppose.

I've been thinking about the dog grooming thing and I'm still excited and am growing very anxious for the day I can have my own business. While Shawn's gone during the day, after doing my cleaning, I watch a lot of Animal Planet. Shawn used to "hog" the TV, so now I get a chance to watch it and I love it. There's a lot of dog shows on and it makes me happy to think I'll get to have a job involving something I enjoy so darned much.

I even was thinking about the type of dog that I want to get and decided on a Japanese Chin. I wanted a Pekingese, but noticed when looking at photos I favored the short-haired ones, obviously trimmed since they're long-haired dogs, and the Japanese Chin looks basically the exact same as that. It's funny that I'm so big into Japan and end up loving a Japanese breed the best. But I didn't stop there. I have a notepad that I doodle in, or write stuff down so I don't forget, and have been using it a lot lately while playing Pokemon and I started to draw up a house. Not anything extravagant, but something like what I want to strive for.

Shawn and I both like the idea of an Oriental theme and I want to cross traditional with modern, having the futon on the floor to sleep and the table on the floor that you see people eating and having tea at, and some paper screens between the kitchen and living room, but then also have some sort of modern lighting and storage and some doors to some rooms. There would be too much chance of the cats destroying things if we had too much for them to destroy.

I thought about the landscaping and how I want a big wooden fence around the whole area/yard for the dogs I groom and my own when that happens, even for the cats to go outside. I thought of Grandma Margaret's yard, her fence is really tall, so cats couldn't get out and how I want a rabbit hutch in the corner of the back yard with chain fence around it so when dogs are out, they can't hurt the rabbit(s).

I even thought about how I need a top on the pen so cats don't get in and still need the fence turned out at the top, too, so cats can't use it to get up and over the fence. I thought of it all; outside landscaping, inside décor. Heck, for lunch I had green tea and some rice with egg I was so much in the Oriental spirit. Not only is it delicious, it's fairly good for you, too.

I finally stood up to my dad more firmly, saying I'm pursuing the dog grooming thing for sure and that's it. I really want my own business and still plan to have a couple years at a pet store to get practice and save up some money for getting the whole house thing.

I used to think I didn't have goals in life and I didn't want anything big, but getting the time to slow down and think about it, I really do have big ambitions. I even spent time thinking about grooming dogs and how I'd handle customers and how I'd organize the schedules, including thinking about what hours to have the business open, etc. I thought about how I'll take my own dog for a walk and also how I'll play with the customer's dog a bit beforehand to wear off some energy so they're more cooperative for grooming and everything. I really want this.

May 9

I can't get a dog after graduation, they're not allowed in the apartment, so it wouldn't be until this winter when the lease is up. That's only if we could afford a small house or trailer; preferably a little house that can be slowly fixed up and converted to my ideas. I may change my idea about what breed I want by then. I showed Shawn some pictures, including the little Japanese Chin yawning, and he liked them.

In about three or four years I want to have my home set up, hopefully also the grooming stuff to have my own business started. I'm considering starting grooming school in the fall, assuming I can have the funding figured out and then applying over at *Petco* and/or at some local vets that offer grooming. I'll work a couple years to get the experience and slowly build things up at home. Then when I feel ready, I'll break away and start my own business. I'm not going to Japan. I want to, but I don't think I can afford to do so.

We haven't written our actual expenses out in list form, but we have gone over them with a calculator before, that's how we know we can afford them and will have a couple hundred left over. I want to look how I feel. I'm young and want to look good while I'm young. As I get older, I'm *supposed* to look like this. So to me it makes sense to fix it now, with the surgeries, and leave it go later.

The schooling I can stick to since it's something I want. If I get a job, too, which I am trying to do, then I can pay off the loan and the surgery payments. Shawn is supportive of my decisions, but I wouldn't doubt him eventually saying he'd rather not pay for it. *If* that happens, I'll worry about it then. I'm not going to worry about that now and quit before I get anywhere.

I think support will continue if I start in the fall, but only until I'm done with school. I wouldn't expect the lack of a Japan trip to affect my job opportunities. It's not like everyone else goes and it's a requirement. I would like to go someday, but that's a big trip, one I'd like to take with Shawn and spend a while there, not have to worry about school. So I'm okay not going now. I'm sure Dex the cat will be happy about that; he may die just having me gone six weeks for school.

May 10

Shawn and I talked a lot about houses and dogs and he told me how he doesn't like to make plans. But today, instead of talking about a dog, we got talking about a "baby brother" for Prince Dex. As Dex dug in my cookies (I gave in and let him chew at one; he decided he didn't want it and then came back later for more anyway) we started to talk about it. I have to fill out an application for the one we want. He's in a foster home, I assume he's rescued, and the cat won't be fixed until next Friday.

I think I'm going to scratch the idea of a rabbit hutch from my future house plans; we don't need more than the cats and a dog at some point.

My cat that passed last year was 17 years old; we got her from the pound when she was seven. She was a couple months older than me; I called her my Elder Cat. I know they live a long time, which made it really hard when she was put down. Part of the reason I love cats is they live a long time. They're like my kids and you get to see them grow up to be in their teens and then they pass, which is like them going off to college and never calling again. Adding another cat is a lot to handle, but I'm up to the responsibility, as is Shawn. It's sort of weird how much more we're into animals than we are into children. We're up to this responsibility, but not that of kids. I'm in no way ashamed of that, though.

I have a difficult time going to an animal shelter, especially going near the dog kennels. I revert back to that little kid in me that keeps screaming she wants a dog and it's hard to walk away. When I was younger I wanted a dog really bad, and my dad and I used to go to the shelter but I got to the point I'd leave tearing up because I couldn't have a dog (mom always said no) and my poor dad would've gotten me one if he could afford it.

I still haven't had a dog that's *mine*, so I don't plan to go near sheltered ones until I'm able to take one in and even then I'll probably go through a rescue site so I can get the breed I want. Dex came from an animal shelter and when I was there waiting for Shawn to fill out the papers, I walked around and looked at all the cats (the dogs were in the back) and they meowed a lot and then were silent. As I walked around to each one, they'd meow and rub on the cage. Then you'd hear a meow from a cage across the room of a jealous cat wanting to show off for a chance to go home, too.

It's really tough to leave with only one when there's so many, but I realize I can't give them all a home. I don't plan to become a hoarder. Now that we can afford another, we'll get one and this is *it* for cats. No more pets until we have a trailer or a house and then it'll be a dog.

I just got another email about Tango the cat. I have to let the woman know when we've talked to the landlady and the lease is updated for having cats. We tried calling yesterday and today with no luck, but left a message. She asked the names of the vets our cats went to so she can check that they're up-to-date, but I told her honestly that they all came from other people, so I have yet to personally take them in for shots, but explained I will be doing so next month as well as getting Anaki spayed. My dad's going to help pay for it if not cover it completely, and then I know they are for sure up-to-date. It sounded a bit "fishy" and I'm sure she won't like the sound of it, but I'm not going to lie. I can't anyway if she's calling the vets to check. Hopefully my honesty will be rewarded.

I was talking with Shawn more about this home situation and he and I really want to get a trailer this fall. I told Shawn I'm willing to put the surgery stuff on hold if we can get a trailer when the lease is up and he said he likes the sound of that, especially since a trailer around here would be less expensive.

I'm going to see how I do losing weight and then maybe I won't need as much surgery anyway. I mean, the boob job ended up not having to happen. I got some of my aunt's bras from my dad and they are getting tight now, too. I think the growing bust, on top of me losing weight, assuming I can lose some decent weight, may make me all right in the end.

It's really hard to think about not getting surgery, but at the same time Shawn claims he loves me no matter what and I don't need it anyway. Although the surgeries are for making me feel better, it's easier to wait with him on my side saying I don't need it.

May 12

I'd really like to get Tango, but I don't know if Shawn is responsible enough for another cat. Whisper, the past couple of days, has been being a little troublesome again and he still insists on treating her like a dog, which I get mad at him for. So we'll see.

I "blew up" this evening. I'm not sure what triggered it. Maybe it was the constant Girls Gone Wild ads or the ad for the new "cleaner ladies" for your cell phone (text something to some number and get these chicks on your phone that "clean" the screen). It made me really aware of how badly I want to be back to my normal size. I dug in my boxes of clothes and pulled out the smallest pants and t-shirt I fit in before getting pregnant and brought them to the living room to show Shawn. I know he felt bad, especially when he asked how long ago I fit into them and I told him right before I was pregnant.

I ended up drinking half a jug of flavored water and then cried on Shawn's shoulder a bit. He was somewhat flustered, saying he doesn't know how to deal with "this," referring to me when I get upset about my weight. I told him all I expect is for him to hug me and tell me I'll get there, like he always does. I don't expect more because I know he can't do anything.

I shouldn't be so worried about it, but it does really bother me. I went through being pregnant, which I hate that it ever happened. I had two kids I don't want, and now although they're gone and I can forget that they ever happened, I still have my physical self screwed up. I'm seriously two to three sizes larger than I was before getting pregnant. It didn't help that, while hanging out with Grandma Margaret while Shawn was at work, she mentioned I shouldn't be too much bigger now than I was before I got pregnant and should be about back to normal.

I feel really crappy when people say I should be there and I'm not yet. I do want to try to lose weight on my own, I do want a home that's mine before I worry about surgery because of pain and cost and it's healthier to get in shape anyway. But at the same time, I want so bad to be back to how I was. I really don't know how to explain this in another way.

My dad called yesterday and said he went to the doctor, something about getting checked for a heart attack, and they hooked him to a monitor and if something slopes up, he's okay, and if it slopes down, he's not okay. I guess his sloped sideways. So he told me he *might* have a heart problem. We giggled at the fact he sloped sideways. It is a bit scary to think of and last night I dreamed of dad in a hospital bed and it's just not pleasant.

May 13

I joined an online diet club and started to set up a customized nutrition and exercise plan, substituting if I don't like or don't have certain foods and substituting exercises if I am lacking equipment. Tonight I'll ask Shawn if we can go grocery shopping tomorrow to get some fruits, chicken, yogurt, and veggies. It seems complicated but the more you set it up and think about it, it's easier because it tracks calories and stuff for you.

I like a lot of the foods they list for around dinnertime, it's just a matter of me learning to make it or Shawn being willing to do it for me. I'll show him what I have set up since I have tomorrow and the next day planned and ask him what he thinks. I wrote down some of the key things they listed, fruits, veggies, skinless chicken, yogurt, etc. We still have $280 on our food stamps card so we can afford "the good stuff" although I really don't plan to spend that much.

I look forward to eating healthy, knowing that besides good health it can get me to my old weight and I would like to learn some of the exercise dance stuff to "surprise" Shawn with. I told my friend Andrea that while losing weight I'm going to wear t-shirts and sweatpants so when I'm where I want to be it'll be even more shocking to show off because I'll go from all that frumpiness to some nice, fitted clothing.

I think I'm getting sick today, my throat is a bit "weird" and I have a headache. I hate getting sick, especially now that I'm starting all this eating and exercising. I'll try to sleep well tonight to make it go away.

May 14

I do need to work on how I feel and sometimes I feel okay about wearing decent things, but a lot of times I don't. I feel good about this whole process, as I told Shawn last night. I'm excited to lose weight and as long as we have the resources I think I'll do okay eating. Today will suck because we won't shop until tomorrow, Shawn says, so I'm lacking a few items for snacks.

I feel better today. Shawn and I are going to go bike riding tonight, assuming his mom will let me use the air pump on my tires. I sent an email to my mom saying "Happy Mother's Day." I was going to ask about the fact that the Clarks paid her and she owes Shawn and me $160, but figured if she didn't mention it in response to this email then I'll ask her. It would be rude to ask today.

I just got an email from the woman who has Tango. Once there's an approval from the landlady (still waiting to get hold of her, we keep calling) we can adopt Tango. I sure hope the landlady doesn't require more of a deposit. She knew there'd be at least two cats coming in. We asked if the price is the same for multiple cats and she told us yes at the time, so she can't change it now. I guess we'll find out.

I think my physical, mental, and emotional "me" are clashing right now. I sometimes feel okay emotionally, but a lot of times I think my emotions are still that of a twelve-year-old while I feel my mentality is higher, even with my memory troubles lately. Physically there are times I get cocky with myself and still feel like I'm some slim slinky little thing, like I used to be, but then I see myself and there it goes. I feel one way, look another, and my emotions still like to fly around.

May 15

I got an email from my mom responding to the email I sent yesterday for Mother's Day. She replied "Thanks!" and signed it "Mom." So I guess it's something. I replied again asking if she's doing anything special, but no reply. I have to ask her about the Clarks payment, but didn't feel it was right to ask yesterday, so we'll see if she replies and then I'll ask.

Shawn said I should email because mom *did* have a college fund for me and it would cover my schooling and I want to get my papers filled out soon for school and loans, if needed. So I went ahead and sent an email asking about the Clarks and about the college fund and at the end added that I hope she had a good Mother's Day. I probably should've waited.

The college fund I think was actually set up by my step-dad. He had $10,000 for each kid and mom pointed out that by the time the two younger kids go to school they'll have more saved up because they're younger and I'm going sooner. But I don't know if I still get that since, according to my mom, Robert isn't happy with me and he wanted me to move out, which is hard to imagine he felt that way since he seemed more concerned about me moving out than mom did. I guess we'll see what she says.

Mom replied about the Clarks and the college fund. She said I'm on my own for the Clarks, so Shawn is going to ask his mom for their email and if she got reimbursed. I have a feeling my mom got it and expects me to be too chicken to find my money, so she thinks she can keep it for some expense that she thinks she put towards me. And she said that my college fund was spent between the other kids, as I assumed would happen, so she told me to do the loan. I can't really do anything about that since it was Robert's money, not hers.

Mom wouldn't ever invest money into me and probably not many other people because she's greedy like that. I still wonder how she figures she used child support on me. I know I didn't eat $250 of food in a month and even if I did, half of it should be coming from her like my dad pays half, so either way where'd the rest go? I really wish *she* had a fund for me. I guess that's what loans are for.

As I told Shawn about the college money, it was Robert's money anyway. Medical and dental weren't common, I'd go to the dentist once every six months and most medical is covered by insurance because my dad has to have that for me and then whatever costs there are, Dad still had to pay half. My mom almost never bought me clothing though every now and then she'd bring home some underwear or a shirt that was on sale somewhere, but most of my clothing I got when I was with my dad.

My dad tended to be my mom *and* my dad, even when it came to bras and underwear and dresses for dances, even for going to get birth control and eventually my IUD. I know this last year of school mom almost didn't pay. She had Shawn cover it and then paid him back, but I think she was tempted to ignore paying him back just like she's ignoring the fact that I should've been reimbursed the same time she was and probably was. I get a strong feeling she has my money. She can't expect my dad to pay for everything and she pretty much did anyway.

We have the meeting with the landlady tomorrow and then will call the lady fostering Tango. But, assuming the landlady approves (not sure why she wouldn't, cats are allowed, one flat fee), we can have Tango. We pick him up either Friday morning or Monday morning, which I won't be here Monday through the week after. I'll be staying with my dad through graduation and then Shawn will bring me home that Sunday night. So, Shawn may pick Tango up and I won't even see him. Although that sucks, it would be good for Shawn so they can bond and Tango will be really his. Dex, though, may come with me. Shawn can handle taking care of the cats without me, but I don't think Prince Dex can handle being without me.

May 16

Shawn liked that I looked nice for him last night. I even talked him into a backside massage since I heard that'll help break down any cellulite and make it a bit smoother, and I realize it won't go away completely. Not sure of my exact size right now. I'm guessing an awful 13 because I have a pair of size 11s that are too tight when I get them on. I was a size 9, but it was always too big in the waist. Size 9 fit my butt and thighs and my waist was that of a 5 or 7. I liked my little curvy figure. I wasn't thin but I was normal (well, for my height, a little thick) at 135, but I was okay with that so at 120 I should be good.

I browse eBay a lot for clothing, especially Japanese streetwear styles, and also for cosply outfits. I hope to get small enough to feel confident in an anime outfit and go to a convention someday. That's another little goal of mine. Shawn wants to go, too, but he's already in shape.

We are approved for Tango. The landlady asked if this was our second cat because supposedly only two are allowed and we said yes although it's the fourth. Luckily they don't ever come over to our building and if they do, they have to notify us beforehand. She never told us the two cat rule when we moved in, so we were shocked but tried not to show it. We'll hopefully be moving out around December, so we're halfway through the lease.

I just talked to my mom over MSN using microphones. I think she spaced that I have a cell phone and she actually took my number at the end of the call. She told me about her new job she starts soon and about the kids and my step-dad and we chatted decently. She said he is having surgery for two hernias (he had surgery three years ago for one, now there's two more) and I explained more about Shawn's hernia stuff since she didn't get details at the time and she didn't say anything bad about him either.

Tomorrow we get to pick up Tango. Sunday is the open house assuming Shawn is home early enough. He thought he had a parade Monday, but remembered that's next Monday, so Sunday night I'm headed to my dad's with Dex.

May 18

Right after getting Tango from the vet, we got him to the car and opened the cage to put his collar on and then Shawn took him out for me to hold on the way home. Tango was okay with that until I closed the door, before Shawn got in on his side. Tango scratched my arm, and then bit my thumb pretty hard. I chased him around the car to put him back in the kennel and finally got him in so Shawn could get in the car. I told Shawn that's why I didn't want to let him out yet. Tango slept off and on all the way home and is really nice now that he's indoors. Shawn left for drill, so it's just me and the cats for a couple days.

Rosemary from the adoption agency emailed me and is going to stop by tomorrow because I guess some papers got lost so I have to sign something quick. The fun never ends. I can just imagine what it'll be like when I get a job and start school, etc.

May 20

I seriously think I can see some changes already from this dieting stuff. I notice it around my stomach/waist because it was so stretched there and my waist near my hips is actually fairly even now. I first noticed last night when I was sitting in bed. I still had the stretchy bits flopping in front, but on the sides it didn't do that really at all. I can't wait to add exercise tapes to the routine and see what the next week and the next bring.

I just checked my online banking and when I asked Shawn to withdraw $130 he withdrew $150 even though I only had $133 in there. The bank charged me for being negative and now my balance is -$47. He's at drill, so when I called I got voicemail, but I left a message and sent a text saying I'm angry.

The bank charges $31 for overdrafts, and he took out $20 more than I had. We talked on the phone, though, and he was very apologetic. He said he thought he only took out $130 and he'd put $50 in tomorrow before work.

Graduation will be such fun (sarcasm).

May 24

I'm dying my hair again, but to what will be a surprise. It involves two steps/colors and I already had it "approved" by Shawn, mainly so he wasn't surprised when he saw me Sunday.

I'm going to call the local vet on Monday to see if they need an assistant, maybe get a job there.

May 27

I *was* going to bleach my hair and then just have pink bangs, *but* I ran out of bleach because of my hair being so thick. I even asked at the store if it would be enough for my hair or if I should buy two things of bleach, so I covered it all with pink. Its *very* bright pink with some black streaked in, which doesn't look bad even with being an accident. I guess this pink lasts a couple months before fading, so when it does, I'll fix the bleach. If the vet is willing to give me a job on the conditions I change my hair, then I'll dye it back to black or something.

We stopped at my aunt Shirley's to print the new pictures of the kids for my great grandma to see at the nursing home.

Graduation is tonight.

May 28

Well, graduation wasn't *that* exciting, but my mom did attend and actually gave me a card with $50 in it. I have a nasty cold, so afterwards when Shawn and I went to Darlene's open house, we didn't stay too overly long.

Shawn's in a parade today and I was going to watch, but he suggested I stay home because of my coughing and sniffling and after a little bit of thinking it over I agreed. It looks like it may be chilly outside this morning and not a good thing for a cold.

Dad was going to give me his scale, but it's messed up. I thought I had the dial in the middle, making it say I weigh about 148 (having lost weight), but when Shawn got there and tried it, it said 125 and he knows he weighs 145, which means I actually weigh a lot more than I thought I did. Pretty depressing, but at the same time I do think I lost a little weight from whatever my starting weight was. I'm going to avoid a scale for a while and go for physical results, not numbers. I told Shawn that the scale would just make me upset more often, so I'm not going to put myself through that.

Shawn has some caffeine pills he said he used in basic for energy, but I guess if you take one after every meal, not exceeding three a day, then it'll help to lose weight. Shawn's normally picky about weight loss pills, especially ones with Hoodia in them, but he "approved" these and said I should try them. If there's caffeine involved, maybe it'll help me avoid drinking pop at least until we get some diet pop in the house. Hopefully it keeps me from getting a headache.

I just want the cold to go away.

May 29

Most people liked my hair. We visited Grandma Margaret, after going to the movies, and she said she didn't like it. She wasn't mean about it, I didn't think, and then called later to tell Shawn to tell me she was sorry for being so blunt because I guess she felt bad. I didn't expect her to apologize, so it was a nice surprise. She also gave me a $100 check for graduation, another nice thing she didn't *have* to do.

My cold is still sucking, but I got some Sudafed for it today, so I'm hoping it makes a difference although I'm not big on pills/medicine, making even the caffeine pills a challenge to take.

Shawn got an application for another job because his boss is starting to cut his hours. We blew a tire today on the way back, so unfortunately we'll have to talk to Grandma Margaret. It's just not a good day.

May 31

I didn't call the vet yet; I've been talking back and forth with the woman at the grooming academy about getting school stuff squared away and dealing with Shawn and his job. I really hope the other job works out instead. Maybe I'll call this afternoon. Plan Bs are nice to have, but sadly we don't at the moment.

Shawn decided to quit his job and really hope for this new one. He'll be leaving next week for active training, so he wouldn't be working anyway. Either way we need Grandma Margaret to help us with this month's rent and he gets part of his bonus after active training, which will hold us over a couple months. He came out whistling and shouting "I'm free!" So he's happy about it; I'm undecided.

He'll be in active training for three weeks. I think the people where he put in his application that he knows from working there the summer he was 17 would be happy to hire him back, at least that's the impression they've given. While he's gone, I think I'm supposed to be taking care of Nora's two dogs while she's gone and then Grandma Margaret's dog in July some time. But that won't take all day, just have to feed them and let them outside.

Nora emailed Shawn and asked how I was feeling because he said I wasn't feeling well which is why I wasn't at the parade and then she asked if I was pregnant. It really pisses me off that she assumes me not feeling well means I'm pregnant. She knows I have an IUD. I think she talked to Grandma Margaret, who knew I had a cold, so I really don't know what her quizzing was all about. She continued to mention visiting the twins and how they're doing.

Shawn showed me his phone bill for this month and I can't say I'm happy. I guess he didn't delete a couple things and got charged some fees, so there's about $16 at least that could have been prevented. I'm trying hard to "count to 10" and not get snotty with him, mainly because I don't like when he gets "mean" back. It's like his only defense, he doesn't know how to apologize and suck up like most men, yet. Right now, I'm so mad I want to cry.

June 1

I have considered adding dog walking to things I can do; it's not out of the question. We have to talk to Nora sometime soon to get things straightened out although Shawn has told her about ten times that I'll be here and want to take care of her dogs. I don't show interest unless she starts talking about me, but I guess I should ignore even that. I already know that she "likes me as a person, just not dating

Shawn." So I assume that's why she likes to pick at everything, because she doesn't like me being with her son. At least if Grandma Margaret picks, she's not trying to be mean, she's just honest like that. And she did a good thing by calling the other day to apologize, so even that I think is fading. Maybe she sensed I'm "sensitive." I didn't say anything, so not sure.

The phone bill *should* be better for next month.

June 3

Well, last night was a good night. I was a bit emotional because of things being on their way, which isn't the good part, obviously, but then asked Shawn to marry me in the most serious sense I could. He ended up looking me in the eye and saying, "Will you marry me?" Of course I said yes, but told him if he meant it then to get the ring out before bed and get down on one knee, which he did and it's even more appealing to see it the "official" way than any other. Needless to say, I'm wearing my ring again. We still won't get married until I'm 21, but it's very exciting that he feels *ready* this time.

June 4

Shawn keeps referring to my ring as my "happy button." I haven't told anyone else yet. I'm sure Nora will figure it out when she notices the ring on my finger, my dad I may tell later. I want to enjoy it myself for right now. I have a lot to do before I'm 21, but that's good. Better to know I don't need to worry about marriage until then.

I've talked to Shawn about moving, but he's not sure; he's like my dad and said he doesn't like to plan too far ahead. This winter we still want to move out of the apartment, but not sure if we can afford that.

June 6

Shawn just got done gathering his stuff for AT, with some help from me. He'll be leaving *really* early tomorrow morning and will be back on the 23rd. Today I'm starting my cycle, so I keep kidding him that he's leaving at my emotional time.

Sometime today we have to see Nora so I can get a garage door opener to take care of the dogs. I don't think she's leaving until a couple days before Shawn gets back, but she wants it squared away before he leaves.

Shawn called to check about his job application and they said that they looked at his application, but the position was already filled. The lady said to call back in a couple weeks, though, because the people normally don't last long.

I keep putting off calling the vet because of my pink hair. I'm pretty certain they wouldn't "approve" of it. It's starting to fade fast, though, so once it does I'll bleach it so it's even and then call. Platinum blonde/white hair shouldn't be considered "wrong" in any way.

Shawn had a tire blow last week. He ended up getting four new ones, thanks to Grandma Margaret, and has to pay back half when he gets back from AT because that's when he gets his three year part of the bonus. Also, when he gets home, he's going to pay off the rings. He said he'll be getting enough for a couple months' rent, too, so he can easily afford to search for a good job.

My child support will last until around X-mas when I get done with school. I'll be starting in September. I'll be sending papers in soon, doing loan stuff after I turn 18 and should be done in mid-December.

June 7

Shawn seems to be good at getting work when he needs it and getting by when he doesn't have a job. It's amazing, I think, how lucky that boy can be with that sort of thing. But of course if someone mentioned luck to him he would laugh because he doesn't see it that way.

He left about 45 minutes ago. Woke up at 4:30 a.m., which I did as well, and left earlier than I thought he would. He said it was in case he forgot something and needed to come back even though he was given a list and yesterday I helped him gather his things. So I helped him carry his laptop and another bag down and said my goodbyes.

I took a shower, although I'm tired and should sleep but can't since I'm one of those people that gets up and is *up*. I called Shawn a little bit ago because he forgot his gloves, one of which I had to hunt down for him because I remembered seeing it and he couldn't find it himself.

He said he didn't need them badly enough to turn around, and would get another pair from his locker. So now it's me and the cats.

I just got done doing the first part of my exercise DVD. It was about 30 minutes long and for someone that hasn't worked out in a while, it definitely was tough! Tomorrow I'll do the lower body section of the DVD and if that's not too long, I'll do the upper body part, too. I think alternating will help keep it from getting old too quickly. It was a good workout. I worked up a major sweat, and now am tired.

The only problem I came across with the DVD was one exercise, lying on my side and lifting my hips, and I hope I can improve on that. My hips are my largest part of me and I couldn't lift more than half an inch off the ground because they're so full. The easier the exercises become and the smaller I get, the more encouraged I'll feel.

I hope to lose five pounds this next two weeks while Shawn is gone. I'm stocked up on frozen meals and now with exercising I can actually eat a little more so I don't get less than 1200 calories. I'm tired, but feel good that I stuck with that whole section of the DVD. I was going to try to go on, but as soon as I lifted my leg for the first lower body exercise I felt the other turn like Jell-o. So I though I shouldn't push it.

June 8

I talked to Nora on AIM and gave her my cell phone number and she'll be calling next week to let me know about the dogs so I can take care of them for her. Also, I've been reading up on Hoodia and may start taking it. I want to talk to Shawn first, although as Nora said "it's my body." But I'll feel better having his "approval" first.

June 11

I talked to Shawn and he asked me if I'd rather him go to Iraq or Egypt. I guess next year he for sure has to go somewhere and he already told them Egypt, but asked me in case I wanted him in Iraq instead, which of course I don't. I guess Egypt would just be a peacekeeping mission for a year and he wouldn't really have to do much of anything whereas Iraq would bring up more chance of him getting hurt and he'd have to work a lot.

I still don't want him to go at all and won't count on anything until it happens, but I guess we can talk about it more when he gets home. I told him I didn't really like it being brought up while he's already away for a bit. Two weeks is still a long time, I think. I don't want to think of him being away that long. It feels like I just got him and he'd be leaving again. I really am getting tired of long-distance stuff, but love him to death. Maybe that's what the psychic meant I'd get tired of, the long-distance. I still think about that sometimes.

June 13

Well, my new GameCube ended up at my mom's house because I, like an idiot, forgot to change the address on my PayPal account and didn't realize until it was too late. I called DHL and ThinkGeek, but because I got 2-day shipping I didn't have time to correct it. So, my mom will pass it on to my dad, eventually, and it'll get shipped to me. I have done a lot of waiting for that darned thing.

Waiting for Shawn to get home takes forever. There are still 10 (or 11 if they keep him an extra night) days left. He told me to call him when I wake up this morning, which I did at 7:00 a.m. (since I didn't go to bed until 1:30 a.m.) and he said he was eating and he'd call back. Twenty minutes later I called him and he said he had to get some stuff together, told me to take a shower and then we could talk. So I showered for 20 minutes, waited about another 15 minutes and called again and he said he was still busy. He promised he'll call when he's done since he's *supposed* to have this morning off, but it's 10:30 a.m. and here we are.

Today, assuming I can get hold of Grandma Margaret — she goes to church all the friggin' time it seems — I have to mail out Shawn's phone bill for him, because, although I told him to do it before he left, he forgot. Hopefully I can go grocery shopping this afternoon, too, because I'm out of dinners.

I'm a bit frustrated with Shawn being gone and how it's making things go. The lack of communication feels terrible and the cats, though I love them, seem to be more anxious with Shawn gone as well. They seem to get into more; maybe because I can't give the attention that two people can. I have no idea. I know that a lot of times if they hear someone in the hallway they perk up and sit and wait thinking Shawn might be coming home. So I guess we can all be disappointed together.

In a way I feel sort of bad because the lack of communication and attention has me leaning on an online friend (male) that happens to have a thing for me. I know there's nothing wrong with flirting a bit or liking him, considering I love Shawn no matter what and he'll never be replaced, but at the same time I feel bad.

I have a problem with seeking attention all the time. I tend to blame it on my mother, not getting enough from her, but that could just be an excuse for me being messed up. Whatever the case, I just want 10 days to go faster and, right this moment, want to be able to talk to Shawn. And I really don't want to go out with Grandma Margaret and have him call because I want to be able to talk to him, alone. Not that we talk dirty or anything, but I feel more comfortable having my few minutes of "us" together.

It's like magic, I no sooner write and then he called. He talked for a minute, but then it was windy and he said he'll call me back, so now I am sitting again. He got a chance to explain that he's been put in charge of a lot of stuff that he shouldn't be, so they have him doing a lot of work. I said that sounds backwards, normally the joys of being in charge means everyone else does the work, but I think they gave him the fancy title of "in charge" so they didn't feel bad about making him do stuff.

So, now we wait again. We're getting *somewhere*, although I get a bad feeling that this may take a bit. At least we got to talk for half an hour. He apologized further for being busy and I apologized for being upset. He was a bit grumpy and it gave me bad vibes.

I told him how I was and how I feel and told him about the cats and my plans for the day, just the usual up-to-date sort of thing. Someone asked him in the background who he was talking to and he said, "My girlfriend," to which I questioned, "Girlfriend?" He corrected himself and told the other guy he was talking to his fiancé. I told him he said he was serious, so I do expect to be called by the appropriate title. He said, "You know I love you," and it felt better. I hate to be so protective of the title, but at the same time it was taken away from me once already. He was really tired sounding and was playing his video game, so towards the end of our chat he was zoning out a bit. I told him he should take the next half hour of his hour break to relax and play his game. I love talking to him and told him that, but I also don't want him to pass out or anything and he already had a caffeine headache.

He is supposed to call tomorrow evening. He said they should have things under better control then so his off time is really that. I told him I won't call and bother him; I'll wait for him to call and plan on getting my stuff done for the day in the morning. I feel better having talked to him, and although we had a moment of sorrow of missing each other, it was still a nice feeling to have him agree with me.

I applied to be a sales clerk at a clothing store, nothing special. It's at the mall and one of the few places Shawn and I go in at the mall, there and the video store, so I figured why not. They called today regarding a job and I told them my situation with Shawn gone and asked if I could start in July, since it's just summer help they're looking for. They said okay, but asked if I could get in for an interview now. I told them I'm sorry, but I can't, so maybe I'll get lucky and they'll call back in July. Shawn said I could've asked Grandma Margaret, but it's really hard to plan around her because she's such an active church member.

I do feel that I'm getting better with it all, but at the same time it's like every time I turn around, one of us has to go somewhere for a week or two, then I'll go to school for six weeks, then he'll most likely go to Egypt for eight months to a year.

For the most part, I trust him again (although I'll admit, my mind still tends to wander) and I believe that he loves me and we'll make it, but it just sucks when we have to revert back to the long distance, even for a week. I guess I still have that fear that if he's far away, another Victoria will come along and seduce him. I don't care how much you love someone, I still think there's always a chance for things to happen. That was proven to me when he did it with Victoria. And, I totally trust him; I just don't trust other people. I still believe there are people out there manipulative enough that they could talk him into doing something that would hurt me, even if he didn't intend for it. I'm trying to get over it, though.

I realize I can only rely on myself, but I feel like I've done that long enough that I want to be able to invest a lot of feelings in someone and get them back and feel secure about it. I have a lot of emotional issues that need to be addressed and I plan to talk to Shawn about them when he comes home. He's not doing anything wrong, and I'll tell him that, it's just that I want to overcome a few fears and want to make sure he understands what they are.

Now that I got all that sappy stuff out of my system I think I'll drop it until Shawn is home. I'll talk to him directly about it, but don't want to while he's away. And when I hear him in a better mood, then I feel more comfortable to wait for him to call me. It's just when he's grumpy, although ninety-nine percent of the time not at me, I feel like I have to fix it and I hate letting bad feelings set.

June 14

Shawn sent me a text message at about 5:30 p.m. saying he has to go to bed early because he was put in charge of something-or-other and can't talk tonight and told me he loves me. I sent back my okay with a smiley face and said I love him, too. Then he sent back that he'll explain it all tomorrow. I assume he figured I was upset, although not showing it. And I said I'm not mad, it's fine, I trust his judgment. So he said he'd call around 9:00 a.m.

I handled it well, haven't called him at all last night or today, actually wasn't concerned about it, and was kept busy enough that I didn't even see the time go by. Normally I would assume that something is up besides what he says, but I just let it go and took it for what he said. I think I took a good first step in trusting and not clinging.

June 15

Oh my Gawd!! I went online to check my bank account, which is the easiest way for me to keep track of it, and I knew that I had withdrawn money for Shawn's phone bill, but left $3.45 in there so that it wouldn't overdraft me. I was checking because now that it's getting into the second half of the month child support will be coming and also to see if Columbia House credited my money back since they like to send and charge me for things that I already said no to *by the deadline*, so I'm getting a couple DVDs when Shawn gets home and then being *done* with it. There's an overdraft charge and an $11.99 charge from some company I don't even know.

I called the bank and they said to call the company, then call and file a dispute through the bank's 800 number. I called the company and it was really noisy and hard to hear, then the lady gave her spiel of "my name is so-and-so, may I get your name?" I said my problem and she said she can't help me with that, and immediately went on about saving money at thousands of restaurants and hotels and basically tried to sell it to me.

So I hung up and called the bank to file a dispute, which the guy ended up saying it's fraud and to cut up my debit card, they'd send a new one with all the paperwork and get me a new number. So, someone tried to rip me off.

I swear I'm going to live through everything there is in life, bad at least, before I get to age 20. So, PayPal is pretty much "offline" for now because I'll have to put a new card number in and I'll have to somehow deal with Columbia House and tell them I had a fraud issue and my card is dead.

I'm just glad I caught it. If I had more money, I may not have noticed an $11.99 deduction, especially if I recently took money out for something else. So, in a way, being broke helped. On top of all that, I got up early this morning to talk to Shawn and texted and he said he's taking a nap, but will call later and that was basically it, besides him saying his love, etc.

He texted before and said he heard a song that made him think of me ("Momma I'm Coming Home" by Ozzy Osbourne), which was really sweet. I said thanks, but texted back a little later because some of the lyrics seemed a bit not nice. But then I looked up further and found out they are, so I'll have to tell him whenever I talk to him that I found out more. It was nice of him, especially considering I didn't get to talk to him much lately, but, maybe getting put in charge of stuff means something good.

June 16

I got to talk to Shawn for a few minutes last night, it was all very pleasant and I explained the song confusion to him and he just laughed.

I talked to my friend, Luann, who is about Shawn's age, and told her about Shawn maybe going overseas and how he says we'll get married when I'm 21. She told me about her friend who is dating a guy that goes overseas a lot and they've been together three years and have a house, but they're not married. She said it's really hard on her friend and I should ask Shawn about marriage before he goes overseas.

She said that I can still drink at the reception if I'm 18. I may ask his thoughts about it. I honestly do think that being married would make me feel better, so I would be a stronger support system. If I'm married, then he's "mine" as much as can be and it'd take a lawyer for him to leave me. Okay, bad joke.

June 18

Last night I talked online with my Aussie friend, Zack, and he did a phone call over the Internet for a few minutes because he didn't have to work for an hour and Lemmy, a friend of his who has a band and is trying to get a CD out, said hey which I thought was so cool because I really like the music and Lemmy seemed neat from pictures I've seen. I ended up chatting with Lemmy for a while on MSN Messenger. So now I have Zack and Lemmy telling me to visit Australia.

I think being online has played a big part in my life and I've never found a problem with meeting people online and then in person, as long as I'm careful, of course, and actually think whenever I can afford to go to Australia I surely will. In a way it's sad how many friends I have online compared to how many I have in real life, but at the same time it's better than nothing especially since I can't really go anywhere without the car and wouldn't know where I was headed if I went.

I guess the people that share my interests are just like me in the sense they don't like to go outside much either. I really need Shawn to come home so I can get out more. I've been trying to get hold of Erica, but she is still off with her family.

I have no idea where my GameCube is at the moment since it got picked up from my mom's house, I assume to be redirected to me. If I don't see it today I'll have to make some calls. Today, also, I hope to get the paperwork to get my debit card stuff straightened out.

I still don't know my exact weight. I'm hoping when I watch Nora's dogs (assuming I'm going to, she still has to call me) I can just hop on her scale. I'm to the point that when I lay down flat on my back, my stomach is as flat/thin as how I want it when I stand up. It helps me see I'm getting somewhere, but of course it's still not where I want to be. I woke up and looked in the mirror this morning, especially since I noticed it the most this morning, and honestly do think I can see some improvements already. Even if it's in my head, it's still good motivation. I always worry, though, that by my birthday I won't be down near where I was hoping by that point, or that I won't get to my goal at all.

I didn't sleep well last night because I let the cats in, which I hadn't been doing the few nights before. Tango likes to roll around on me a lot and Dex is obsessed with my puppy stuffed animal that I sleep with. Anaki was actually by my feet a lot of the night, which scared me a few times when I moved and felt some little furry thing.

June 19

Before Shawn left he promised to take me to some hang-out place, and I'll have to remind him when he returns. Hopefully I can meet new people and gain real friends. I have a few people I know from high school that may be attending the college in town, so if they have free time I should have them to hang out with. My friend Lindsay already said she wanted me to hang out with her when she's up here.

Shawn has a lot of female friends anyway. I think he has mainly female friends whereas I have mainly male friends. His best friend even is female. I know he has spent a lot of time online in the past talking to other girls, some overseas, but he's made me come to realize that nothing will happen. As far as my Aussie friends, they both are in relationships, so it's not like that's what it'd be for, and if I went to Australia, I'd take Shawn. I've thought about going there before, this would be a good excuse and give me a free place to stay. It'd be fun to see Lemmy's band *with* Shawn. If Shawn had friends in another country and wanted to visit I wouldn't care so long as I'm going too.

Going out is fun with Shawn because it's spending time doing something with him other than sit around, but when it's just me by myself I don't have interest in other stuff. I don't like going outside much, I don't like reading, and there isn't too much to actually see. Most of the stuff is in the next town which is a college town. I really am just an Internet geek. That's why back in my home town I didn't do much. I didn't have anyone around that made doing stuff feel worthwhile. If I liked going outside, it'd be different.

I think Nora is going out of town tomorrow and she still hasn't called about the dogs. I can't remember if it's tomorrow or the next day, so if I don't hear anything tonight I'll assume it's the next day or she found someone else. I don't like talking to that woman, mainly because she asks me about Shawn and our plans so much, so if she wants me she has my number. I've even gotten on AIM more often lately, to give her more opportunity to catch me, but she's never on.

One more thing about real friends: Back home, a couple months into pregnancy, I hung out with my friends Jimmy and Kirk. It was in the evening when it was dark; we went walking along the train tracks through the woods, down to the bridge, etc. Just hung out and it was a lot of fun. I hope to find a couple of friends to do that sort of stuff with here. Just roam around and hang out. I don't want a group; I want one or two people that are as unenthusiastic about the daylight as I am. Not that Kirk and Jimmy completely hated sunlight, but they both liked video games a lot and were inside doing that often. And I don't limit myself in saying Internet friends can't become real life friends. I met Shawn online and I know he met Erica on MySpace and she's great.

I'm not very self-motivating. I used to be very driven with art. I loved drawing and coloring and was the kid that told my parents I wanted to be an artist when I grew up. My mom said you don't make much money that way, so I slowly just got to where I am. I still love drawing, but don't do it nearly as often as I used to. I loved soccer and gymnastics, too, and always wished I got the chance to stick with them, but soccer got "old" for me, especially when my mom never wanted to go to the games and she stopped helping pay for gymnastics.

I guess I feel that a lot of stuff I could've done and had interest in was "taken away" when I was still young, so I it's hard to find something to invest a lot in now. I'm "afraid to commit" to a subject, in a way. I wouldn't run off somewhere without talking to Shawn and giving him a chance to come with.

I haven't done much with the exercise DVD this past week. I've been online to the point where it's 2:00 p.m. and I realize I need some lunch. I think the Internet is the only thing I get that absorbed in.

I like vampires and have a "thing" for that sort of thing. I like to be bitten, and bite, and like a lot of the dark Victorian-styled attire and homes. I hate the sun and tans, I like pale and pasty skin and if I could afford to get my teeth filed to be sharp I totally would. I like their eternal youth and gothic style. If only they were real.

June 20

Tonight I got another text from Shawn saying he won't be able to talk to me and I keep thinking about when/if he goes overseas. I love him, more than anything, but I really don't know if I can wait forever for him. I say I can, convince myself I can, but I really have to wonder how much waiting I can do for a person.

I've never been unsure of Shawn before and lately I sort of have been. It really upsets me to think that way because I have it set in my mind he's the one I want to marry. But, a small part of me lately keeps thinking, "You're 17 and there's other guys you may still want to meet." I do *not* want to talk to Shawn about this, but at the same time maybe I should. But, being unsure like I am, I'd hate to open that all up. If I can figure it out on my own without having to discuss it, I'd rather.

Am I happy with Shawn? Sure, ninety percent satisfied with what we have and where we're going. But it's that ten percent, which I actually find quite large (I think it's been growing), that makes me wonder. I assume it's normal to question things. Now that it's more *real* that we're engaged and have plans for marriage and I *know* he's in it this time I guess I know how he felt before, when things get real and you notice that "this is it." I used to feel this way a lot dating guys, always felt panicked with commitment of any kind and didn't keep a guy around long. But, then I got to here and felt like this was great and I had no fear and no interest in running. Until now, that is.

I guess I really have to think about *why* I'm in this relationship because I always tell my friends not to be with someone just due to history. Be with them for who they are now and how you feel about them now, sort of "live in the moment." I need to evaluate if I'm doing that. If I feel, from moment to moment, I'm satisfied, or if it's not enough to be worth it.

This all sounds so terrible. And I keep thinking of that darned psychic every time I have doubt. About how Shawn and I won't last a year and how I leave him. I don't want to make her right, but I don't want to commit to something in life only because I didn't want to make everyone else right. I know I love him, I guess I'll start there.

It's really hard to think about. And I wouldn't be getting out of it because of inconveniences. It's just a matter of noticing certain things that I know I'd have to live with forever. What this has gotten me to see is that I should talk to Shawn. I was scared that talking to him would mess something up, but if we can't communicate then that's a dead sign we shouldn't bother. I'm not sure why I was worried about talking to him; I know he'll understand, especially since he went through similar feelings before.

I still have three days until he's home, so I'll know more when he gets here and we talk about it. Right now I don't want to think too much about it, it's making me upset. And, I shouldn't stay because of nowhere else to go or because everyone expects me to stay. And I just want to be sure I'm not with him for reasons like that or reasons of history. I really want to be sure.

I talked to my dad and he said to talk to Shawn. He told me about military breaking up a lot of relationships with people having to be away, because I told him about not being sure if I'm willing to wait around for a year, and said Shawn and I will have to discuss it. I'll talk to Shawn and tell him my anxieties, which could just be from him being gone for a while now, as my dad suggested, and see what he says.

Well, I got a chance to talk to Shawn. He actually had a free minute, it was nice. I told him how I felt and at first he sounded a little worried because I sounded upset even though I tried not to be. And I told him that he didn't do anything wrong to make me feel like this, I was just scared and the idea of him leaving and having to wait around was scary. He said he loved me and I asked if he was sure he wanted to marry me and he said yes.

I told him I think I'm sure I want to marry him, but we're waiting until I'm 21 at least. He said okay, he likes our plans anyway, which is sort of big for him because he hates making plans. It ended well with him saying he'll be home Saturday about noon and he wants me waiting naked for him. I still hope to talk to him a bit more when he's home, but for now this was nice so he knows how I feel. The more I think about it, I think it could just be jitters but I'll know more as time goes on.

My parents were married about five years. They were married a year before they had me and then divorced when I was three. I know the divorce rate is high, that's why I don't want to be like that. Maybe he will think more. I hope that if we do ever get to the point where we don't want to be together, we'll at least be civilized about splitting up. Talking feels good, he's great at being reassuring. Saturday seems far away.

June 21

I think child support runs out when I turn 18 unless I fill out papers proving I'm in school, but considering it's only four or five months, I don't think I'll bother.

June 22

Shawn came home early! He has to go back in the morning for a few hours, but it's still nice to have him home tonight. We went out to eat with Grandma Margaret, got a couple games for the new GameCube, took a shower together, and are now relaxing. Tomorrow when he gets home we'll go grocery shopping and he can go pay the bills that are due.

I like having things back to normal. I talked to Shawn a little more about being scared and he said he understands. I asked if he was scared about it and he said sometimes, but didn't really say why other than "because he can be," so not sure if he was just saying it to reassure me or not. Either way, he said he understands.

I told him that I think I'm sure about marrying him and wanting to be with him forever, just concerned a bit that he'll back out again, but he says he won't and we left it at that. It was discussed to the extent we felt it should be, and now we're fine.

June 23

For all the hard work Shawn did at active training, he got the highest medal you can get while there. This is pretty neat, he's proud of it and is telling everyone, which he should. As he said, he was very unlucky and at the wrong place at the wrong time and that's the only way he ended up being lucky and getting this medal.

I'm tired. I didn't sleep well last night with Shawn, actually, because he sprawled and had me on the edge of the bed a lot. Then I closed my eyes after he left for his last bit of reserve stuff this morning and some Arabic guy called me (he did yesterday, too) from 888-888-8888 saying I won some $1,000 shopping thing and a vacation. Even if it is real, they woke me up.

Today I actually listened to his spiel, although I don't trust a number like that, and told him I was sleeping and asked if there was a way for me to not accept this "prize." He said something about how it's all free, I just pay shipping on something of $1.95, and that's when I hung up on him again. I'm not giving him a card number; I just got done dealing with fraud although I still haven't received paperwork on it.

Tango really ticked Shawn off this morning. We love the little bugger, but he insists on peeing outside the litter box, either on the kitchen floor, right out in the open not even near the litter box, or on clothing. Not long before Shawn left I had a clean batch of clothes in the basket on the couch and Tango ended up ruining that. This morning, though,

Tango peed on Shawn's uniform jacket he needs for today. Luckily we got some fabric freshener spray last night and Shawn just cleaned the spot and sprayed it for the day.

So now I have to look up why the cat is peeing on stuff. I am guessing he's marking interesting smells, like the jacket from Shawn, and the clean clothes. But I don't know why he'd be marking or anything if he's fixed; I thought that took care of that stuff. I think Dex has done it once or twice, but has "grown out of it," so hopefully Tango does as well. In the meantime, I'm going to find out what I can do. We tried finding a place that sells a spray to discourage peeing in the same spot, but there aren't any specialty/pet stores around here, we would have to go to a larger city.

I guess in a way it's good that guy woke me up with his phone call; I got the laundry going and hope to have it done by the time Shawn gets back around noon. And, I got my new debit card in the mail, but still not the paperwork to fill out to fix the fraud stuff.

June 25

That Arabic guy may be part of the previous scam although they never called me before the fraud, nor did I give a number to anyone before. I noticed on my phone this morning they tried calling again. Good thing I left my phone in the living room, so it didn't wake me.

I did some research about the peeing. One of the solutions is have him fixed, but he already is. It could be from a bladder infection that he won't use the litter box, but we saw him use the litter box last night, and he's been doing it since we got him. It also said it could be a territorial thing due to having multiple cats. Considering what he marks fresh unmarked laundry and Shawn's uniform after the scent of being out of the house a while, it sort of makes sense. He's getting in and marking what he can since the others have their smell everywhere. I'm trying to think like a cat. It may help to encourage them when they play together by praising them, encouraging them to clean each other, since Tango actually never gets in on the group cleaning, etc. So, last night when Tango was sleeping near me and Anaki came and laid on me, I praised them both for being near each other, petting them equally.

Today I get to take my fraud papers to the bank to get them faxed. Our new GameCube game, Asterix & Obelix XXL, is out today, we get to pick it up, plus we're getting some stamps so I can mail my school papers. I didn't realize we had old stamps instead of the new ones until recently.

I got a call from an Arabic woman, different number, but same company. I hung up after she said the company name.

June 27

Today Shawn informed me that the army will financially support starting your own business. So, if he's still in when I start my dog grooming business, as long as he's a part of it, which he would be, we'd have financial support which would be great.

June 28

I've been taking care of Nora's dogs for the past week. Grandma Margaret does the stuff in the morning, I let them out in the afternoon and then in the evening when I feed them and give one his pills. I like taking care of the dogs and hope to start spending more time with them. Shawn often gives me a ride over to take care of them, but he likes to leave right after they're fed and taken outside. I asked him if we can spend more time over there and he said "we'll see," so I think tomorrow I'll just hang out with them a bit while he plays his GameCube.

I don't think Tango peed on anything last night, so that's good. I told him I wouldn't call him "Pee Paw" anymore if he stopped peeing. So, maybe he likes that idea.

Shawn and I have been talking more about eventually getting my business going and he says he wants to start a landscape or lawn care business since there's only one similar business locally and he thinks it'd be a good business to have. We also looked at a car today. We know it won't happen for a while but it was fun to look. It's a *Zenn* electric car. It only goes 45 MPH, but for in town stuff or the little bit of highway driving we'd do, it'd work just fine. And it's small enough I'd feel okay driving it.

June 30

Monday Shawn has an interview for the job he put in an application for. He called a couple days ago asking if they had a full-time opening yet and the lady said no, but one of the guys called back saying the secretary didn't know what she was talking about and he's supposed to call them Monday. That'd be a 9-5 job with even better pay than his old job. He thought he was getting his bonus and still hasn't seen it, so he has to have his mom look over his papers when she gets home to see what's up.

Last night we went to Cheri's birthday party. She was in town from her father's house with her boyfriend and they had a gathering at her mom's house. Afterwards, a guy named Sam had another party for her which did involve drinking, smoking, and smoking weed, which I didn't partake in; Shawn took a couple hits from a bong. The party at Cheri's mom's house lasted forever. There were a lot of people I didn't know, but luckily Shawn's and Cheri's friends are people I've met, and I did enjoy talking to them while they were there.

I got to meet Cheri's cousin, who is 15, and she did nothing but give me looks while talking to Shawn and hugging him. She followed me around, and she openly said in front of both of us that she and her "boyfriend" broke up. We told Cheri later, but she said "that's Steffie," which wasn't very satisfying since it helped bring me down the whole five friggin' hours we were there. After I mentioned it to Shawn he ended up agreeing that he noticed it too since he wasn't paying attention before I pointed it out.

Also, I got to meet Cheri's sister, Pamela, who is a few months younger than me. And I found out that Shawn and she dated for a month and Shawn slept with her. I was upset at first because all I was told is one of his friend's little sisters liked him, not that he dated her and slept with her. Shawn said sorry a lot for not telling me because he thought he did, but I explained that I really knew nothing about it. Since it was in the past, I just didn't feel comfortable seeing her for the first time and finding that out at the same time.

I told Shawn it's hard for me to put trust in him again when I keep finding out stuff from the past. After each new "discovery" I ask if there's anything else and he says no, but sure enough... I just feel like he's hiding stuff from me when I only get half the story. Anyway, at the second party, Mark was there and Shawn asked him, "Where's my money?" and Mark looked a bit worried, but Shawn then laughed and said he was just kidding because I told him specifically not to bug him about it right now. Other than Mark, Cheri and her boyfriend were the only people I knew. I spent a good part of the night talking to Cheri's boyfriend as Cheri ran off talking with other people and Shawn sat next to me watching the TV while high. Her boyfriend drank and was buzzed, but still managed to hold decent conversation about music and video games.

Driving home we saw cops a couple times and Cheri was concerned since she lost her driver's license. We ended up back at her house, because we left the car there and rode with her, and then drove home. We got home about 2:30 a.m.

I asked Shawn if he likes parties and he said yes and I asked if I had to like them and he said he'd like me to. I told him I don't, because I really don't like drinking or smoking or weed and feel uncomfortable around a lot of people, especially ones I don't know, and he said I don't have to like them it's not a big deal. But hell, if we're invited to another one, I have no clue how that'll work. I don't want to go, but also don't want Shawn drinking or smoking stuff while I'm not there and just don't like the idea of staying home and wondering what's going on at the party.

July 1

Shawn said he's not sure about the new company's drug testing of job applicants. He said for the army he can drink water and, as long as he doesn't drink too much water, can get by on those, but if these are digital then he doesn't know.

I think as I get to know more people, I'll be more into going to parties. That was a big part of it, the other being that there was weed. The drinking I could tolerate, it's not in my face and the air or near as illegal since everyone there was at least 20 except me. I think Shawn and I will have to talk about it more, because I don't mind going, almost as a babysitter until I know people, as long as there's no weed and just drinking.

He and I are fine now as far as his past, why do I need to know more? Between last night and this morning talking with him I think I got over finding out about Pamela. I think I'll tell Shawn that if there are any more "surprises" to just not tell me unless it'll affect "us" and now and I need to know.

I don't mind looking uncool as far as saying no to weed; I just don't like making Shawn mad. And, sadly, if I say no and then tell him no, he gets upset. I told him this and I think part of the problem, since it has been getting worse, is his lack of Prozac. It helped keep him a bit happier and lately he's been depressed more and angers easier.

Yesterday he was "gloomy" all day until last night as we were goofing around in bed. And he got mad at me yesterday because the cats knocked over his ashtray he had on the arm of the couch and I asked him if he was going to pick it up. He was mad because "he was using it," although he was done smoking and I always tell him not to put stuff, especially the ashtray, there because it gets knocked over a lot. I didn't see why I should stop what I was doing for that, I pick up after him enough as it is. So I boiled it down to he was having a bad day.

July 2

Shawn's interview is either today or tomorrow. The secretary called and said today at 4:00 p.m., but the guy who interviews has something to do, so it could be later.

Yesterday I got to wait around all day while Shawn played his video games. I kept saying I wanted to do something with him or play, but it never happened until about 11 last night when I got to play my *Pokemon Ruby* for an hour because I was getting tired by then.

I understand he really likes his new GameCube, and he has a new toy to play with and I'll get less attention, but that didn't get me. It bothered me that he waited around for Cheri to get online so he could play *UNO* with her. I know she's his best friend, but she sometimes makes me feel like I have to compete. I talked Shawn into a game of Scrabble in the afternoon and he wanted to leave the GameCube on so he could see when she got on. He text messaged her during that time, and it pretty much ruined the game for me because he didn't really want to play. Not that it went badly, other than he won as usual, but I kept thinking about the damned TV on right next to us. I don't know if this is good or bad, but I'm going to tell him that today he's not playing video games all day, not unless I'm included.

I have a possible job opportunity. It's nothing big, but I could work every other weekend cleaning some rooms at a nursing home. I haven't put in an application yet, still unsure if I will or not.

I mailed my papers for the dog grooming academy and I also emailed Lynda telling her they're on their way and she said she'd watch for them. I asked for and received a link to bus routes and Lynda says there's a taxi service, too, but most of the things are within walking distance and she said normally a student or two brings a car, so she's sure someone would let me tag along sometime as well.

Shawn just called; he's on his way home from his "interview." I guess he got the job just by walking in. So, he starts tomorrow morning and has to be there at 8:15 a.m. And, today I actually got him to play video games with me and include me, so that's a good thing, too.

July 3

Shawn started the job this morning, and works until about 5:00 p.m. It'll be a full-time, 40 hours a week job, and he'll get paid $9 an hour. So, we'll definitely be able to get by. After expenses we'll have a little left over until our food stamps card runs out, then we'll be "just right" and then still have my child support, which I'm saving for another GameCube game. He was supposed to get his bonus; he looked at his paperwork yesterday at his mom's. So, if it doesn't show up today, he may have to speak up at drill.

I forget when Nora gets home, so I'm just taking care of dogs until I hear otherwise. In a week or so, Grandma Margaret is leaving for a couple weeks and I said I'd take care of her dog. So, if nothing else, I'm getting a few bucks for this stuff although not sure what Nora will pay me. And I get exercise from riding Shawn's bike, it'll be even more so when I ride over to Grandma Margaret's. Sometimes Shawn takes me over in his car, which it's good for the dogs to have more people to see, but I like getting out on the bike. I ask Shawn to just go outside with me. Even though it's sunny, I try forcing myself out, and he just won't do it. When he starts complaining about his PT test or his "lack of ab definition" I'll have to bring it up.

This afternoon after taking care of the dogs and eating some lunch I promised Shawn I'd pick up the bedroom. I don't really mind doing it, it goes faster than he thinks, but I do get annoyed when it gets messed up all over again.

I hope Shawn sticks to this job. I love him, but it doesn't look good when he tells me he wants to quit a job. It's just unappealing. He says he doesn't like asking his grandma for help, but it makes me wonder sometimes.

I found out today that he's going to float his dad $100. Shawn insists he should help his dad, but I really don't like it. I feel we have to worry about us getting by before we take in anybody else. I'm going to tell him that if he expects me to put in $100 of my money for bills, he can forget it. If he wants to help his dad, it's his paycheck. I'm trying to save for my Morinaga tamagotchi and, and, considering he bought himself *The Legend of Zelda: Four Swords Adventures*, I think I should be able to buy myself a thing or two. But, I'm almost afraid to say too much because I know how his temper is. I just mentioned again about saving for my new tamagotchi and he was like, "I know, but it's my dad!" in a very defiant tone.

July 4

Well, Shawn didn't want to ask his mom to help his dad because he knows she would hold it over him forever. He said he may ask Grandma Margaret to help his dad instead.

The closer I get to my birthday, the more I don't expect my turning of age will change much, other than I get my tattoos and can go in Pleasure Zone when Shawn does. I just thought of that because we stopped there on the way home today to get a vibrating ring. I still plan to apply for the cleaning job. Shawn was going to take me there, but now he has a job, so hopefully Saturday morning I can go pick up an application.

July 5

Shawn's mom either gets home tomorrow night or the next day so I'm almost done with her dogs. The time flew.

Shawn did end up getting the money for his dad from his grandma, so that's good because we have the electric bill to pay.

July 8

Lynda from the grooming academy called and said I can send in my loan papers now and she can hold them in my file if I want, so I'm going to finish filling them out tomorrow and send them in. She said to get the loan for $9700, plus whatever I wanted to take out for expenses. Hopefully I can get something worked out that I don't need to do that, either save some money or get a bank card for Shawn's account. It's all through Sallie Mae; I don't know what all it goes through other than that. Dad will co-sign if he has to. Worse case scenario, I ask Shawn to sign with me although I don't think he has any credit.

I actually don't think I'm going to check into that cleaning job. If it weren't for taking care of Dolly, Grandma Margaret's dog, I might, but I wouldn't be able to let her out in the afternoons on a couple days if I did. This dog sitting stuff is almost becoming a job anyway.

Shawn had a dream two nights ago and told me about it. He never remembers his dreams, so I thought it was weird when in the morning he told me he had a dream about me. My first question, was it a good dream? He said yes and said I was really skinny but not unhealthy-like and that I was in a bikini and we were walking around. He said he doesn't remember why we were walking or why I was in a bikini and had a tan, he said he was probably showing me off. Me, with a tan? Well, if I was as little as he described, I just may suck it up and get one. I liked his dream; I was very enthusiastic and excited after hearing it. It still makes me motivated.

July 9

I just got done cleaning the kitchen. There's a row of cardboard pop boxes that have built up because they don't fit in the garbage and nobody takes them down until they get to be like they are now. I know our living style isn't perfect as far as cleaning goes, but we do clean once it gets to a certain point. It's becoming more and more me cleaning and doing the dishes and picking up after Shawn.

I know I'm not perfect, but I also know that three-quarters of the stuff lying around is not mine and at least half of it I have told him to pick up or put away including his work shirts that are in the dryer now I had to wash because Tango peed on them. I told Shawn to put stuff in the bedroom so Tango doesn't get in it.

I'm wondering how to get it through Shawn's head to pick up and put his own stuff away. Not only will it make it easier when I clean for him, but also benefits him because the cats won't dig in it or anything. I don't want to sound like I'm nagging by repeating myself or come off as a selfish wench that wants him to do everything, because I know that's how it would probably sound, but I want him to understand that if he puts a little more effort in, it'll be better for everyone.

I sit here, as the dishes are running, typing and looking around the living room and it just amazes me how terrible it is, especially compared to how it was when I last cleaned. I'm not saying it was immaculate, but it was definitely presentable. I told Shawn that if I had time I'd clean the living room, too. Do I have time? Well, sure I do. But will I clean it? No. I want him to see the kitchen compared to the living room since they were on the same level so he can understand a bit better. Maybe visuals will help. Then, after he puts his clothes away and picks up his food in the living room (he'll be thrilled to see what the cats did to the bag of chips he left in here), I'll do the rest.

I feel mean, but at the same time, I feel a bit used when it comes to this stuff. I think he's used to his mother just getting tired of seeing it and doing it for him. I love him and don't mind cleaning up some, especially since he goes to work to support us, but at the same time he makes my job a lot harder than it needs to be. I guess I'm not very good at "training" a man.

July 12

I think Shawn's car will need a gasket changed because it is leaking tranny fluid. But, besides that, Shawn went to the doctor yesterday morning because the night before he was having shortness of breath and was light-headed and it persisted into the morning. They did some tests and said he needed to go to the hospital and do more tests because it could be a heart attack or a clot.

We ended up spending all yesterday through this morning at the hospital, in a room where I didn't get a place to sleep or a pillow, since Shawn was getting better and wanting to leave. They took his blood three times, gave him the setup for an IV that they never used, and had him wear an oxygen mask. In the end they told him he needs to quit smoking and the slight chance it's from chemicals he works with or asthma, but they weren't certain and we got to leave. It was the biggest waste of 24 hours.

July 13

Today's going to be a long day! Between 11:30 and noon I have to ride over to Grandma Margaret's to take care of Dolly and I'll probably play with her a bit since she needs the attention. Then I have to come back home and wash all of Shawn's army clothes, minus his coat and Class A's because those are dry clean only. He needs all of that for tomorrow, which it would've been nice if they told him sooner so it wasn't a mad rush to get it all washed up again.

Then I get to pick up a few things in the living room, again, because although Shawn said he'd pick up his cans and at least put them by the sink, they've yet to move along with some other things including a glass that was just knocked over and broken by the cats.

Yesterday we caught Anaki peeing on some of Shawn's things on the couch. Good thing I told Shawn to not blame Tango for all of it and only scold him if he sees him do it. I don't know if Anaki was marking something Tango already did. I know he's peed on some things in the past because I'd seen it, but we went a few days without anything or if she was in heat and doing it. I didn't think female cats marked things like males unless she felt she had a scent to cover.

The laundry won't be so bad because you put it in and wait to swap loads, but it'll take time because he has a lot of stuff and the washers can't hold too much, especially thicker materials, and the dryers won't dry if you put too much in them although they can fit a lot.

And the fun continues. I just got home and got some laundry going. I went down to get the bike and it was missing. I called Shawn to ask if he moved the bike and he said no, he hadn't touched it, so I explained how it just wasn't there. So, we're both thinking someone took it. There are two other bikes on the rack that I've seen there before, but ours is gone.

I ended up walking over to take care of Dolly. It took a little over an hour to get there, let her outside, play with her a bit and then walked home. Walking is good for me; I was just hoping it wouldn't take so long. Luckily I think there'll still be plenty of time to do Shawn's laundry for tomorrow.

July 15

Shawn's aunt asked if they checked his cholesterol when he went to the emergency room. I said no, I didn't think so, and she told me about another person in the family that had a "cholesterol attack" and I told her the way Shawn eats, I wouldn't be surprised. I don't know much about cholesterol, but I do know that Shawn isn't a healthy eater not that I'm always much better, but I'm trying. Shawn laughed and said that was probably it. So, if he has a problem again, he'll have to bring that up. Hopefully hearing that will make him a little more conscious of what he's choosing to eat. Because he has a high metabolism and is so skinny, he just figures he can eat whatever he wants even though he knows it's not that good for him.

July 17

Last night, at about 3:00 a.m., Shawn woke up coughing and was unable to lie down. He tried to sit straight up for a while, but he had a hard time breathing again. After talking to his mother, he called the help line for the emergency room and they said he should take cough medicine. So, went to get some from his mom, came home, took it and went to bed.

This morning he didn't go to work. He slept and then I made him breakfast. He said he'd go in later if he felt better. He did have to run a truck key over there, but was ready to pass out when he got back home.

He said that his boss wasn't too happy, but he's not mad. I hope Shawn's health stuff improves because I'd really hate for him to lose his job over it.

July 18

Shawn is home again, he took cold medicine last night but was still not right this morning. He's on title 19 still, so he has full coverage to go back to the doctor, I think he just doesn't want to have to stay overnight again for no reason.

Last night we went out to eat and he made the comment he hopes he's not just making himself sick and it's just all in his head. I said that I had to be honest, I kind of thought he was and he says he doesn't want to be, so he doesn't know why he would be doing it. I asked him if he didn't want to go to work and he said no, he likes his job, so that's not it. I told him that I think when he's playing his video games or something he seems fine because he's doing something he wants to do.

He's pretty good about knowing when he's truly sick and when he's not. And I do believe if it's "all in his head" that he's not trying to put it there. I guess we'll see what tomorrow brings. If he's still "sick" he can go back to the doctor, if not then it's back to work. I don't think he has a history of problems like this.

July 19

Shawn just left for work. He might be a few minutes late because he had a hard time getting up when the alarm went off. I told him to just tell them his medicine took a little longer to wear off than he thought. I mean, not complete truth, but it'll make him look better than just plain late, I think, because they know he's been sick. At least he's ready to go back to work.

Everything's fine. He came home for lunch. He said he made it to work on time.

My bank account was credited the overdraft charge from the fraud, so I suppose that means things are on their way. Eventually they'll take back the temporary credit they gave me of $11.99 and give it again, but I assume as a refund from the company that caused all of this.

Yesterday through last night I was thinking a lot and I feel re-motivated to use the exercise DVD. I probably won't start while still walking to take care of Dolly, but I just feel ready to exercise. I saw a bunch of people biking and Shawn said some bike thing is coming up where people bike across state. I told him I want to do that and hearing him explain how it would be biking all day for a week and the tone in his voice making me feel I can't handle that, which right now I probably couldn't, makes me want to get in shape.

I mentioned to Shawn about working part-time where he is since he'd be able to give me a ride over, but Shawn said he didn't think I could handle it because there's a lot of heavy lifting and carrying stuff. I know he's not trying to be mean when he doubts me, but I really wish he wouldn't be such a guy about it. So, needless to say, I'm feeling ready to go.

As far as the twins are concerned, I get updates on rare occasions and photos, but don't request more than they send to everyone. I think Nora gets more frequent ones, but she asks for them. I think the Clarks have it under control now, but the twins did go through some strep throat or something for a while and I know they struggled at first with two kids. Honestly, I don't like hearing about them. Call me heartless, but I still am trying to forget I ever had them and still wish I would've aborted.

July 25

My dad finally has Internet at his house, so we'll be able to email to stay in touch more. We talk on the phone; it's just not as often as it was when I first moved.

Whisper is living in the bathroom as of last night. She came down from her normal spot and I picked her up. She smelled terrible, so I took her in the bathroom to dry bathe her as I do occasionally with the cats to keep them smelling clean and I noticed how light she was. Shawn asked me if I put food up there for her, which I did, and asked if I put water up there for her recently, which I didn't. He and I figured she must've not come down the past few days at all. So, I brought a bowl into the bathroom and gave her water, which she immediately began to drink. I opened a can of tuna for her, put a few pieces of dry food on it and gave her that, which she ate part of and this morning I see she ate all of it, which is a lot for Whisper, since she normally doesn't eat much at a time.

I made her a makeshift litter box and there were already a few towels and a pillow on the floor, so she made herself at home on them and slept. I also noticed she'd been sneezing and her nose was red and a bit slimy, which is really odd considering it's summer and even with the air-conditioning on, her curled in her towels in her nest in the kitchen would be plenty warm. I'll see how she does today living in the bathroom, but she may end up having to go to the vet again. Good thing I have some money for the vet. I'm going to call today and also ask how much it costs for routine shots for cats so I can get the other three in sometime soon for that, too.

I'll be talking to Shawn tonight about taking Whisper to the vet tomorrow. Her nose is still really red, although she did get up and purr and rub against me when I spent some time in the bathroom with her. She did that yesterday, too. When it's just her and me, she's great. She'll lay on Shawn and prefers him over me in the living room, but I think that's because he is more firm sounding with the other cats than I am, so she feels safer with him out here, but likes me better when it's alone time. I'll probably see if Grandma Margaret can take us tomorrow because I don't think they'll be open late enough for Shawn to go.

I was in the bathroom, checking on Whisper, and stepped on the mat by the shower and it felt uneven. I looked underneath and there's the porno magazine that I told Shawn to throw out and he had agreed he didn't need anymore. I tore it up and put it in a plastic grocery bag for Shawn when he gets home. I wasn't happy. If he and I were having sex as much as I wanted, I wouldn't care if he cranked one out on his own sometimes, but we're not.

I asked him about the magazine when he got home and he said instead of waking me in the morning, he just does that. I told him he should know I'd sacrifice sleep for us to have sex considering he's now "too tired" from working to do it and always expects me to just give him head instead. I'm still a bit upset, but I've cooled down for the most part. I told him from now on I'd like to be a part of things, considering it doesn't seem to happen otherwise.

I think I have a fever. My face is flushed and warm and I just feel sort of blah. I hope it's something that'll pass by tomorrow so I am not too run down to work out.

July 26

I feel better this morning, so I'm trying to get Whisper in at the vet. I called the vet, they're only open until noon, and I can't get hold of Grandma Margaret. So, tomorrow I'll try again. Whisper is eating and drinking water and using the litter box all right, so she seems fine, just stressed.

I may be making a mistake with Shawn. I don't mind him masturbating (hell, I do it), it just bugs me that he's always too tired to do it with me, yet he can do it with himself. I mean, I know I take more energy than his hand does, but I offer to be on top quite often even though I don't enjoy it as much. As I told him, if he and I were having sex more often, I wouldn't be as bothered by it. It's just that I feel I don't get it ever anymore.

I'm sure my frustration got the better of me yesterday. I won't say anything more about him masturbating; I guess that's his business. I just wish he wasn't always too tired to be in the mood for sex. I know I shouldn't think this way, I just always feel "undesirable" when he turns me down. Which is why I got mad when I found out he was jerking it to some magazine. It's not even a good one, which made me feel worse. It's just a bit depressing.

I know that my drive is a bit "overactive" and that I tend to connect having sex with love, which they aren't the same. And I know Shawn is tired a lot and that makes him not want it as much as I do. I mean, when we get old and feeble, we need more to fall back on than sex anyway. So, as much as I wish he had more of a drive, I'd rather have him as he is than not at all. I have faith that things will even out at some point.

Last night we had a talk about the doctor. Shawn needs to get back on his Prozac, we can both tell. He's very quick to anger, especially now that he works. When he was on Prozac, he was a bit more rational about things instead of jumping into being irritable. We also talked about me getting checked for depression. We sort of laughed at the end of the night when I said at least we can have problems together.

This morning, Shawn was "friendly." We didn't have sex and he wouldn't let me touch him down there because he has a sore spot from when we fooled around. I was glad to at least get the kissing and attitude that I did this morning; it's just that sort of attention/affection I guess I was looking for. I think I'll try my hardest to not ask for sex or anything like that. And if he was affectionate like this morning more often, that would be equally satisfying in a lot of cases.

I asked Shawn about working where he does. I asked once before and he didn't think I could handle it. I said maybe there was another opening so I could make some money and get the exercise since it'd be carrying stuff, but he said that they don't need anybody. I actually would like to find something local that requires some physical labor. His job's not really local, but I could ride to work with him on the days they needed me. Hopefully my age isn't too big an issue.

July 27

I apologized to Shawn yesterday evening for getting upset about his magazine and told him I understand how it takes less energy for him to do it himself. I told him we'll get him a better magazine. Sometimes I have browsed porno magazines with him.

I tried calling Grandma Margaret, but no answer, so I'll have to try later and see about getting Whisper in to the vet.

July 28

Last night Shawn decided he was "in the mood," which made me happy. I didn't think he was going to be, but then he said he thinks his sore is okay and sure enough, one thing led to another. Unfortunately for him he has to work today, but I doubt it'll be a full day and he still has tomorrow off.

I tried to get Whisper to the vet yesterday, but they didn't have an opening. Grandma Margaret seems to be busy until early afternoon almost every day, so I couldn't get hold of her. I still have to give her keys back and get paid, so hopefully tonight I get hold of her. She called Shawn last night and asked if we wanted to come over for ice cream, but he wanted to stay in and I didn't get to talk to her.

I think Whisper is feeling a bit better, she isn't sneezing as much and her nose isn't quite as red. She jumped to her feet the moment I went in the bathroom just a few moments ago and was rubbing against me a lot. I brushed her and petted her for a few minutes. Any time I stood up to do something, like brush my hair, she would rub against my legs and meow at me to pet her. She has a raspy meow from her previous owner chain smoking. So we hung out for a bit. I won't let her out until she's done sneezing in case she has something contagious besides being stressed. At this rate, we may not have a vet bill anyway.

After we pay rent in a couple days, I'm going to schedule all the cats for shots minus Tango, since he got his before we got him. I wanted to get it done sooner, but it was a matter of affording it since Shawn tends to talk me into frivolous things instead, but we have plenty of money this month.

Grandma Margaret just brought over some corn and my payment for watching Dolly, and I gave her back her keys. She handed me a small wad of money, I saw a $50 bill on the outside and figured there were a few ones inside and just tucked it in my pocket. She said she hoped it was enough and I told her whatever she felt she should pay I'm sure is fine and I didn't even look at how much it was. I think it's rude to inspect the money in front of people. I got upstairs and saw she had given me $125. I think that's a lot for little Dolly, especially because it wasn't that big of a deal to watch her. The part that really was funny is when I went to put it in my wallet I found $43 that I have no clue where it came from. I feel rich, temporarily.

August 2

Shawn and I have been talking about apartments and we've decided to stay here another year. We were going to switch, but figure this would be good until next year. We've also been talking about phone services, since my contract probably won't be going for much longer.

I never did get bike tires tonight. Shawn says it'll be tomorrow night because he doesn't work Saturday and he wanted to stay in tonight. I think we may invest in a small grill, too, for the deck. He's wanted one for a while and I finally said okay because his grandma gave us rib-eye steaks. I love steak and I'll encourage him to cook meat instead of carbs any day as I don't need the carbs, though I love them.

I guess the good thing about not having my bike is I started my cycle today, so I don't feel "obligated" to ride it on the first couple days when I feel icky the most. I keep forgetting to ask my dad, but I really should get checked for depression. I don't want to get on any pills, I don't like taking medicines, but at the same time I know I feel sad over things I shouldn't.

I still want to get checked for ADD, but that's not as big a deal. I'm pretty sure I have that, reading what I have: inability to focus (which I truly can't sometimes, even though I try really hard to, such as when a friend is talking to me), plus sometimes dyslexia and an inability to remember things. There were other symptoms, too, but those are the two I have. Dyslexia mainly with numbers, but I mess up letters at times, too.

August 3

My dad finally figured out Windows Live Messenger. I got him to download it, so we're talking online. And he's talking to the cellular people about my contract.

August 5

My bike tires are pumped, although I may try and get them a little firmer at the gas station, but this'll get me there. Shawn cussed a lot over trying to get them pumped with the little hand pump and over trying to get the speedometer on, but he managed.

I talked to my dad about insurance covering me getting checked for depression and he said he's not sure but will call tomorrow and ask what they cover. So, soon I may be getting that taken care of. Hopefully with me trying to pursue this, Shawn will be "inspired" to get back on Prozac.

I finally convinced Shawn that we need to go through all of our stuff, including his clothing, and figure out what we should keep and not keep. Hopefully we'll lighten the load here a little bit. I know the couch that Mark left us is a hide-a-bed that we don't want, so we plan to clean it up and sell it, but that won't be today.

After we make some room by getting rid of what we don't need/use/want maybe we can fit a couple shelving units here or there to put the rest of our stuff on. I really like the cube-looking ones that are shelves, but separated into cubes. I think there are drawer things to buy for them, too, which would be a good idea for at least the lower ones so the cats don't get in stuff. Anyway, those are what I'd like to get eventually.

Shawn's car I think is dying. He said that his brother ran the car too hard when it was his, and "raced" it with his friends, which is why it's crapping out now. We still use it, but it's leaking tranny fluid a lot and Shawn thinks there's more wrong with it although neither of us know much about cars, so I tend to ask my dad these things. Something about a U-joint, which is what broke before, but it feels like it when we turn sometimes. I'm not sure.

Instead of investing in a normal grill, Shawn fell in love with an electric griddle. Surprisingly it was only $20 which is what won him over most I think and we cooked our steaks on it last night. It worked great, which surprised me. It's easy to clean up, too. I asked him if we can eat more meat now that he has his new "toy" and he says "we'll see," as he does with most things.

He was up watching the weather last night (I asked him if we could because of lightning) and I ended up going to bed because of feeling ill. I have no clue when he came to bed; I zonked out. So, in case he wasn't smart and stayed up past seeing the radar, I'll let him sleep a bit right now.

I guess we are settling in. We cleaned the kitchen and the living room today. He wasn't very ambitious, but still helped between getting lost in the TV. For the most part it is what I want and I am happy. There are still things that need to happen like school, me finding work, my losing weight, Shawn deciding on a career path and sticking with it. But, right here, right now, I'm content. And tomorrow we'll find out about the insurance.

We had steak in the freezer because Grandma Margaret gave it to us. I love chicken, which we have in the freezer and I hope to get more and we have a bunch of hamburger left to eat. Sometimes Grandma Margaret gives us the hamburger, so we're "stocked up" at the moment with about five pounds of it. Grandma Margaret gave me a cook book this past Christmas, so I can always use that to learn how to cook. She explains some things to me at times, too, and I know I could call her if I didn't understand something. Besides that, I have the Internet.

I hope the car lasts, but Shawn really just needs a new one whenever that's a possibility. Eventually I need a car, too, so I can get to work. He does have insurance, though. I think it's the basic stuff not covering being stolen or such, just if he gets hit.

August 7

My dad told me today he heard from my aunt Shirley. She said my great grandma isn't doing very well. She was recently moved to another area of the nursing home. When I told Shawn he said that's where they go when they don't have long left to live. My dad said she was fine, I assume to not upset me. I don't know if she's going to pass soon or not, especially since I haven't seen her in a while. My dad said he'd let her know that I'm thinking of her. She's 85, but I always felt that's not that old, at least not to the point of dying, 90+ is when people should be passing.

She did in a way help raise me, so I am attached quite a bit. Before she moved to assisted living then to a nursing home, while she still lived in the house my dad now owns, when I visited my dad, we played cards and she showed me how to cook the very little that I do know. And she did pretty much raise my dad, as his mom died when he was little and my grandpa couldn't always afford to take care of him.

On a lighter note, in a few weeks I can get my tattoo and Shawn will get his.

My dad found out about insurance and said if I ask them to bill it as a regular office visit instead of therapy, it'd just be ten percent copay and that's fine. So I'll talk to Shawn and see about getting an appointment. I asked him when my insurance runs out and he said in two months, which is good, because next month I'm due for another visit to the gynecologist. I can get on title 19 like Shawn until I get a job with insurance or something independent, which won't happen because I've heard that's pricey. But, title 19 can provide full coverage. Actually, on the recent monthly slips Shawn gets for it, my name's been on it. And, because I'm not yet 18, there was a letter from them saying I can get free school lunch. I laughed.

August 8

I promised Shawn that today I'd stay in and clean the bedroom, besides walking to the store to get the money order for his phone bill. Starting after lunch, when I'm awake, I'm going to do 25 crunches every hour to make up for it.

Shawn seems a bit concerned about paying bills this month for some reason, but I just figured it out and we're fine. Worse case scenario, we can't get our tattoos until next month. But, I can live with that. Not that I'd be happy about it, but I'd rather not be in debt. He was also a bit grumpy this morning since he had to get up early for work. So, maybe his negative attitude towards going to work had something to do with it.

Last night Shawn and I had sex. Yesterday was my first "free day" after my period, so I showered and shaved my legs and my "bits" and told Shawn we're having sex tonight, to which he just said okay. We went to bed; he turned out the lights, and immediately started things. I was very impressed with his drive, especially since he knew about getting up early today. And, on top of that enthusiasm, he just seemed to have the right attitude that I haven't seen in a while. He was really into it, which that alone can improve things so much. I don't know if this means his drive is "better," but getting that enthusiasm more often would be great. Maybe he likes the small changes we can see already from my diet and exercising.

He called today to ask if I got the phone bill taken care of and I told him yes. I rode up and got the money order, then sent it out. He was very appreciative and pleased. So, maybe with me taking initiative to do these things, such as take care of myself and take care of the apartment, it really is appealing to him. We'll see how he likes what I did to the bedroom tonight. As soon as I can get my cube-shelving things I can do more such as move stuff to them and use the plastic containers/tubs for his army stuff.

I've been doing crunches and a simple move with my legs for my inner thighs today at various times. I left my mat out, which the cats had to wrestle on to test it out, so I can just go to it. I looked in the mirror at my stomach today and it does look a bit smaller. I think the part about it that's most noticeable is my stretch marks are fading quite a lot. I can still see them, but straight on in a mirror they're not the first thing I notice anymore. So I'm finally doing something right!

Shawn said he got paid from the army, so he has $400+ in the bank right now and it's only week one for this month's work, so he's still got a few paychecks coming as he gets paid every Friday. So I guess we're plenty fine for this month.

August 9

Last night I got half the laundry done, and plan to finish it this afternoon. Luckily, I can ride my bike today because other than laundry I don't have as much to do today. Last night Shawn had equal enthusiasm to the night before. And, again I was impressed. I know this won't last forever, he's got to get tired some time, but it's still really nice for a change.

Shawn has to work on my birthday, and has honor guard for a parade that weekend, too. So, hopefully we will have time together.

August 13

I just took out my eyebrow stud. Lately it's been getting sort of swollen and pesky like my lip ring did and there's a bump almost like a wart, except sometimes it gets puffy and sometimes it's fine, near the bottom hole. So, since it's not very professional looking, it's causing problems now, and I'd rather remove it myself than a dog take it out for me during school or eventually work, it's out. It looks sort of blah with just two little red holes and that one swollen little bump. But I cleaned it and put antiseptic on it, so hopefully it gets better.

I went to the police station with Grandma Margaret today and looked at a lot of bikes they had. One that looked similar to mine was there for three years. I didn't see one that looked like ours that fit the time it was stolen, so that sort of sucked, but at least I have the bike I have now. Recently some cars have been stolen and that sort of thing is getting "popular," so I have to make sure Shawn locks his car tonight and every night.

After looking at the bikes, Grandma Margaret took me to her house as I wanted to see Dolly and I told her about riding my bike to lose weight, since we chat about all sorts of stuff now it seems. And I said how today I wasn't sure what the weather was doing because it's supposed to storm, but it's sunny and really hot right now. So I want to ride my bike, but don't want to get out there and then it starts raining. She said, "Oh, I have a treadmill I don't normally use, but you can jump on that if you want."

At first I wasn't sure, only because I couldn't find my shorts before going out and had thick sweatpants on and that room didn't get much air circulation. She said I could walk without pants if I want, she'll just close the door. So, I went three-quarters of a mile before getting too hot, I was dripping with sweat, and then put my pants on and called it good. I still plan to do crunches tonight, but that's sort of a neat option if it's too hot outside to ride over there and walk. Mix things up a bit.

I did something just a little bit ago that I'm not sure I should have. I noticed the other day that Shawn got a PM on MySpace from a girl he dated in high school, one he's still friends with, and I think it was from a month ago, but he doesn't delete anything. So, I signed on his account and looked at it. It didn't say anything other than something about she likes alcohol and, by the sound of it, he said something against it before she replied, which isn't bad, but then I got sifting back through PMs. I saw a few from Victoria, which my dislike for her is still great, but the only thing that bothered me in reading was a nickname she referred to. I guess he called her "baby girl," and he calls me a lot of little cutesy nicknames and it makes me feel bad if I'm called something that she was called even if I was called it before her. I shouldn't have looked as I pretty much let this crap go, but it's just the nickname that bothers me and makes me think of bad times.

August 14

Food stamps are done for us. Shawn still has to mail in his pay stubs, I think he has ten days, but we got a letter saying that they're done paying unless the paperwork we send in says otherwise. I keep telling him to send it in, but of course it takes their letter to get him "motivated."

I weighed myself and am down by two pounds. It's not much but it's at least something. If Shawn didn't buy me chocolate recently, it'd probably be even better. I had a dream last night that I was really skinny. And, for some reason, I found some Asian chick's purse and was going through it and using her stuff, maybe because I have such a thing for Japan. But it was nice to imagine myself skinny. The dream makes it seem more real. I was wearing lighter jeans and a yellow fitted t-shirt, along with my white belt I own. My hair was still bleached like it is now, which makes it feel like I could get into it soon. I think I'm letting my hair go back to "normal" and not mess with color for a while.

No more snooping for me into Shawn's stuff. It's not like he stays out late and chats on the phone with strange women or anything like that, so there's no reason not to trust him.

August 20

Shawn's working late tonight. There's a lot of water damage from the storms last night. We're supposed to get more storms and, sadly, it was raining a bit throughout the day, so I didn't get out on my bike. Tomorrow will be a "push hard" makeup for today.

Saturday is the big 18! I don't know when Shawn plans to get me in for my tattoo and for his, but I'll have some faith that he has it figured out. I asked him the other day if he has my birthday stuff ready and he said yes, which surprised me considering if he goes anywhere I'm normally there, so I just wonder when it happened. It makes me excited!

Last night I found my bikini. I remembered how cute it is and how much I want to wear it again. I can get it on, which is a plus, but it doesn't fit as well as I'd like. And I can't get my board shorts on. The top is a bit small as my boobs are definitely bigger than they were. I'm sure by the time I've lost weight, they'll be small again. I have it hanging in the bedroom now so I see it on occasion and am reminded why I'm working so hard.

August 22

Shawn just gave me part of my birthday gift. He asked me if I wanted it and I wasn't sure, but gave in because he said it's in the living room and I wanted to know how the heck he got a gift in here. He ended up pulling out $140 and said, "Saturday we're going to spend that for you," which is really sweet because I give him a hard time about always buying stuff for himself when we go shopping. So, I get cake, some "loving," and to go shopping. Plus eventually tattoos; we're still talking about when for that. So I'm in a good mood this evening.

August 24

Grandma Margaret just called me and said in an hour we're going to go out for lunch for my birthday. I think that's pretty sweet of her. There's a local place that's small and only open three days a week and they serve soup and sandwiches and have sticky buns and, on occasion, pie. I've wanted to go there since she mentioned it, so this is really nice although I may avoid buns and pie. I'm hoping they have tea, too. Soup, sandwich, and tea, I like that stuff, as simple as it is. After I get home I'll mess with the VCR and hope I can get it working.

I just got home from lunch. I had a medium size plate that had tater tot casserole and fruit and a biscuit and then a slice of pie. It's definitely an exercise day to work off that pie and casserole. It was really good, though. Grandma Margaret also gave me a little gift bag with two different lotions in it and a card with a $50 check inside.

Tomorrow will surely be a spending day! Other than a robe and a teapot I have no clue what I want. If I were buying clothes I'm sure it wouldn't last long, or video games, but I'm holding off on clothing for now and there aren't any games I really want at the moment. I may ask Shawn if I can put part of it towards the "tattoo fund" so we have a chance to get it done sooner. He has to pay off the rings which he probably will next week after rent and it'll end up being a little bit until we get in otherwise. We'll see. I'm excited to go out tomorrow.

August 25

I'm up earlier than I would've liked to be today. Shawn has to march in a parade this morning and then we can go shopping. He just left and I'm waiting for his mom to get me so I can stand with her. I can hear Shawn having problems with the car while he's trying to leave. He really needs to get that fixed.

Today we're paying off my rings. The jewelers said today's it. I think there's only $100 left though. It'll be nice to have that expense taken care of.

I emailed Lynda from the grooming academy to remind her today I'm 18 and she can turn in my loan papers and to let me know what they say.

I just got home from shopping. I got a new, nicely padded seat for my bike and a small teapot. I wanted a robe, but there weren't any. Probably this fall is when they'll be more popular. I also got an *Angel Tamagotchi*. I have to have some sort of toy, it's a birthday after all. I still have money left, so I'll save that for now.

Nora gave me a card today at the parade with a $20 bill in it. I still have about $90 left out of my original $210, plus my father said he's putting money in my bank account and, shockingly, my mother called and said she'll be mailing a card with some money in it. I was surprised that my mom called. I talked to my little brother a bit, but my sister was at her friend's house and she was gone last time I talked to anybody there, too.

Mom sounded pleasant and said she wanted me to know she didn't forget about my birthday. I told her I appreciate the call and the card that'll be coming. My mom probably does love me, it's just sad that it takes me moving out and being gone for a while for her to start showing it. And I'm not talking about her giving me money, that doesn't show love, I'm talking about the phone call and just plain being nice. I guess it's a step in the right direction.

I'm not sure if, when my dad pays me, he's going to give me "extra" to make up for graduation or not. On occasion he mentions that he still "owes" me for that and I keep telling him it's up to him, I don't expect anything. But, I should have a nice chunk of money in the end.

My head hurts right now which is odd since I thought pop and chocolate cake would be plenty of caffeine, so I may go lay down shortly. I asked Shawn to rub me down, so hopefully my back will get a nice treat tonight.

Katie: My thoughts for the past year...

Mark moving in was a mistake, I still feel that way, but I also think I'm over him owing us so much money; why hang on to that if I know he's never going to pay? His birthday is tomorrow, so I wished him a happy one the other day and he did me the same. We still get along, I still think he's a great guy, just proves how much I do not want other people in Shawn's and my territory.

At first moving into the apartment I didn't know what to expect. And for a while it was rough and there were times I honestly was thinking maybe this was a bad idea, even though Shawn and I were working it out. Now I'm glad I went with that decision and stuck with it, I wouldn't be here if I didn't. And, that was really the only time I ever stood up to my mom and said, "I'm doing this."

Shawn still wants to verbally assault my mom when he gets a chance, but part of me still feels she's my mom and I know if I tell him not to say anything, he won't. I think that her calling on my birthday was a big step. Maybe not living together will make us get along further. My dad always said that's what it took for her and my grandma to get along.

I think there's hope and that things are "just beginning" with her and I. I think that me being away is making my mom relax more about me, especially since I haven't caused any deaths, gotten knocked up again, and didn't come running home.

I think she's realizing that I'm not just an immature girl that looks to get into trouble since getting pregnant pretty much "confirmed" all of the thoughts she had about me. And, at least I'm hoping, me showing I can do all the stuff she didn't think I could, survive on my own or with Shawn, is opening her up. She's more willing to talk to me about her job and tends to tell me about what's going on instead of me asking, on the rare occasions we do catch each other online or whatever. She probably does love me, but I never felt she liked me and I think that may be changing. I still feel towards her a bit hesitant to be too open because I tried for so long to no avail.

I still don't like Victoria and occasionally can't help but think about that whole situation. And, of course, I put more blame on her than Shawn. I don't think about it as much as I used to, which is good, but for right now it's still just a bad memory.

As for the twins and my thoughts about this last year, I'm going to sound heartless again, but I like how things are now. I rarely get photos and actually would be fine not getting any. I don't talk to them or the Clarks, I'm not in the picture at all and I like it. Sometimes I forget it ever happened and I still wish it didn't. I still feel it was just one big terrible experience. One day I'll have to face them, when they find out we're their parents, and hopefully by then I'm a little more accepting of things.

Summing it up, what would I have done differently? Not had sex that very moment and waited until I was on birth control, only because we would've been much safer then. I would've put my foot down more about Mark although that may have pushed Shawn to Victoria even more and I wouldn't have someone nice enough to tell me like Mark did.

As far as having to let go of so much of my game stuff and my electronics, I probably wouldn't have sold so many of my tamagotchis or my PS2 or the Game Boy. A lot of me wishes I were rich so I didn't have to sell any of that, but with interests changing I guess I still also feel it was okay for me to just get down to a few favorites.

I'm haggling about tamagotchis with someone online that has four rare ones I'm after. The rare ones are expensive, but there's one that I could resell later for about twice the price. Tamagotchis are, in my mind, the replacement to a small pet. They're about as exciting as a hamster, with more variety. They "evolve" and, in the new version, can get jobs which basically just opens up new games for you to play and they can connect using the IR thing at the top of them, so they can be "friends" and after a long time can breed.

My tattoos may end up waiting a bit and Shawn seems to be "putting it off," too. I'm pretty set in what I want but I'm waiting to see if the tamagotchis deal goes through. I think he's still thinking of how he wants his tattoos to be.

Things I'm happy about? My decision to move in. The adoption although I still feel an abortion would've been better. I guess I think things played out how they should. Shawn and I aren't nearly done living, I'm not nearly done living, but we're in a good place and I'm glad I worked hard and went through so much to get here; it makes me appreciate it even more.

Last night in the bath I was just thinking: I'm an adult now. It's really weird since I try so hard to be young. It's going to take some adjusting and I can only imagine what everyone will expect of me now that I have a fancy number.

Unless Shawn ends up getting sent overseas, we're still thinking it'll be three years until we get married. We have no plans of it sooner.

Epilogue

Katie's life is far from over and writing an ending for her story is not something I can do even though most people who read the manuscript prior to publishing wanted an ending with enough negative consequences to deter other teens from following in Katie's footsteps. My hope is that Katie's story will make teen readers cautious enough that they won't make the same mistakes she did.

Regardless of how easily Katie seems to have been able to get on with life, unplanned pregnancy dramatically changed the course of her life. Until she became pregnant, Katie planned to go to college and get a teaching degree. Her boyfriend was already attending college. Neither are currently enrolled in college, her boyfriend dropping out at the end of his freshman year and Katie deciding not to go at all. Their current job options are limited to those that don't require more than a high school diploma. Perhaps they will continue their education in the future but day-to-day survival must now be their first priority.

Katie is an intelligent and tenacious young woman. Whether or not she lives "happily ever after" is completely up to her.

—Pat Gaudette

Glossary

AIM: America Online Instant Messenger is the online messenging program released by AOL in 1997.

Animal Crossing: Video game developed by Nintendo for their GameCube console.

anime: Animation in Japan, called Japanese animation outside of Japan. Anime can be hand drawn or computer assisted and it is used in all types of media including television, films, video games, and commercials.

Asterix & Obelix: Game for the PC, made by Infogrames.

booty call: Contacting someone with the specific intention to have sex.

CPAP: Short for "Continuous Positive Airway Pressure," a machine that blows air into the lungs at a prescribed pressure.

CAC: The Common Access Card is a U.S. Department of Defense smartcard issued as standard identification for active duty military personnel, reserve personnel, civilian employees, and eligible contractor personnel.

chibi wings: "Chibi" is a Japanese word that, when used in terms of anime or manga, is of someone or some animal that is small. Thus, chibi wings would translate to "small wings."

cosplay: Cosplay or "costume play" is popular throughout the world and the elaborate costumes are often tied to anime, manga, gaming, or sci-fi conventions.

eBay: Online auction and shopping website. eBay Inc., the company that owns and manages eBay, also owns several other businesses including PayPal and Skype.

email: Electronic mail sent and received over the Internet.

FAFSA: The Free Application for Federal Student Aid is a form used by nearly all colleges and universities to determine a person's elibility for various types of financial aid that might be available.

forum: Message board or bulletin board system on the Internet.

Game Boy: Handheld video game console developed and manufactured by Nintendo.

GameCube: The fourth home video game console developed by Nintendo.

Girls Gone Wild: Videos of attractive young women who may be in spring break from college and generally in a carefree partying mood who agree to expose themselves on camera, usually in exchange for an article of clothing such as short shorts or a tank top. They may also allow themselves to be filmed while engaging in sexual activities.

hacker: Usually thought of as a person who uses computer technology for vandalism, fraud, identity theft, or some other type of crime.

head: Slang for oral sex.

Hotmail: Free webmail service provided by Microsoft.

IM (Instant Messenger): Real-time text-based communication between two or more people. The typed text conversation can be saved for later reference.

manga: Comics originally published in Japan that are extremely popular with all ages and include a wide range of subjects such as science fiction and fantasy, mystery, action-adventure, sexuality. Some manga stories can run for years; the most popular are turned into anime.

Monster Rancher: Game for the Sony PlayStation in which players raise, fight, and breed monsters.

morning after pill: Pills that can be taken up to five days after unsafe intercou5rse to prevent pregnancy and are made of the same hormones as in birth control pills. The hormones keep a woman's ovaries from releasing eggs and thicken cervical mucus which blocks sperm. Also called "emergency contraception."

MSN Messenger: An instant messaging system created by Microsoft now known as Windows Live Messenger.

MySpace: The Internet's most popular social networking site. MySpace operates on revenues generated by advertising. Users create their own page which includes blogs, blurbs, comments, photos, and other personalizations.

Nintendo: Japanese company known for its video games and game consoles including Donkey Kong, Atari 2600, Super Mario Bros., Nintendo Entertainment System, the Game Boy handheld video system, and the Nintendo GameCube.

OCD: Obsessive-compulsive disorder.

PayPal: A person-to-person payment service that allows anyone with an e-mail address to transfer funds electronically to anyone else with an e-mail address. PayPal performs payment processisng for online vendors, auction sites, and commercial users for a fee and sometimes a transaction fee.

pentacle: An amulet used in religious/magical practice. Sometimes the word "pentacle" is used when the word "pentagram" is meant. A pentagram is a five-pointed star drawn with five straight strokes which is often incorporated into the design of a pentacle.

PM: A personal message or private message, shortened to PM, is similar to an e-mail and is sent from one forum member to another member of the same forum.

Pokemon: Video game-based media franchise owned by Nintendo.

pot: Slang for cannabis or marijuana, an illegal drug used by an estimated four percent of the world's adult population. Cannabis is smoked, inhaled through a vaporizer or orally consumed.

preeclampsia: A dangerous condition unique to pregnancy causing a narrowing of the blood vessels which can result in decreased blood flow to the kidneys, brain, liver, retina, and placenta. Symptoms include high blood pressure, swelling of the hands and face, and protein in the urine. Preeclampsia can cause fetal complications such as stillbirthds, premature births, and low birth weight. The only cure for preeclampsia is delivery of the fetus.

PS2: The PlayStation2, considered the best-selling video game console to date, is manufactured by Sony.

Rogue Leader: *Star Wars* video game developed for the Nintendo GameCube.

SuicideGirls: SuicideGirls.com is a website with semi-nude, erotic, pin-up-style photos of primarily punk and goth young women known as "SuicideGirls." As of March 2008, the website featured nearly 1,800 SuicideGirls. Most have piercings, body modifications, non-traditional hair color or styles, and/or tattoos.

Super Monkey Ball: An arcade game, featuring monkey characters, published by Sega for the Nintendo GameCube.

tamagotchi: Small, handheld, digital pet sold by Bandai. Three buttons allow the user to select and perform an activity so that the Tamagotchi does not starve or die.

toxemia: Refers to the presence of toxins in the blood. Symptoms of toxemia include swelling of the feet and protein in the urine (see preeclampsia).

video chat: One-to-one live video communication over the Internet using webcams, microphones, and a videoconferencing program such as Yahoo Messenger, Windows Live Messenger, Skype, or iChat, to name a few.

webcam: Cameras whose images can be accessed using the Internet, instant messenging, or video conferencing software.

Windows Live Messenger: Instant messaging program created by Microsoft.

Additional Reading

Abortion (Introducing Issues With Opposing Viewpoints), Emma Carlson Berne

Abortion (Open for Debate), Corinne J. Naden

Abortion: Understanding the Debate, Kathlyn Gay

Babies, Robyn Gee, Susan Meredith, authors; Susan Stitt, illustrator

The Best Investment: Unlocking the Secrets of Social Success For Your Child, Andrea Goodman Weiner, Ed.D

Birth Defects, Lisa Iannucci

Coping With Teenage Motherhood, Carolyn Simpson

Current Controversies - The Abortion Controversy, Lynette Knapp, editor

Current Controversies - Teen Pregnancy and Parenting, Helen Cothran, editor

Dear Diary, I'm Pregnant: Teenagers Talk About Their Pregnancy, Anrenee Englander

Dear Kate: Letters About a Life Begun Too Soon, Sherri Goggin

The Dirt on Sex: A Dateable Book, Justin Lookadoo

Disciplining Young Children, Kristin Thoennes Keller, Ann Michelle Daniels

Dreams to Reality: Help for Young Moms: Education, Career, and Life Choices, Laura Haskins-Bookser

Everything You Need to Know About Teen Fatherhood, Eleanor H. Ayer

Everything You Need to Know About Teen Pregnancy, Tracy Hughes

Facing Teenage Pregnancy: A Handbook For The Pregnant Teen, Patricia Roles

Hello, My Name Is Mommy: The Dysfunctional Girl's Guide to Having, Loving (and Hopefully Not Screwing Up) a Baby, Sheri Lynch

Hope... Joy (and a Few Little Thoughts) for Pregnant Teens: Consciously Creating Your Legacy, Rachel Brignoni

How Are Babies Made? Alastair Smith, author; Maria Wheatley, illustrator

I'm Pregnant, Now What Do I Do? Robert W. Buckingham, Mary P. Derby

Kerry, a Teenage Mother, Maggi Aitkens, Rob Levine

Kids Still Having Kids: Talking About Teen Pregnancy, Janet Bode, author; Stan MacK, Ida Marx Blue Spruce, illustrators

Listen Up!: Teenage Mothers Speak Out, Margi Trapani

Nurturing Your Newborn: Young Parents' Guide to Baby's First Month, Jeanne Warren Lindsay, Jean Brunelli

Opposing Viewpoints Digests - Teen Pregnancy, Jennifer A. Hurley

Passport2purity, Dennis Rainey, Barbara Rainey

Pregnant! What Can I Do?: A Guide for Teenagers, Tania Heller, MD

Reality Check: Teenage Fathers Speak Out, Margi Trapani

Sex & Babies: First Facts, Jane Annunziata, author; Denise Ortakales, illustrator

Should I Keep My Baby? Martha Zimmerman

Straight Talk About Teenage Pregnancy, Paula Edelson

Surviving Teen Pregnancy: Your Choices, Dreams, and Decisions, Shirley Arthur, author; Perry Bergman, illustrator

Teenage Pregnancy and Parenthood, Roy Evans

Teen Dads: Rights, Responsibilities & Joys, Jeanne Warren Lindsay

Teen Decisions - Pregnancy, William Dudley, editor

Teen Fathers: Getting Involved, Julie K. Endersbe

Teen Fathers Today, Ted Gottfried

Teen Issues - Teen Parenting, Gail B. Stewart

Teen Mothers: Raising a Baby, Julie K. Endersbe

Teen Pregnancy, Michele Alpern, Marvin Rosen

Teen Pregnancy, Patrice Cassedy

Teen Pregnancy And Parenting, Lisa Frick, editor

Teen Pregnancy & Poverty: The Economic Realities, Barbara A. Miller

Teens & Sex, Hal Marcovitz

The Unplanned Pregnancy Book for Teens and College Students, Dorrie Williams-Wheeler

What Do I Do Now?: Talking About Teenage Pregnancy, Susan Kuklin

Young Adults in the Mist: A Survival Guide, Cynthia Trowell

Your Pregnancy and Newborn Journey: A Guide for Pregnant Teens, Jeanne Warren Lindsay, Jean Brunelli

Youth Coping with Teen Pregnancy: Growing Up Fast, Heather Docalavich, Phyllis Livingston

Web Resources

The following is a "short list" of Web sites with information about teen pregnancy, teen sexuality, and pregnancy in general. As this book goes to press, many more sites are currently available, however, due to the constantly changing nature of the Internet, the following sites and links are more likely to remain accessible in the foreseeable future. Inclusion in this list does not constitute an endorsement of a site's programs, services, products, or philosophies.

BabyZone.com – Everything about babies from pre-conception to child care and development after birth. Baby names, baby showers, fetal development, labor & childbirth, maternity clothes, pregnancy week-by-week, safety, twins & multiples, forums, health & wellness. www.babyzone.com

Campaign For Our Children, Inc. – Educational programs relating to preventing teen pregnancy and providing information on adolescent sexual health. www.cfoc.org

Children's Aid Society Carrera Adolescent Pregnancy Prevention Program – Articles, news, resources, statistics. www.stopteenpregnancy.com

March of Dimes - Quick Reference – Teenage Pregnancy Fact Sheets www.marchofdimes.com/professionals/14332_1159.asp

Mary's Shelter – Confidential, comprehensive residential care for pregnant minors who are in a homeless or other crisis situation and who have committed to carry their babies to full term. www.teenshelter.org

MedlinePlus – A service of the U.S. National Library of Medicine and the National Institutes of Health www.nlm.nih.gov/medlineplus/teenagepregnancy.html

The National Campaign to Prevent Teen and Unplanned Pregnancy – www.thenationalcampaign.org

National Network for Child Care — Articles, newsletters, conferences. Also: Child Care Information by State. www.nncc.org

New York Online Access to Health (NOAH) – Teen pregnancy resources and organizations. www.noah-health.org/en/pregnancy/teen/

Not Me, Not Now – Website for teens - "Making Smart Choices about Sex." www.notmenotnow.org

Our Health, Our Futures – Written by two teenage girls who provide information on young pregnancy. Statistics, quiz, initial signs. www.smith.edu/ourhealthourfutures/teenpreg.html

OptionLine - PregnancyCenters.org – Call center located in Columbus, Ohio, formed as a joint venture between Care Net and Heartbeat International, faith-based organizations promoting women's reproductive health. Information about pregnancy options and positive alternatives to abortion. www.pregnancycenters.org

Prepare Tomorrow's Parents.org – National non-profit organization dedicated to bringing parenting, nurturing and relationship skills education to all school age children and teens. www.preparetomorrowsparents.org

Planned Parenthood Federation of America, Inc. – Birth control, Abortion, STDs, HIV, Safer Sex, Pregnancy, Emergency Contraception www.plannedparenthood.org

Power2Relate.com – Parents need to invest time and commitment into teaching children social and emotional skills at an early age. www.power2relate.com

Pregnant & Parenting Teens – Healthy Teen Network www.healthyteennetwork.org

Pregnant Teen Help – Teen Pregnancy Statistics, Prevention and Facts www.pregnantteenhelp.org

Stay Teen – Website for teens by The National Campaign to Prevent Teen and Unplanned Pregnancy. www.stayteen.org

Teen Pregnancy – WomensHealthChannel, articles, forums www.womenshealthchannel.com/teenpregnancy

Teen Pregnancy Prevention – Texas Department of State Health Services - Statistics, fact sheets, prevention programs, health and social consequences. www.dshs.state.tx.us/famplan/tpp.shtm

When Your Teen Is Having a Baby - KidsHealth.org – Information for the mother and/or father dealing with an unplanned teen pregnancy. www.kidshealth.org/parent/positive/talk/teen_pregnancy.html

The Young Mommies Help Site – "Supporting, informing, and connecting young mothers so they can better face the challenges of parenting." Forums, chat, information, resources. created in 1998 by a newly-pregnant young single mother. www.youngmommies.com

Hotlines

Abortion Information: 1-800-772-9100

Adolescent Crisis Intervention & Counseling Nineline - Covenant House: 1-800-999-9999

Adoptions- Rosie Adoptions: 1-800-841-0804

AIDS Treatment Information Services: 1-800-HIV-0440 (1-800-448-0440)

AIDS National Hotline: 1-800-342-2437

Al-Anon/Alateen Hotline: 1-800-344-2666

Al-Anon Family Group Headquarters: 1-800-356-9996

Alcohol & Drug Abuse Hotline: 1-800-662-HELP (1-800-662-4357) 1-800-ALCOHOL (1-800-252-6465)

America's Pregnancy Helpline: 1-888-4-OPTIONS (1-800-467-8466)

America's Crisis Pregnancy Helpline: 1-800-67-BABY-6 (1-800-672-2296)

Be Sober Hotline: 1-800-BE-SOBER (1-800-237-6237)

Bethany Christian Services: 1-800-238-4269

Birthright: 1-800-550-4900

Boys Town National Hotline: 1-800-448-3000

Care Net: 1-800-395-HELP (1-800-395-4357)

Centers for Disease Control AIDS Info: 1-800-342-2437

CHADD - Children & Adults with ADHD: 1-800-233-4050

Child Abuse Hotline: 1-800-4-A-CHILD (1-800-422-4453)

Child Abuse & Neglect, Clearinghouse on: 1-800-FYI-3366 (1-800-394-3366)

Child Find of America Hotline: 1-800-292-9688

Child First Mentor Hotline: 1-800-914-2212

Child Help USA, National Child Abuse Hotline: 1-800-422-4453

Children of the Night Hotline: 1-800-551-1300

Children of the World - To Adopt: 1-973-239-0100

Cocaine Helpline: 1-800-262-2463

Cocaine Hotline: 1-800-992-9239

Domestic Violence Hotline: 1-800-799-SAFE (1-800-799-7233)

Domestic Violence Hotline: 1-800-548-2722

Domestic Violence Hotline/Child Abuse: 1-800-4-A-CHILD (1-800-422-4453)

Domestic Violence, National Resource Center on: 1-800-537-2238

Drug Help National Helplines: 1-800-378-4435

Eating Disorders Center: 1-888-236-1188

Ecstasy Addiction: 1-800-468-6933

Emergency Contraception Information: 1-888-NOT-2-LATE (1-888-668-2528)

Family Violence Prevention Center: 1-800-313-1310

Federal Student Aid Information Center: 1-800-433-3248

Food Addiction: 1-800-841-1515

GED Hotline: 1-800-626-9433

Healing Woman Foundation (Abuse): 1-800-477-4111

Herpes Resource Center: 1-800-230-6039

Homeless/Runaway National Runaway Hotline: 1-800-231-6946

Incest Awareness Foundation: 1-888-547-3222

Independent Adoption Center, The: 1-800-877-6736

IYG-Peer Counseling for Gay, Lesbian, Bisexual Youth Hotline: 1-800-347-8336

Learning Disabilities, National Center For: 1-888-575-7373

Marijuana Anonymous: 1-800-766-6779

Missing & Exploited Children Hotline: 1-800-843-5678

National Abortion Federation Hotline: 1-800-772-9100

National Adoption Center: 1-877-648-4400

National Adolescent Suicide Hotline: 1-800-621-4000

National AIDS Hotline: 1-800-342-2437

National Association for Children of Alcoholics: 1-888-55-4COAS (1-888-554-2627)

National Child Abuse Hotline: 1-800-422-4453

National Counseling Hotline: 1-800-848-LOVE (1-800-848-5683)

National Domestic Violence Hotline: 1-800-799-SAFE (1-800-799-7233)

National Drug Abuse Hotline: 1-800-662-HELP (1-800-662-4357)

National Hotline for Missing & Exploited Children: 1-800-843-5678

National Inhalant Prevention Coalition: 1-800-269-4327

National Institute on Drug Abuse & Alcoholism: 1-888-644-6432

National Institute of Mental Health: 1-888-ANXIETY (1-888-269-4389)

National Life Center Hotline/Pregnancy Hotline: 1-800-848-5683

National Mental Health Association: 1-800-969-6642

National Office of Post Abortion Trauma: 1-800-593-2273

National Rape Hotline: 1-800-656-4673

National Runaway Switchboard and Suicide Hotline: 1-800-621-4000

National Suicide Prevention Lifeline: 1-800-273-TALK (1-800-273-8255)

National STD Hotline: 1-800-227-8922

National Teen Dating Abuse Help: 1-866-331-9474

National Youth Crisis Hotline: 1-800-448-4663

Nurturing Network: 1-800-866-4MOM (1-800-866-4666)

Out Youth Talkline: 1-800-969-6884

Planned Parenthood: 1-800-230-PLAN (1-800-230-7526)

Post-Abortion, National Office of: 1-800-593-2273 or 1-414-483-4141

Post-Abortion Project Rachel: 1-800-5WE-CARE (1-800-593-2273)

Pregnancy Hotline: 1-800-848-LOVE (1-800-848-5683)

Teen Pregnancy Hotline: 1-801-422-6232

True Love Waits, Youth Commitment Programs: 1-800-LUV-WAIT (1-800-458-2772)

Victims of Crime Resource Center: 1-800-627-6872

Women, Infants, and Children (WIC) Hotline: 1-800-DIAL-WIC (1-800-342-5942)

About the Author

PAT GAUDETTE is an author and website developer. She is the co-author of *How to Survive Your Husband's Midlife Crisis: Strategies and Stories From the Midlife Wives Club* which was inspired by her midlife crisis website. She is the author of *Advice for an Imperfect Single World, Advice for an Imperfect Married World, Midnight Confessions: True Stories of Adultery,* and *Sparky the AIBO: Robot Dogs & Other Robotic Pets.* She is the founder of popular relationship-oriented websites including *The Midlife Club* (midlifeclub.com) and the award-winning *Friends and Lovers the Relationships Guide* (friendsandlovers.com). She and her husband, Gerry, live in Citrus County, Florida.

How to Survive Your Husband's Midlife Crisis: Strategies and Stories from The Midlife Wives Club

Authors: Pat Gaudette & Gay Courter

Paperback: 288 pages

Publisher: Perigee Trade. (May 6, 2003)

ISBN-10: 0399528822
ISBN-13: 978-0399528828

You've heard all the jokes about men's midlife crises--the new sports car, the new exercise regimen... and the new girlfriend. But when you're the wife trying to cope, it's no laughing matter.

A midlife crisis can devour a relationship. It may be devouring yours. The Midlife Wives Club is a supportive sisterhood for midlife mates--a chance to vent some steam, share advice, or just get a reminder that you're not alone. In this guide, you'll find wisdom from both midlife wives and experts on:
>*Recognizing* the symptoms
>*Coping* with the threat (or reality) of infidelity
>*Identifying* underlying problems like depression and anger
>*Deciding* when to stick it out--and when to pack it in
>*Protecting* your kids from the fallout
>*Making it through the crisis*... and coming out stronger, saner, and more self-reliant

With personal stories from real women (and men) and a comprehensive list of resources, **How to Survive Your Husband's Midlife Crisis** can help you get past the rough spots--and turn this tumultuous time into a change for the better.

Available in bookstores and online through Amazon.com.

For immediate support for midlife issues visit www.MidlifeClub.com

Midnight Confessions: True Stories of Adultery

Author: Pat Gaudette

Paperback: 251 pages

Publisher: Home & Leisure Publishing, Inc. (Jan 1, 2005)

ISBN-10: 0976121042
ISBN-13: 978-0976121046

Why does a person cheat? What type of person cheats? What type of person loves a cheat? Can adultery be forgiven? Can a marriage survive the adultery of one or both partners? Can a cheater be trusted not to cheat again?

Love and lust are powerful forces but with enough time and tears each of us comes to a point of decision making when faced with betrayal.

If you are the betrayed spouse, do you confront? Do you leave? Do you get revenge by cheating? If you are the betrayer, do you lie or tell the truth? Do you keep the affair going or end it to save your marriage? If you are the other person, do you accept what you can get or do you force confrontation to "get it all"?

Midnight Confessions: True Stories of Adultery examines adultery from the adulterer's point of view, as well as that of the betrayed spouse and the other person. These are their stories in their words. Perhaps after reading their stories and the thought-provoking discussions in this book you will have a better understanding of the decision you need to make to fit your situation.

Available in bookstores and online through Amazon.com.

www.ingramcontent.com/pod-product-compliance
Lightning Source LLC
Chambersburg PA
CBHW071653090426
42738CB00009B/1507